I0793215

IMAGES
of America

DONORA

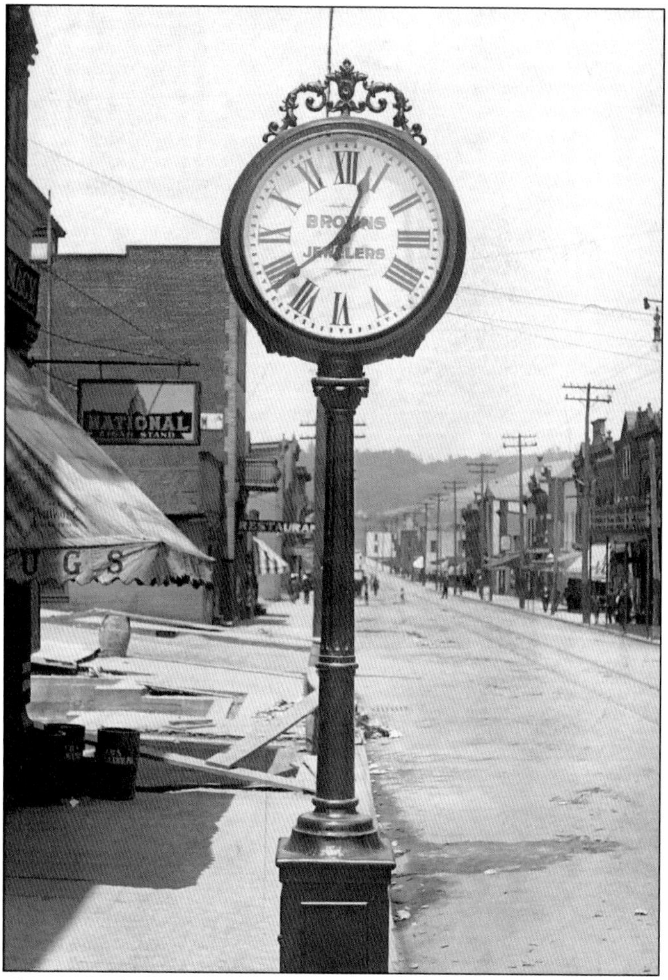

For more than 50 years, the 18-foot-high, 2-ton clock located on McKean Avenue was one of the most prominent landmarks in the borough. The clock's workings were manufactured by the Brown Street Clock Company of Monessen and were assembled in April 1910 at the company's plant in Donora. Originally the operating mechanism of the clock was located in the basement of the Brown Building and was attached to the clock by a shaft that ran under the sidewalk. Before it was electrified, it had to be wound by hand on a frequent basis. The clock-manufacturing plant was eventually converted to Brown's Jewelers, the name seen on both faces of the clock. The fate of the clock is one of Donora's mysteries. In 1967, it was struck and damaged by a truck, and the face and stand were dismantled. Brown's Jewelers eventually went out of business and the building housed a number of companies over the years. Thorough searches of this structure and other likely places in Donora produced no evidence of its whereabouts. Speculation that the clock has been sold and now stands in some other community has not been verified. (Courtesy Donora Historical Society.)

On the Cover: In this 1921 Bruce Driesbach photograph, workers pour molten zinc in front of the retorts at the spelter furnaces. The Donora Zinc Works was an example of Andrew Carnegie's vertical integration philosophy, "Make everything needed for production . . . don't buy anything." Zinc was used to galvanize nails, wire, rods, and fences and was sold to rustproof ship hulls. When the zinc works was built in 1915, it was the largest in the world. (Courtesy Donora Historical Society.)

IMAGES
of America

DONORA

Charles E. Stacey, Brian Charlton,
and David Lonich

ARCADIA
PUBLISHING

ISBN 978-0-7385-7206-2

Published by Arcadia Publishing
Charleston, South Carolina

Printed in the United States of America

Library of Congress Control Number: 2009927291

For all general information contact Arcadia Publishing at:
Telephone 843-853-2070
Fax 843-853-0044
E-mail sales@arcadiapublishing.com
For customer service and orders:
Toll-Free 1-888-313-2665

Visit us on the Internet at www.arcadiapublishing.com

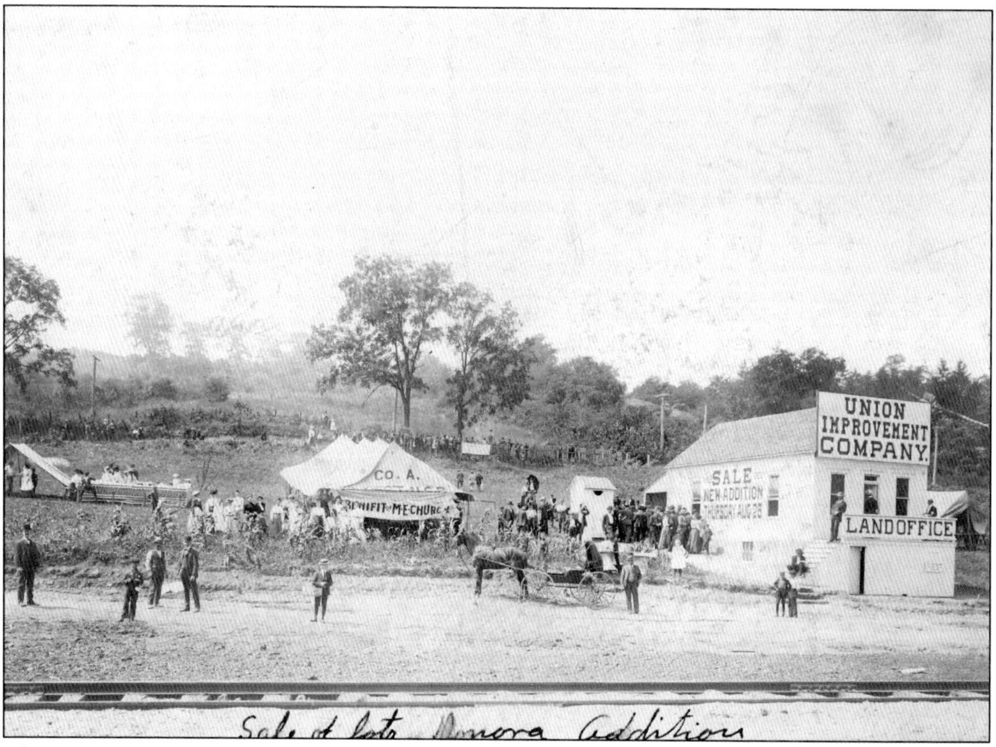

The Union Improvement Company prepares for a lot sale in 1902. In the photograph, a band warms up for a concert and the Methodist Episcopal Church prepares to sell food, which as the sign indicates, will include beer. The Pennsylvania Railroad rolls in the foreground. (Courtesy Donora Historical Society.)

Contents

Acknowledgments

The authors would like to extend extra special thanks to Deb Cheplic, whose expertise, skill, hard work, advice, and patience were invaluable in the creation of this book.

Thanks also go out to the following: Nancy Charlton, Holly Tonini, Ruth Miller, Ruth Yatsko, John Clark, Norma Todd, Rev. Andrew Slade, Patricia Shawley, Justin Shawley, the Donora Historical Society, the Donora Smog Committee, Pearl Williams, Dr. and Mrs. William Frantz, Scott Beveridge, Mark Pawelec, California University of Pennsylvania, Albert Pokol, Dr. Michael Brna, Nicholas Roberts, Casey Perrota, Don and DeAnne Pavelko, John McCans Jr., the Donora Chamber of Commerce, the Donora Downtown Committee, Mayor John Lignelli, Kathy O'Connell, Debbie Schulz, Harry Loftus, Albert Kovalik, Ray Beresh, Glenn Howis, Sally Huhra Phillips, Wallace Zielinski, Dr. Devra Davis, Alice Uhriniak, Janet Walsh Olenik, Adrian Huebner, Robert and Rita Turnbull, Stan Musial, Anthony and Theresa DiDanato, and Diane Martin.

Unless otherwise noted, all images are courtesy of the Donora Historical Society.

INTRODUCTION

The borough of Donora is located on the western banks of a horseshoe bend of the Monongahela River 25 miles directly south of Pittsburgh. It had its origins in 1863 as a small whistle-stop village called West Columbia, located on the river docks of the Gilmore Steamboat line near the Pennsylvania Railroad. The area remained mostly farmland until the Industrial Revolution transformed the Monongahela River Valley into one of the largest steelmaking centers in the world.

Donora was founded as a consequence of the building of a steel mill on a 380-acre site along the river. The site was deemed to be ideal for such industry because of its topography, existing rail and river transportation facilities, and the nearby presence of necessary raw materials. The borough was incorporated as a self-governing political entity in Washington County in 1901.

The naming of Donora was unique in 1901, and even to this day, it is believed that there is no other community in the world so named. The town's designation was a melding of the surname of the industrialist William Donner with the first name of Nora McMullen Mellon, the wife of Andrew W. Mellon, hence Don-Nora, or Donora.

Donner was the planner who proposed and supervised the building of the steel mill on the Donora site. Andrew Mellon, who later became the U.S. secretary of the treasury and ambassador to Great Britain, provided much of the funding for the development of the mill.

The steel plant was built in 1902, followed by the addition of blast furnaces in 1908 and the creation of the largest zinc works in the world in 1916. Over the years, the steel plant evolved into a horizontal manufacturing unit. Raw materials entered the facility at its southern end, and completely finished products were turned out in the component departments along the river. Eventually the wire produced in Donora was woven into cables that supported many of the great suspension bridges of the world, and the products of the nail mill can be found in homes and buildings around the globe.

The ancillary economic development of the borough kept pace with the major industry through the establishment of banks, insurance companies, realtors, and lumberyards. Restaurants, coffee shops, hotels, groceries, and shoe and clothing stores also sprung up. A significant professional service community of doctors, lawyers, pharmacists, carpenters, plumbers, and mechanics moved into the town. As a result, Donora came to be a very prosperous community, and its residents, for the most part, enjoyed a high standard of living.

These developments had a positive impact on the municipal population. Drawn by the numerous prospects of employment, people of many different racial, ethnic, and religious backgrounds poured into the region. The churches, fraternal organizations, and social clubs they created generated a diverse value system and fostered a tolerant political climate.

One of the major downsides of the nation's industrial growth was the indiscriminate pollution of the air and water. In this regard, Donora again followed a common pattern but demonstrated a tragic uniqueness. In October 1948, a temperature inversion trapped the discharge from the Donora Zinc Works furnaces and held it over the town for five days. More than 20 people died and thousands were sickened in this episode that came to be known as the Donora Smog. But again, Donora residents, demonstrating their spirited commitment to service, resolved to turn the incident into something positive and began the process that culminated in the Clean Air Act of 1970. Today community banners justifiably and proudly claim, "Clean Air Started Here."

In one sense, the history of Donora is reflective of the pattern of development common to many industrial communities, but from its inception, Donora also displayed an individuality that separated it from its counterparts. This combination of similarity and uniqueness is manifested in the lives of the citizens of Donora and in the service these residents have provided to their home community and to society at large.

Donora is exceedingly proud of these sons and daughters. Very few communities of Donora's size can claim so many people who have contributed so much in so many significant ways as can Donora. Donora natives have achieved outstanding success in the realm of religion, business, government leadership, military service, education, science and medicine, athletics, and the arts and entertainment. The community has consistently imbued its young with a strong work ethic and nurtured a robust desire to succeed among its offspring. The result is that the title "Donora: The Home of Champions" is an appropriate and earned appellation for the town.

Therefore, it is the people of Donora upon whom this book is focused and to whom it is dedicated. In recent years, the demise of the steel industry and economic downturns have negatively impacted Donora, as they have other small towns around the country. However, in the spirit of resilience that has historically been present, the residents have continued to look and move forward. Building on this mind-set, the people of the town truly believe that "Donora, next to yours, is the best little town in the country."

One

In the Beginning

At the dawn of the 20th century, Donora became the last of the great steel towns built along the Monongahela River, and it all seemed to happen overnight. When William H. Donner moved his Indiana-based National Tin Plate Company to the newly built industrial town of Monessen in 1898, the area that would be Donora in three short years was mostly farmland owned by the Castner, Heslep, and Allen families. Also on that horseshoe-shaped flood plain sat the village of West Columbia, then little more than a whistle-stop on the Pennsylvania Railroad. Across the river was the thriving village of Webster with a grain mill, farms, and mines.

Donner quickly impressed the industrial elite, who in 1899 formed the Union Improvement Company with Andrew Mellon, Richard B. Mellon, Henry Clay Frick, and others focusing their eyes toward creating another industrial complex. Donner's name was joined with Andrew Mellon's 21-year-old bride, Nora McMullen Mellon, to name the new town Donora.

As the mill and infrastructure of the town went up, the population exploded with new arrivals, growing from 12 official residents in 1900 to nearly 4,000 by 1901. The Union Improvement Company thought of nearly every need of a new community except for housing for employees, which created a booming hotel and boardinghouse business. Bed space was at a premium—the legend of three workers renting a bed and sleeping in eight-hour shifts did not originate in Donora, but it was certainly put into practice there.

A large and diverse population poured into Donora to not only build and work at the mills but to also take part in the "American Dream" by starting businesses. Individual entrepreneurs opened everything and anything a new town might need or demand. The newcomers also built churches, a synagogue, ethnic and national social clubs, political and beneficial associations, and fraternal and civic associations. The community put a priority on education, building schools and offering Americanization classes for immigrants. Donora public and parochial schools were a source of pride and community unity for citizens.

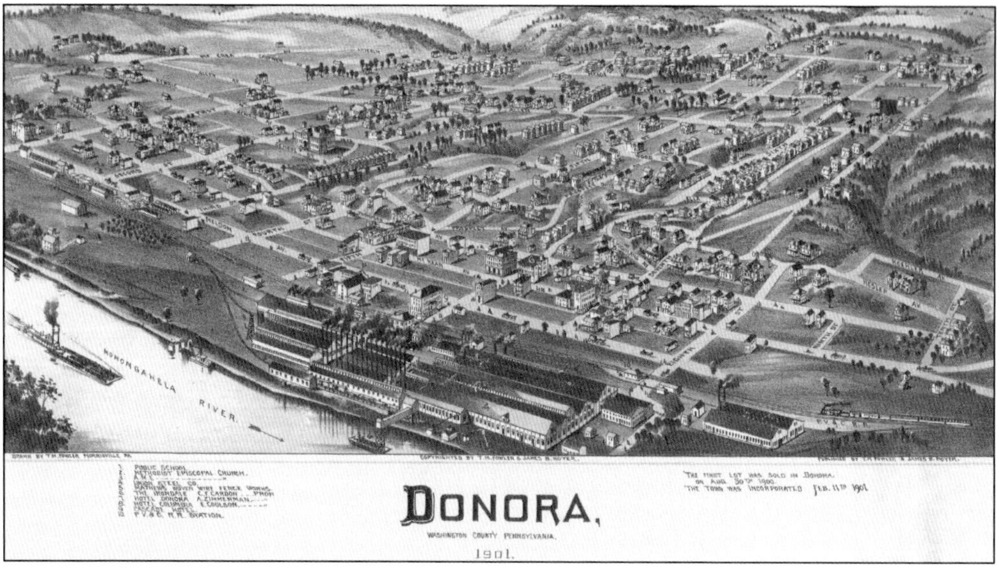

By 1901, when this image was drawn, Thaddeus Mortimer Fowler was nearing the end of a successful career as a bird's-eye illustrator of Pennsylvania towns. He solicited subscriptions for his maps door to door, and sometimes nonsubscribers had their buildings excluded from his final product. This may therefore be historically unreliable, but no less interesting.

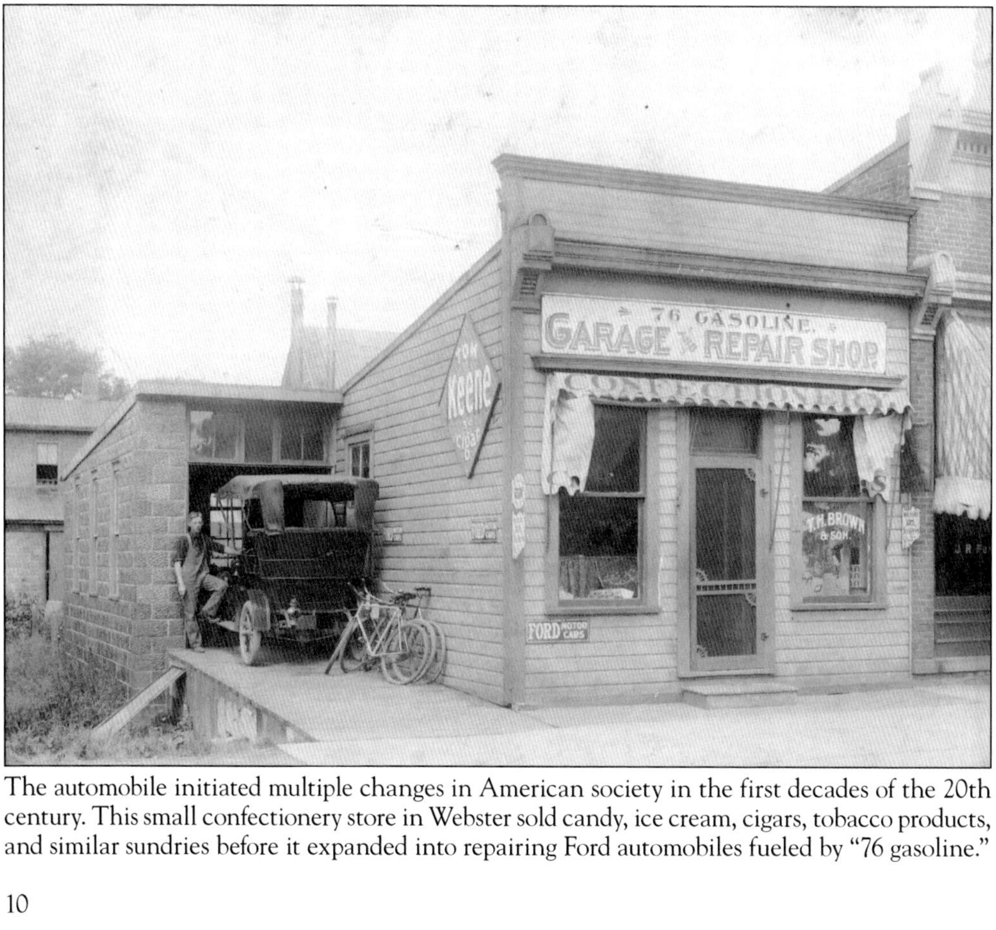

The automobile initiated multiple changes in American society in the first decades of the 20th century. This small confectionery store in Webster sold candy, ice cream, cigars, tobacco products, and similar sundries before it expanded into repairing Ford automobiles fueled by "76 gasoline."

In 1898, William Donner moved his Indiana-based National Tin Plate Company to Monessen. In 1899, he helped form the Union Improvement Company and, along with Andrew and Richard Mellon and Henry C. Frick, created the industrial community of Donora. Donner died in 1953.

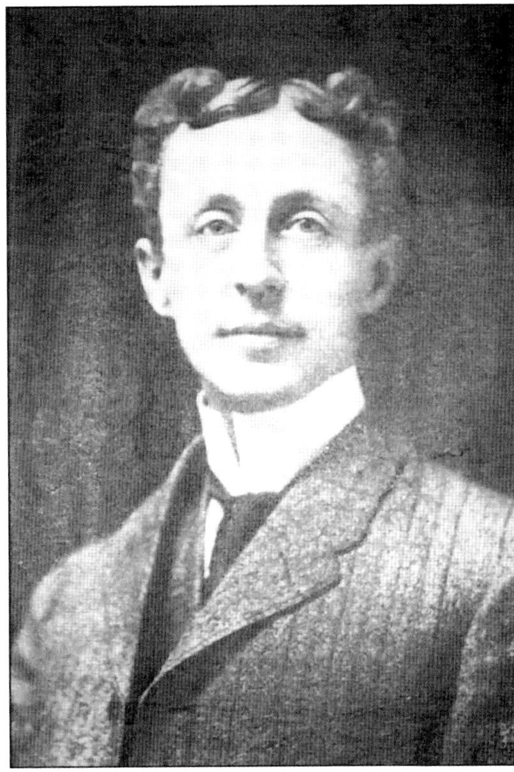

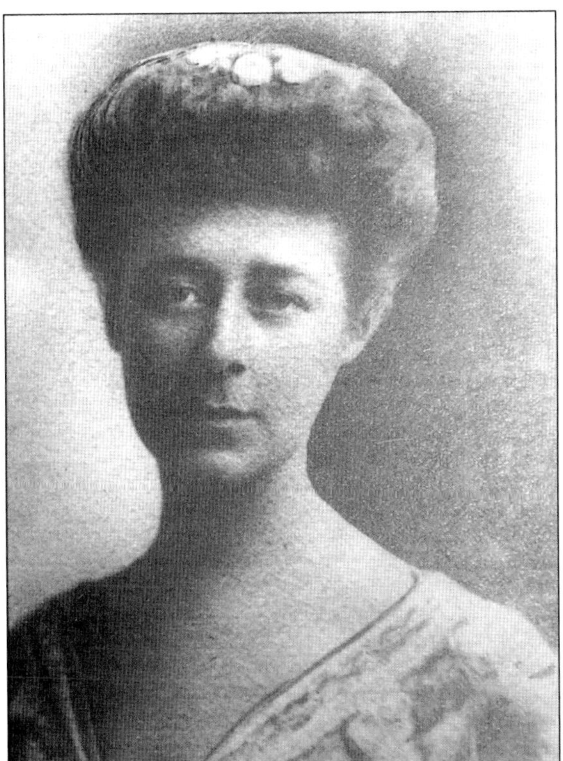

In 1900, Nora McMullen, a 21-year-old Guinness brewing heiress, married 44-year-old Pittsburgh financier Andrew Mellon. Their marriage ended in divorce in 1912 but not before her first name was combined with Donner's last name to create the name for the newly formed borough of Donora.

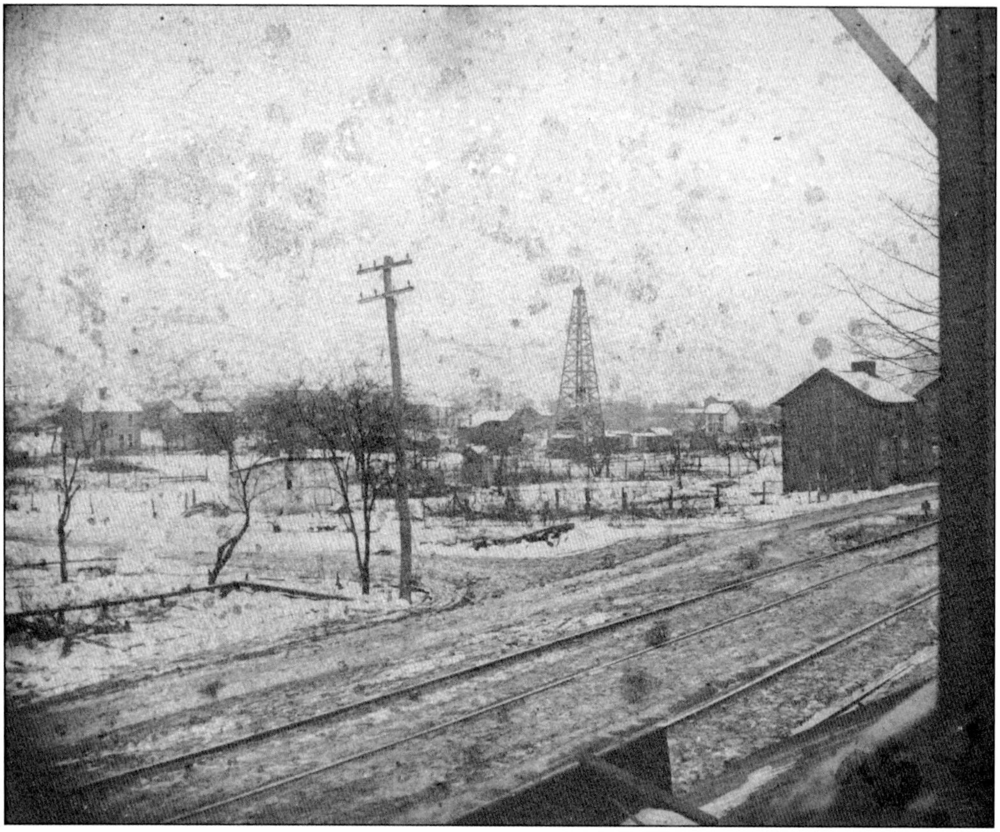

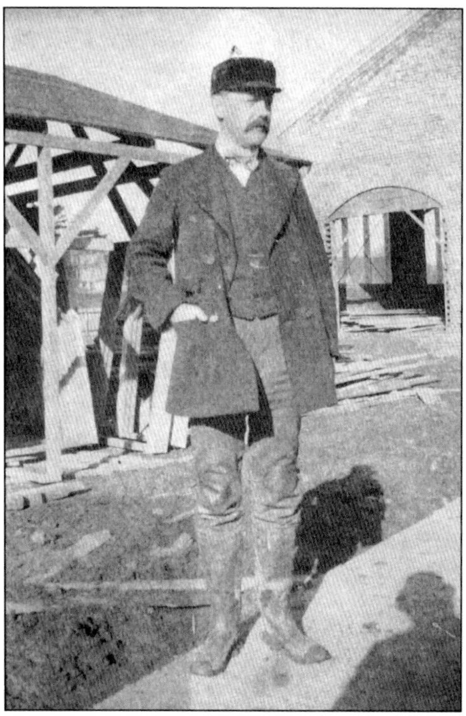

This photograph records one of the Donora Oil and Drilling Company's wells, located along the Monongahela River near what was West Columbia. Although the well seems to be producing a gusher, the oil industry had a short history in the borough. This was probably because of the overwhelming financial success of steel production.

John Parke was hired by the Union Improvement Company to survey and lay out the community of Donora. He also served on the borough council and was employed as the borough engineer. He is remembered for his heroic efforts in trying to warn Conemaugh Valley residents about the dam burst that led to the infamous Johnstown flood in May 1889.

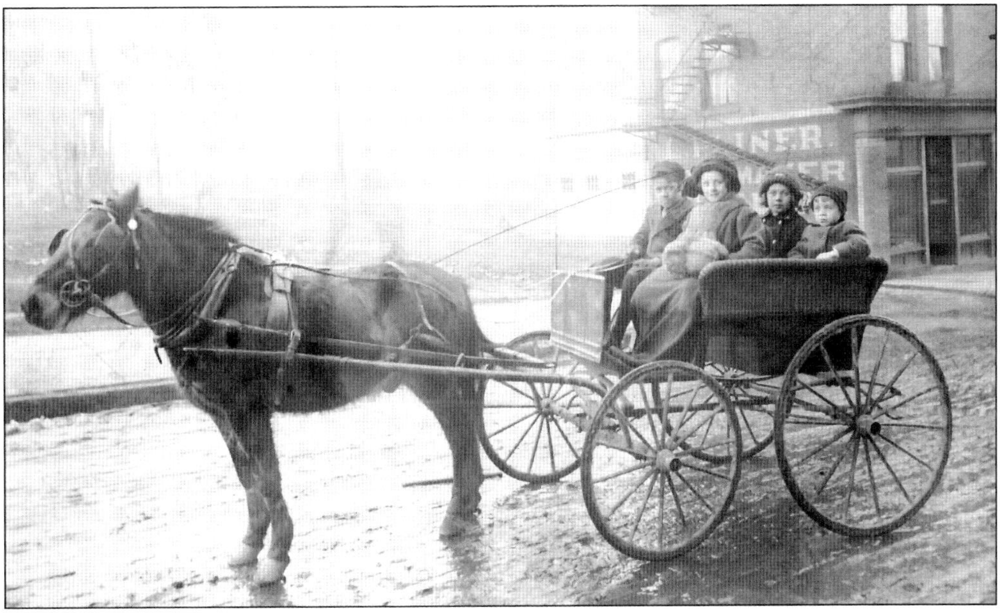

Peter Castner, a German immigrant who fought in the American Revolution, received 370 acres of land on the frontier for his service. His deed was not filed until June 3, 1794, but he began farming on the plot in 1784. This 1905 photograph shows the sixth generation of Castners riding through the muddy streets of the rapidly growing borough of Donora.

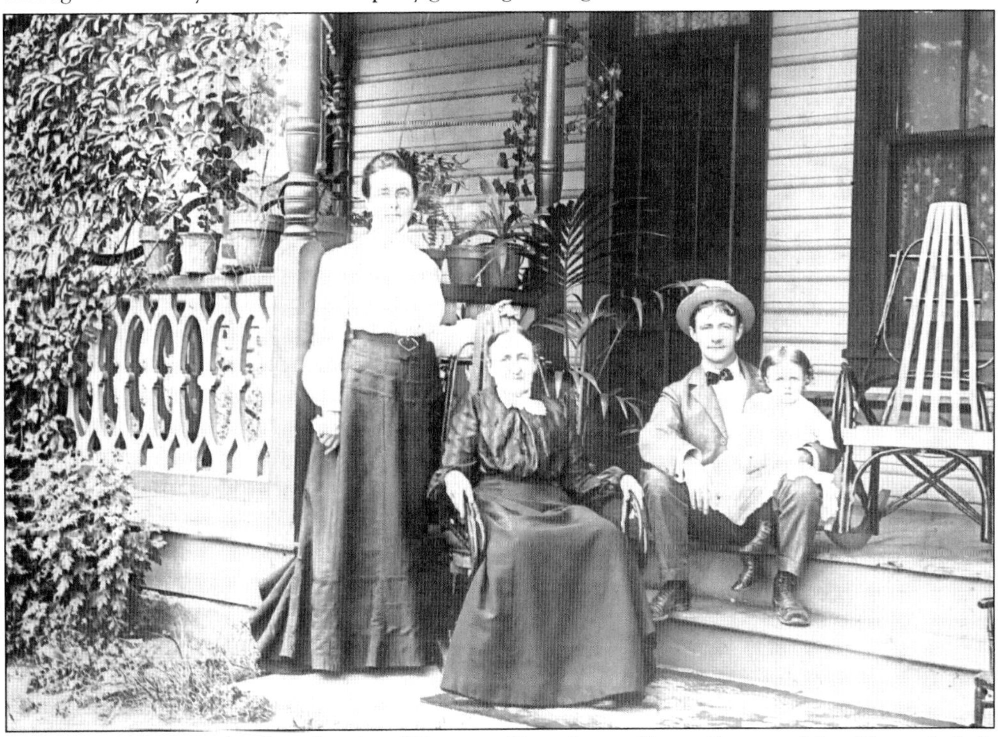

The Castners were the first family of Donora. Here James Percy Castner, his wife, and their daughter Rebecca Donora Castner, the first child born in the borough, pose on the front porch of their home with J. P.'s mother. Castner's father, Bert, was the first burgess of the town.

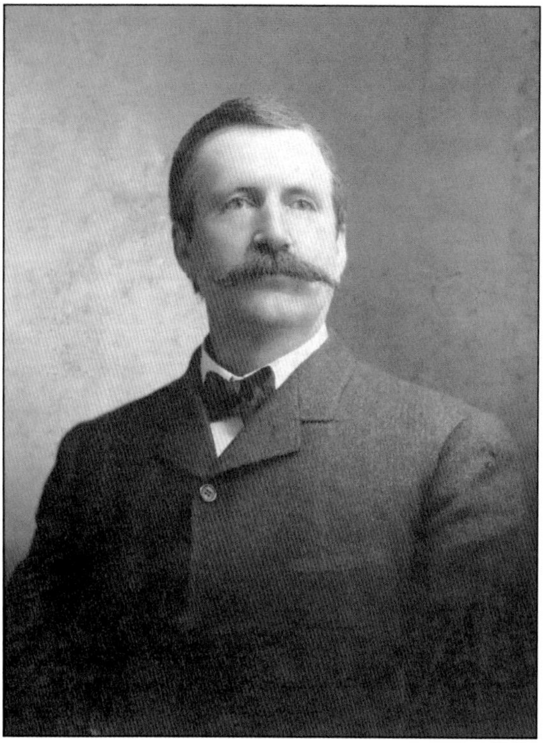

Bert Castner, pictured here, served several terms as justice of the peace and was elected the first burgess of Donora. The contributions of the Castner family were memorialized by the naming of Castner Avenue and Castner School.

Castner, one of Donora's most distinguished founding fathers, sold much of his family's property to provide the land needed for both industry and homes in the new community. Castner was a director of the Union Improvement Company, vice president of the First National Bank, and he and his son James operated a real estate and insurance agency.

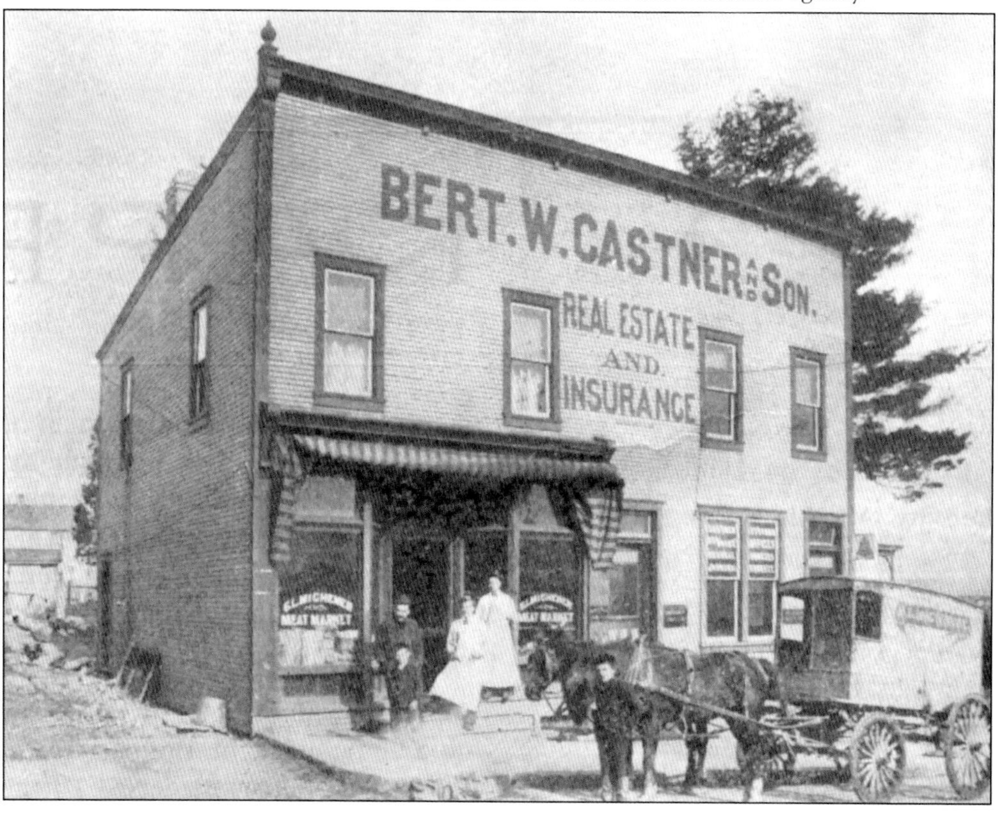

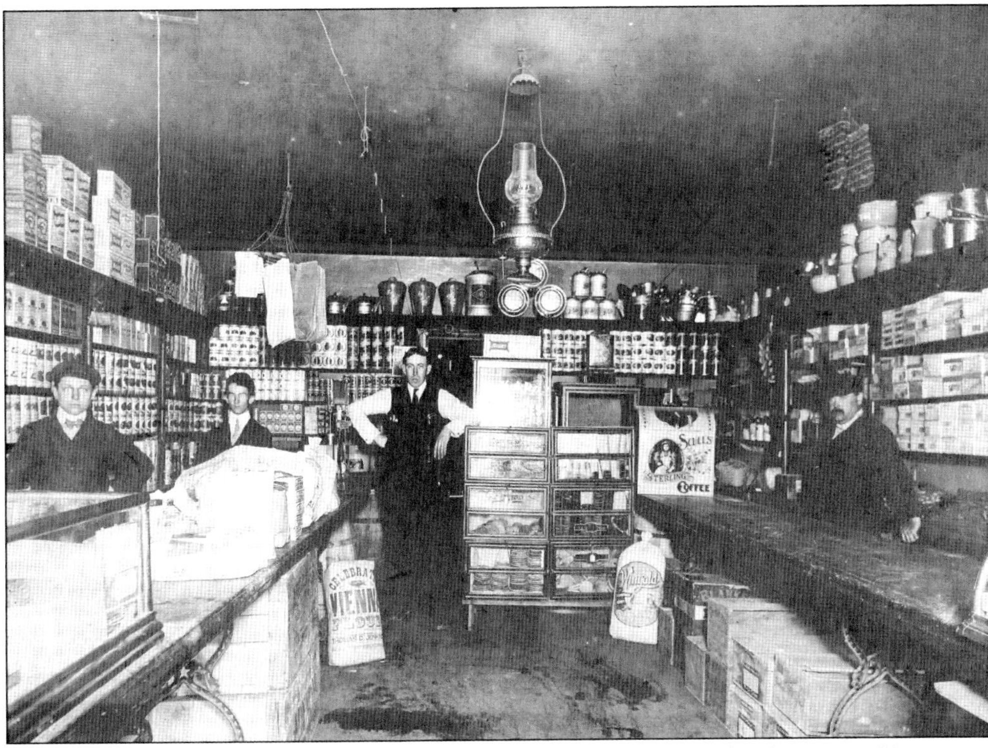

Watkins General Store was a center of commerce in West Columbia and early Donora. Here owner George Watkins (center) poses with his employees and a sample of his goods available for sale.

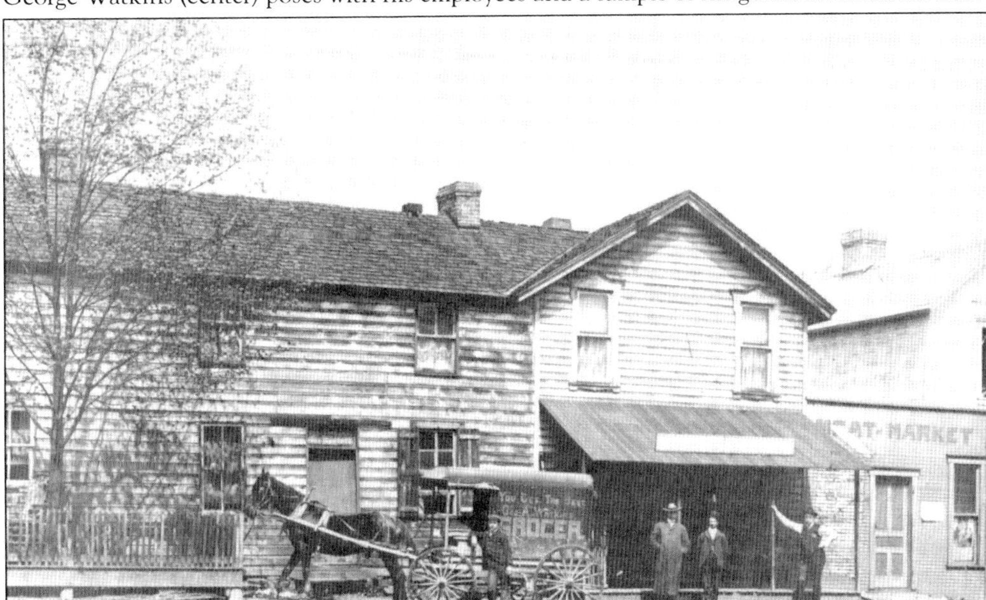

The village of West Columbia, built around a stop on the Pittsburgh, Virginia and Charleston Railroad, dated to 1814 and included a schoolhouse, about 50 homes, and a general store called West Columbia Station. Watkins purchased the store in 1900 and renamed it after himself. Much of West Columbia was razed around 1907 to make room for the blast furnaces.

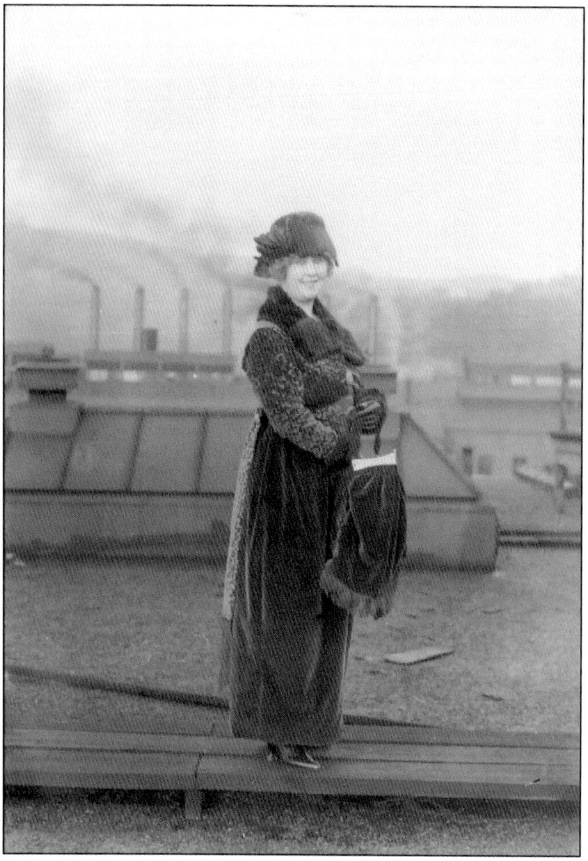

Lulu Dreisbach was a favorite subject for her husband's photographs in early Donora. Bruce Dreisbach worked as a photographer for the American Steel and Wire Company between 1906 and 1930. Here she poses on a rooftop along McKean Avenue with the wire works in the background. She passed away in 1986 at the age of 104.

The area shown was known as both Walnut Bottom and Horseshoe Bottom in the 18th century. After the mill was built, it was sometimes called Hell's Bottom. Note the shadow of the photographer in the foreground and the wire works and open hearth taking shape in the remnants of West Columbia.

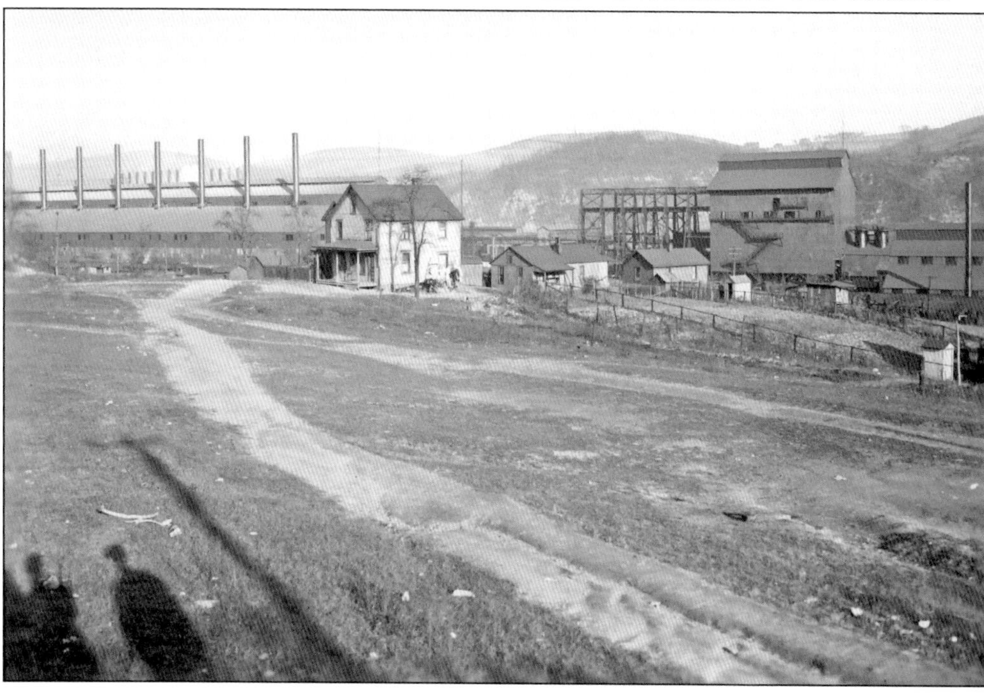

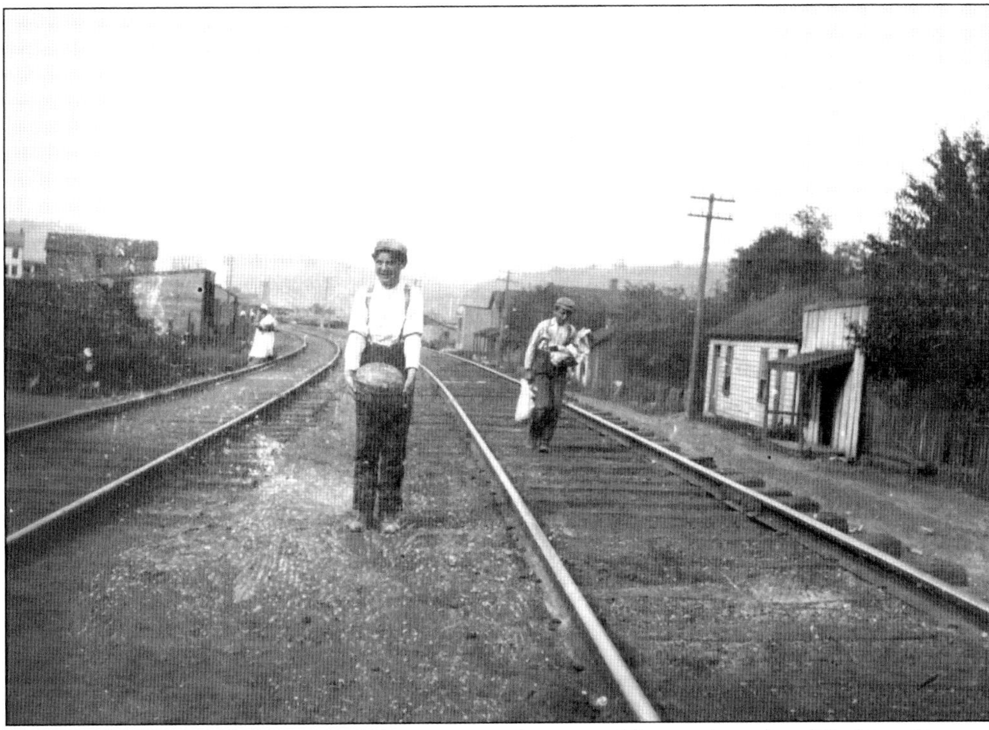

A young man proudly poses with his watermelon, possibly purchased at Watkins General Store, along the Pennsylvania Railroad tracks in West Columbia. By 1908, West Columbia disappeared to make way for the blast furnaces. The stacks of the open-hearth furnaces are visible in the background.

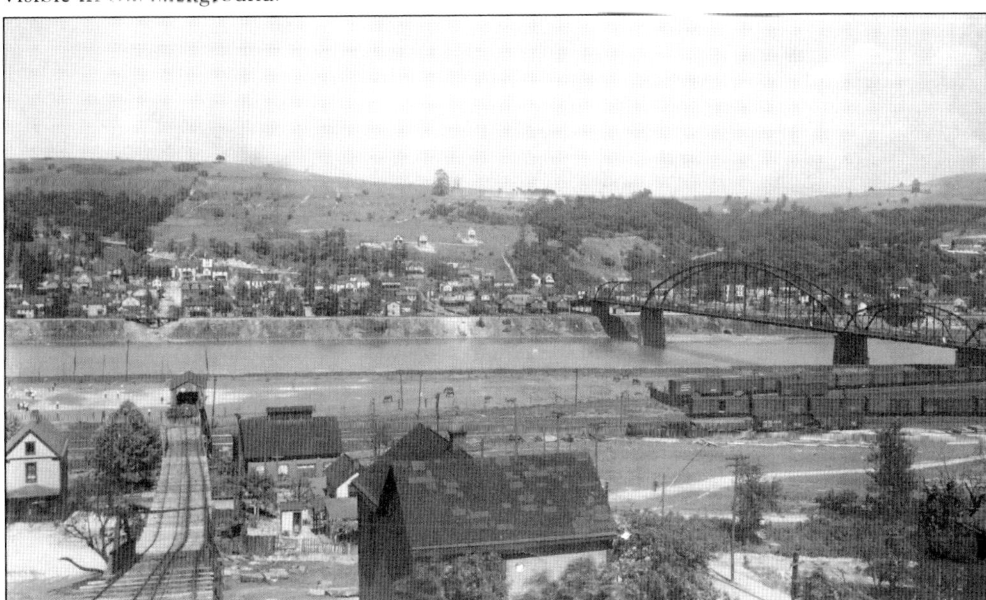

The first toll-free bridge across the Monongahela River connected the village of Webster and the borough of Donora. In this picture, taken before the zinc works was built, the vegetation on the hills of Webster is clearly evident. A pick-up game of baseball is taking place on Gilmore Field.

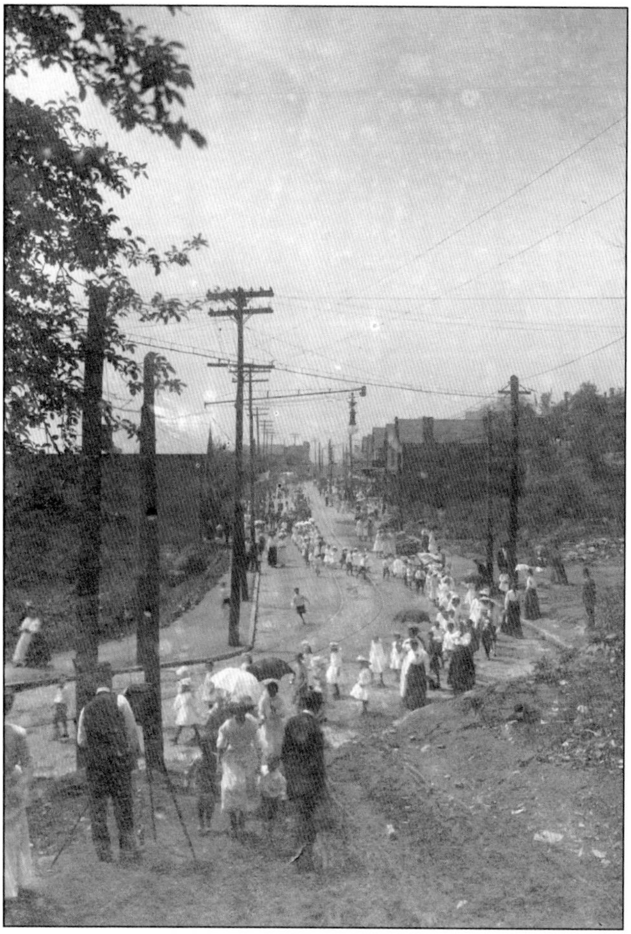

This August Siren photograph captures a Decoration (Memorial) Day procession as it makes its way along McKean Avenue between Tenth and Eleventh Streets on its way to Gilmore Cemetery around 1920. Note the number of white outfits, a traditionally acceptable summer color.

August Siren was born in Finland in 1880. He took some of the earliest photographs of Donora and the mills. He took this photograph from the eastern shore of the Monongahela River looking southwest. One of the Union Improvement Company's first goals was to prevent flooding by raising the riverbank by dumping slag.

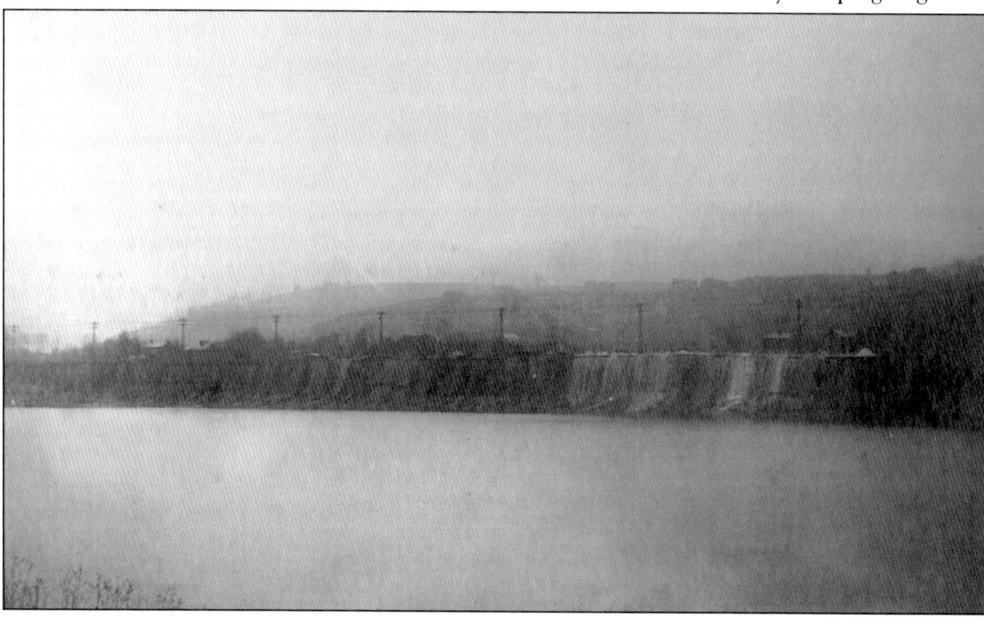

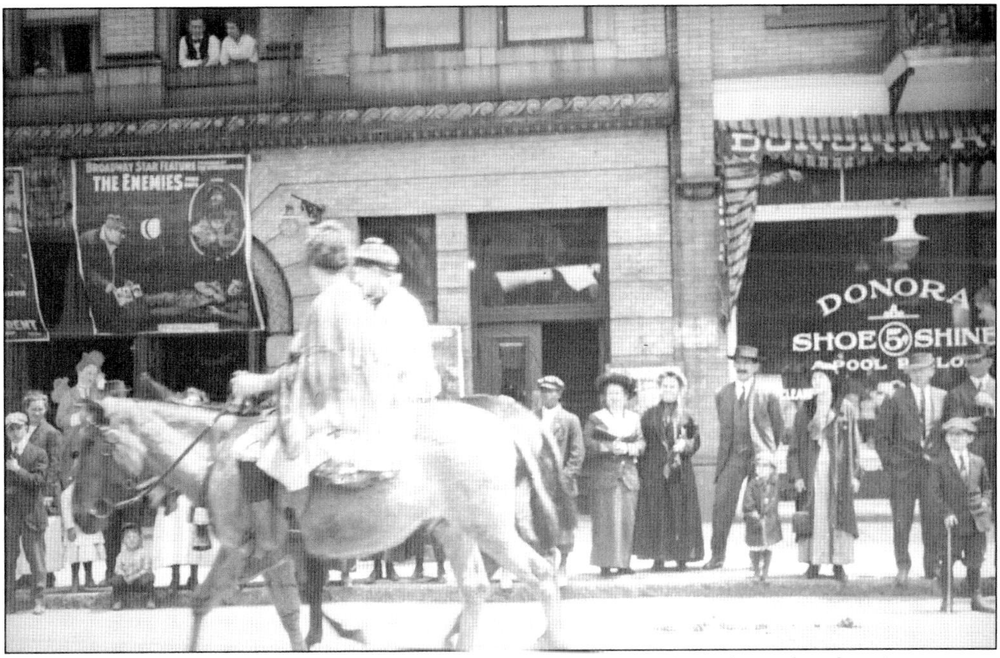

The arrival of a circus was a big day for any town in America. Residents dressed in their finest attire line McKean Avenue to watch Howes Circus parade through town. Here the procession travels north between Sixth and Seventh Streets past the Grand Theater and the Donora Shoe Shine.

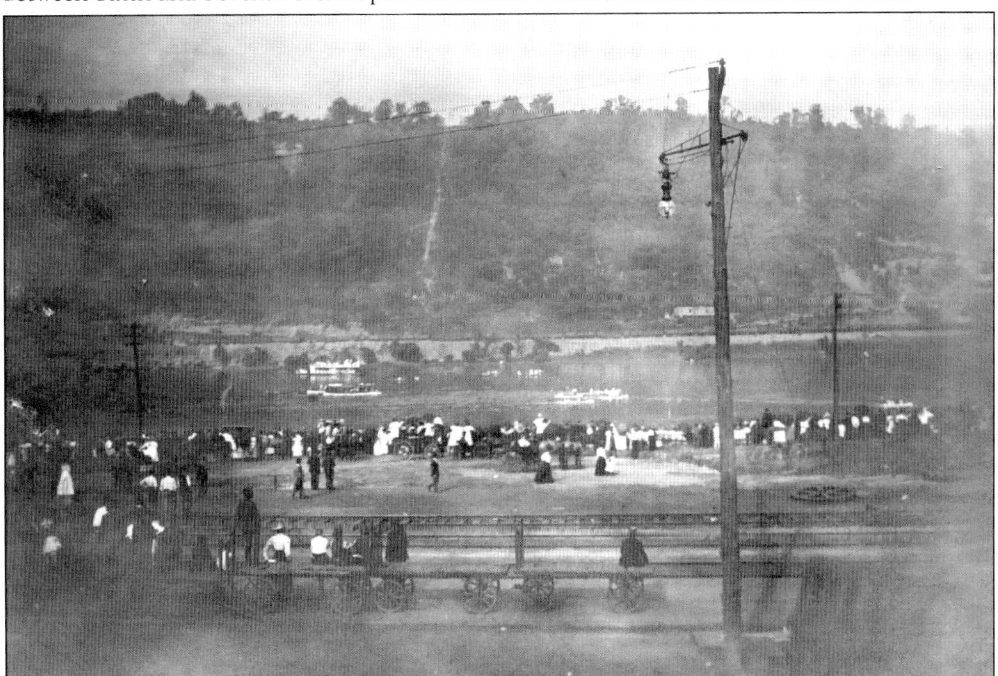

Beginning in 1863, steamboat captain John Gilmore docked his eight-vessel line at the northern end of what became Donora. In this photograph, people stand on Gilmore Field, now Fourteenth Street, around 1900 to watch boat races on the river. Gilmore, who first lived in Webster, then Donora, had his name attached to a cemetery, school, and avenue.

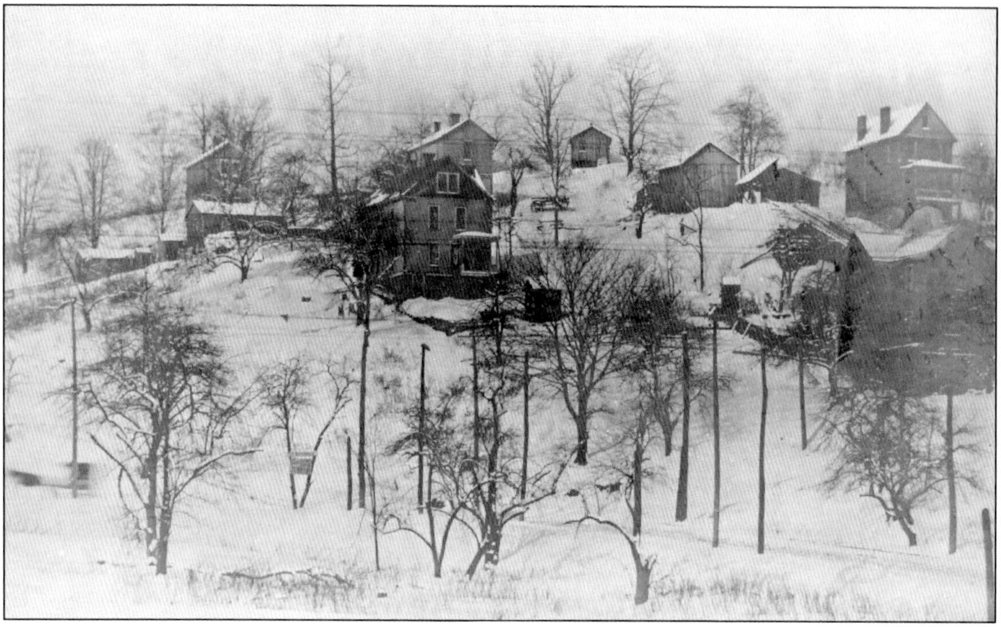

Here is a tranquil winter scene on the hills of the Monongahela River Valley in what later became Donora. The floodplain was reserved for the mill and business district, and homes were built on the slopes with long steps for pedestrian access. When this photograph was taken, people were more likely to travel by horse and buggy than automobile.

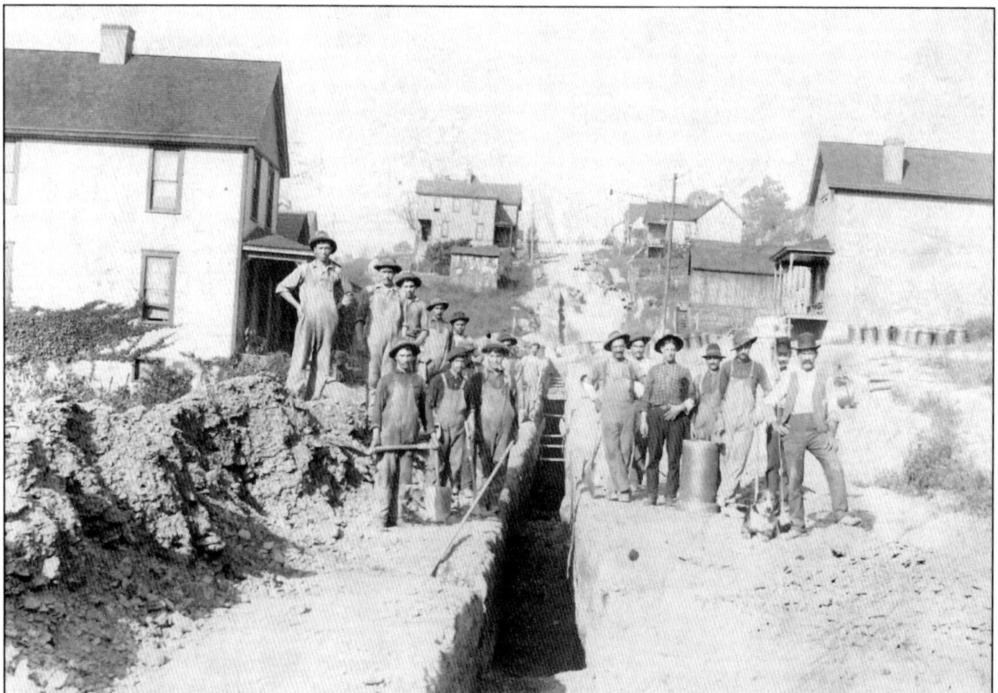

Here workers hand-dig a sewer line down the middle of Third Street around 1905. Building the infrastructure of a growing mill town like Donora provided almost endless employment opportunities.

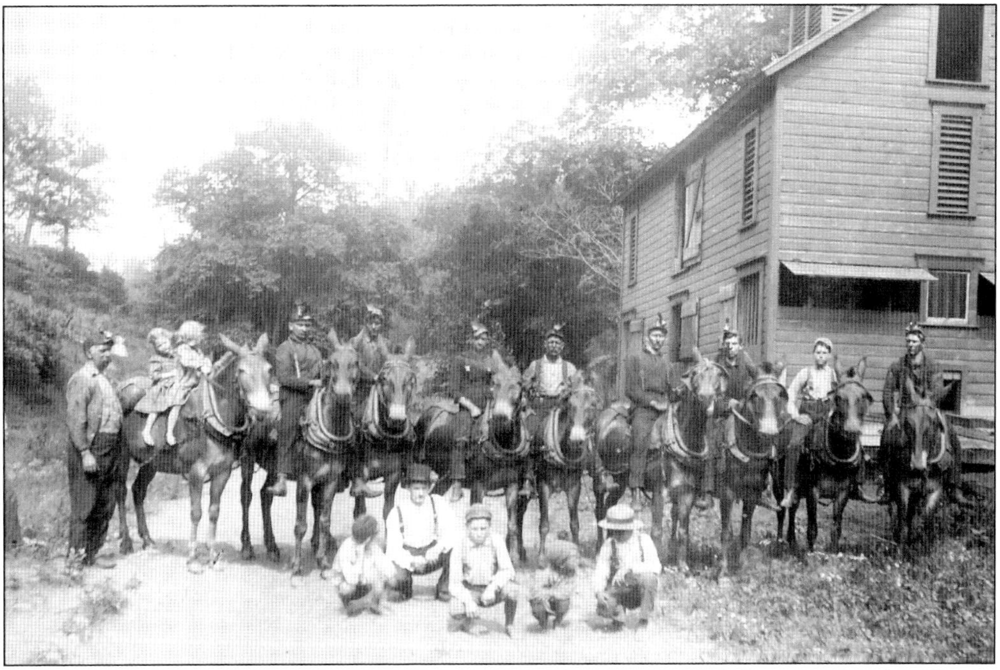

By the dawn of the 20th century, the Pittsburgh Coal Company and the Jones Brothers began to control coal mining along the Monongahela River. This photograph shows stable boss Lewis Gillingham (far left) near the entrance to Daggs Hollow mine. The young girls are most likely daughters of one of the workers.

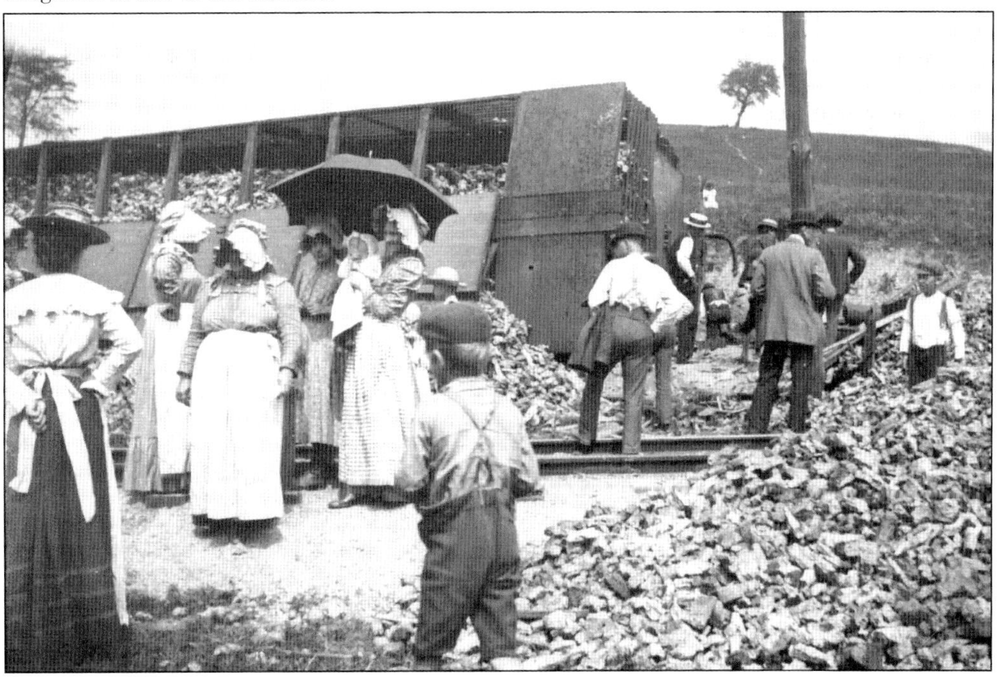

West Columbia villagers turn out to inspect a 1901 coke train derailment. The formal dress of the men on the right suggests it may be a Sunday or holiday, but the attire of the apron-wearing women implies an ordinary workday. Humans in every time period seem attracted to disasters.

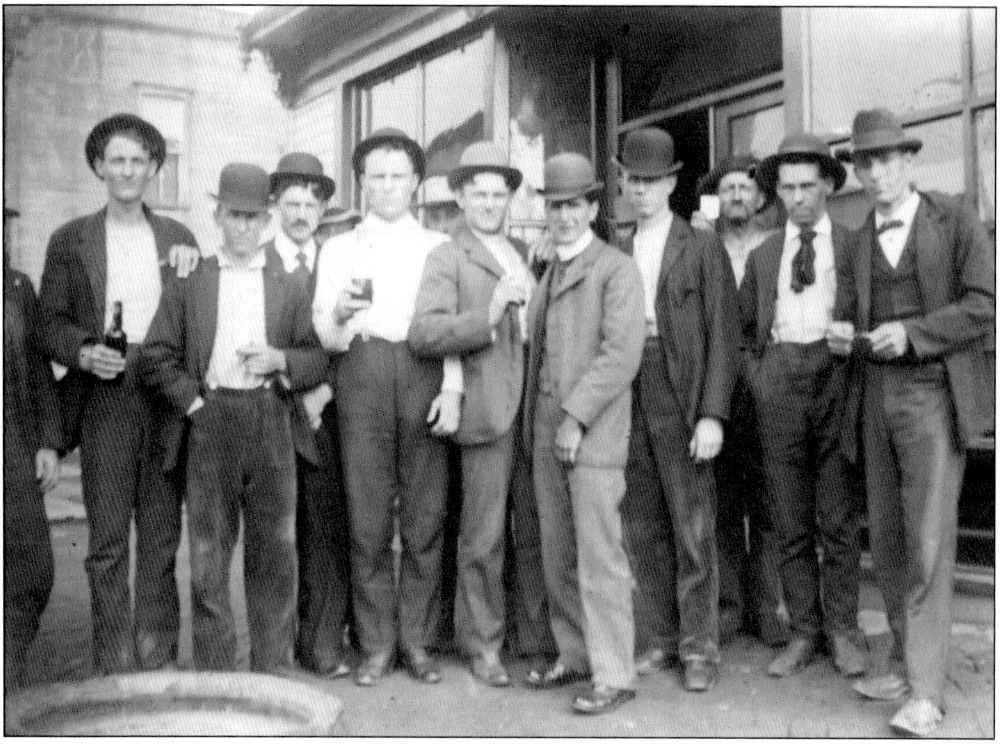

Here an unidentified group of Donora's residents dressed in their Sunday best pose in front of one of the town's numerous watering holes. Bars and drinking establishments grew at such a fast rate during the first decade of the 20th century that the borough and mill joined forces to offer workers more respectable leisure activities.

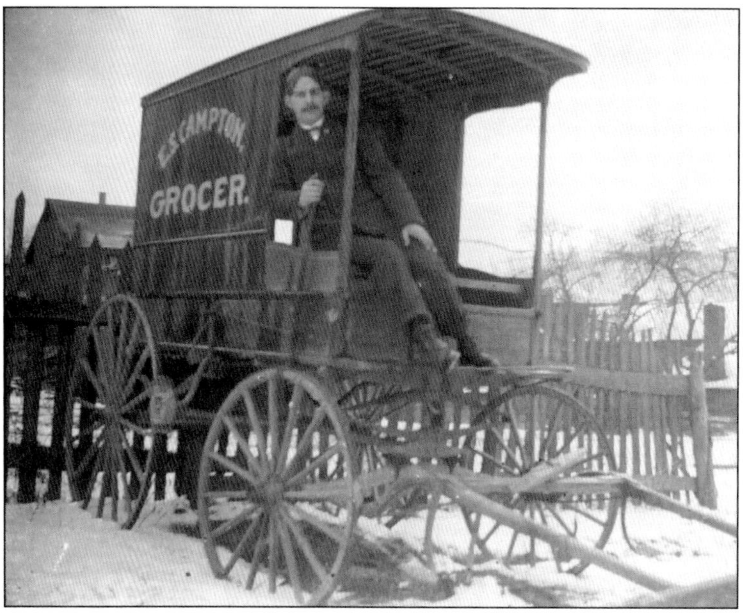

Emmet S. Compton was a former coal miner who moved to Donora in 1900 at the age of 32. Like many others, he saw business opportunities present in the new town and opted for the chance to avoid dangerous work in the mines. In this 1905 picture, he poses with his delivery wagon.

Two

Open for Business

As the 19th century came to an end, there were few people living on the land west of the great horseshoe bend in the Monongahela River that came to be the borough of Donora. A scattering of farms, a few coal miners' homes, and a village known as West Columbia housed the region's small population.

The coming of the steel industry changed the area's demographics rapidly and dramatically. Population swelled from 400 souls in 1900 to over 8,000 by the 1910 census. This speedy growth created a demand for goods and services for Donora's new residents. By the time the municipality was officially incorporated in 1901, groceries, general stores, pharmacies, banks, newspapers, and lumber companies were operating in the newly formed borough. Before the beginning of World War I, motorcycle and automobile dealerships had been established in town. Donora's thriving business ventures were temporarily slowed by the Great Depression, but prosperity returned after the end of World War II. However, the demise of the steel industry, coupled with changing business practices, had dire consequences for the town's economy. The closing of the zinc works in the late 1950s and the steel mill a decade later resulted in thousands of jobs losses. The subsequent decline in population meant fewer local consumers. Almost all of the neighborhood businesses eventually closed, as retailers relocated to concentrated malls.

In recent years, government officials on all levels have worked with the Donora Chamber of Commerce to bring some business and employment opportunities back into the borough. Nonetheless, it is unlikely the town will ever see the great prosperity it experienced during the peak of its industrial growth.

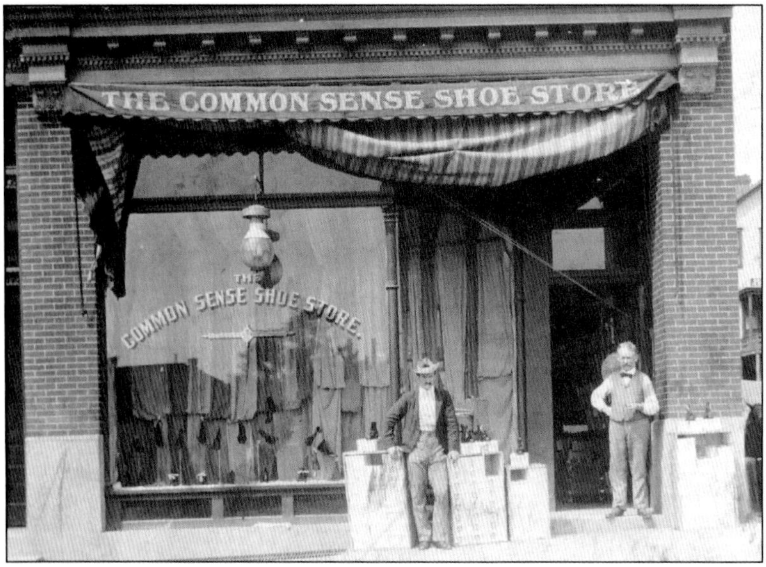

John O. Roberts (right) came to Donora in 1903, put up a building on McKean Avenue, and operated the Common Sense Shoe Store. He lost most of his money in the 1929 stock market crash, and when he died in 1931 his obituary was front-page news in the *Donora Herald-American*. (Courtesy Alice Chase Uhriniak.)

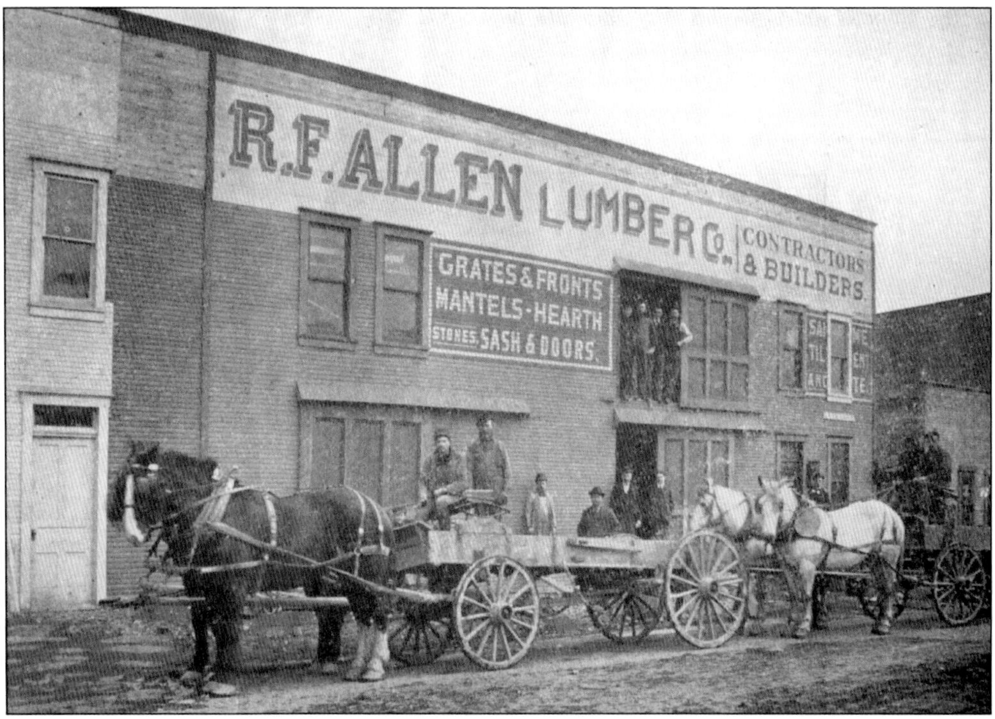

The Allen Lumber Company was founded in 1902 when brothers R. F. and George Allen purchased and expanded the Wilson Lumberyard on McKean Avenue. They were involved in the construction of the Cumberland Presbyterian Church and Methodist Episcopal Church. Allen Avenue and Allen Plan are named for the family.

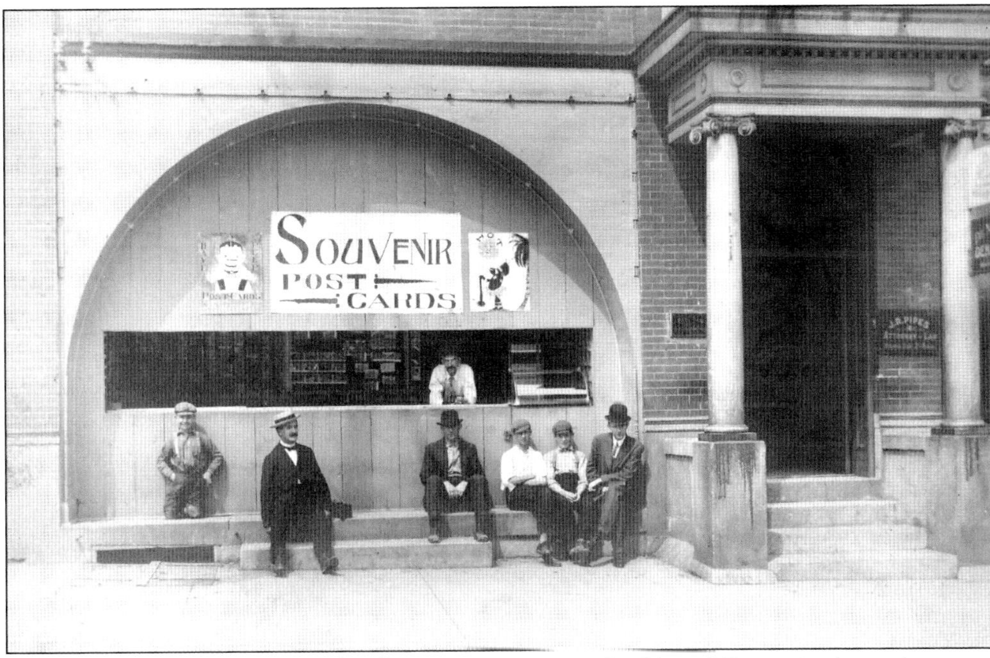

The penny postcard was a staple of communication in the United States in the early part of the 20th century. This store was conveniently located next door to the post office at the corner of Fifth Street and McKean Avenue. Before World War I, most of the cards were imported from Germany.

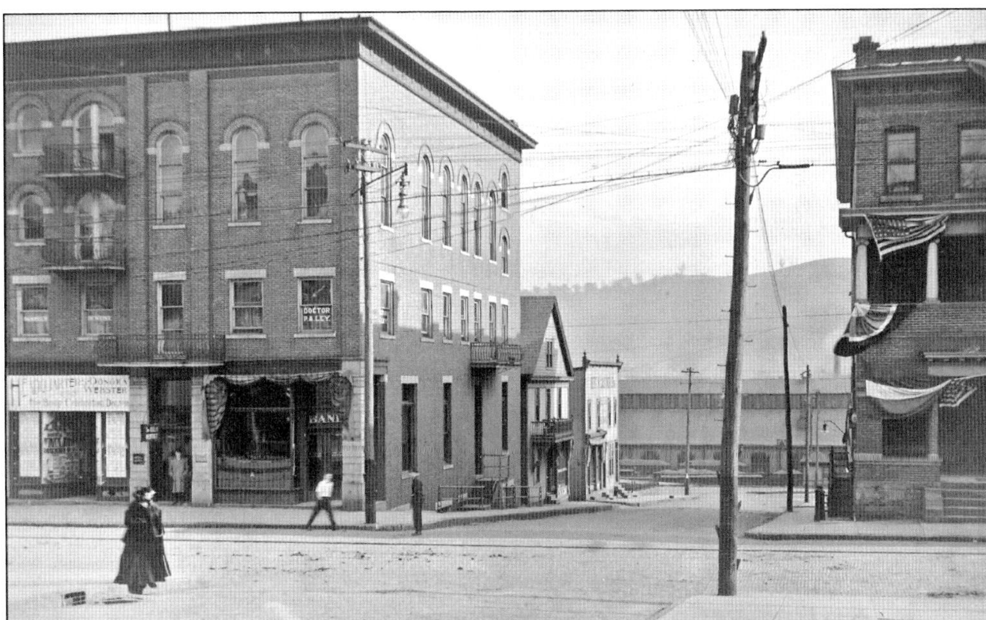

This view shows the corner of Seventh Street and McKean Avenue around 1908. The sign marks the headquarters of the Donora-Webster Bridge opening celebration. The Donora Hotel, visible on the right, is decked out for the celebration. The wire works is in the background.

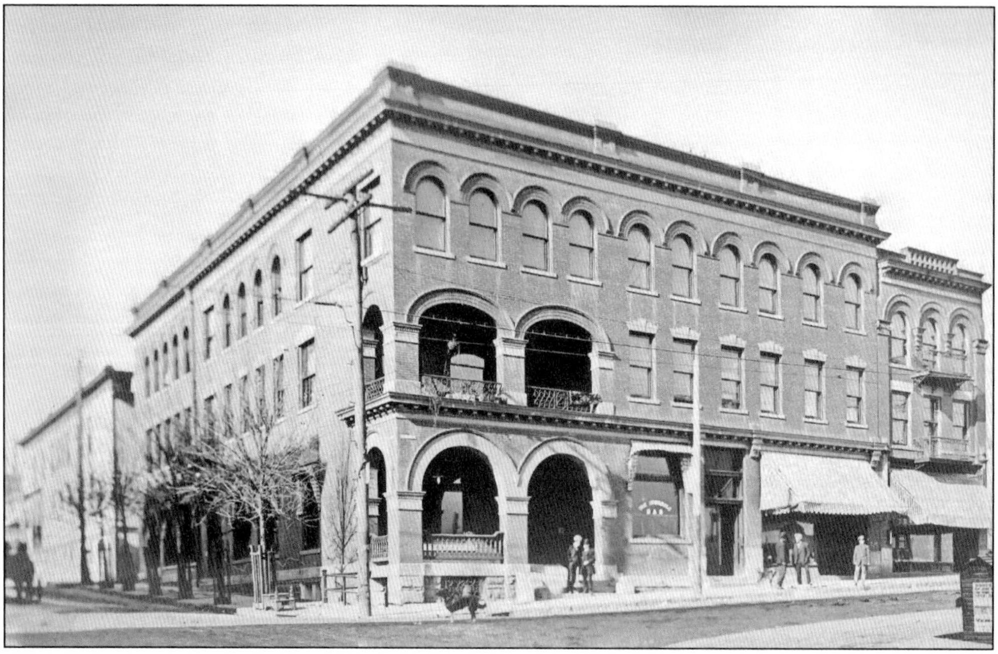

The Irondale Hotel, centrally located along McKean Avenue, provided 40 well-furnished rooms for rent, and its spacious bar was one of the popular gathering places for the town's young men. In the 1960s, the Sabin polio vaccine was distributed by doctors on the hotel's front porch. The Irondale was razed in the 1970s to make way for the construction of the Pittsburgh National Bank.

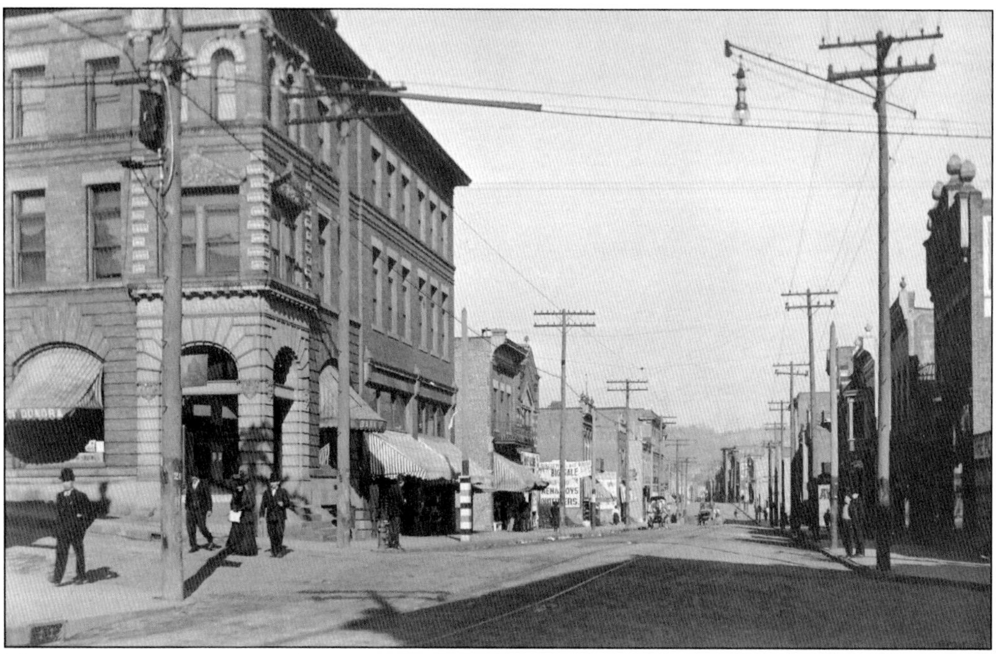

McKean Avenue, Donora's thoroughfare, was named for James McKean, an official of the Union Improvement Company. In 1900, the area was essentially undeveloped farmland. By this 1910 view, the commercial transformation of the area is obvious.

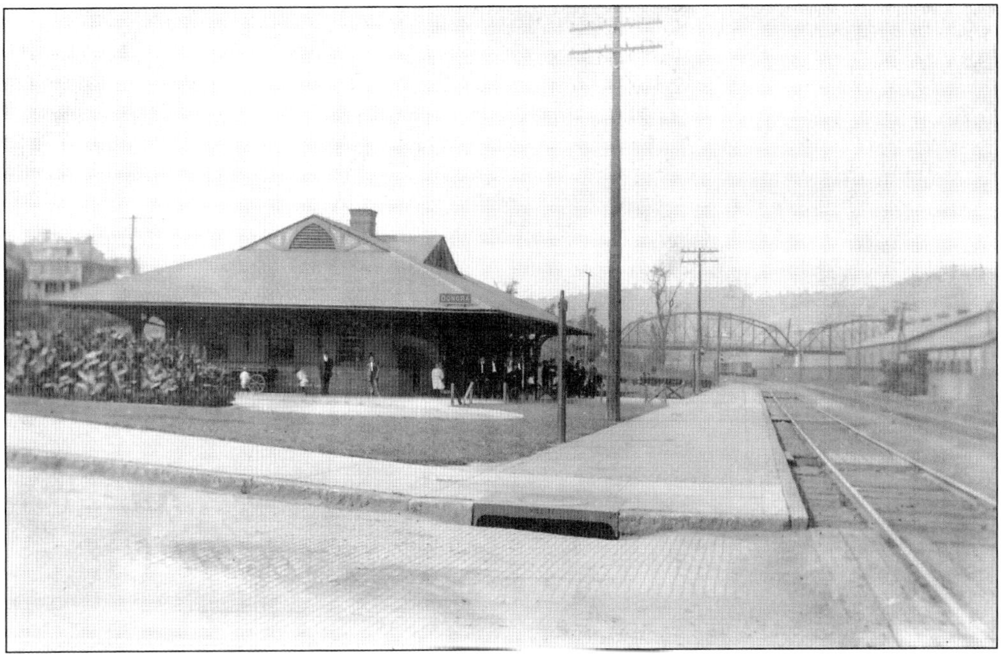

The Pennsylvania Railroad trolley car system provided a vital link between Donora, its surrounding communities, and the city of Pittsburgh. The trolley station was located along Meldon Avenue at Eighth Street. In this 1910 photograph, the newly built Donora-Webster Bridge is seen in the background.

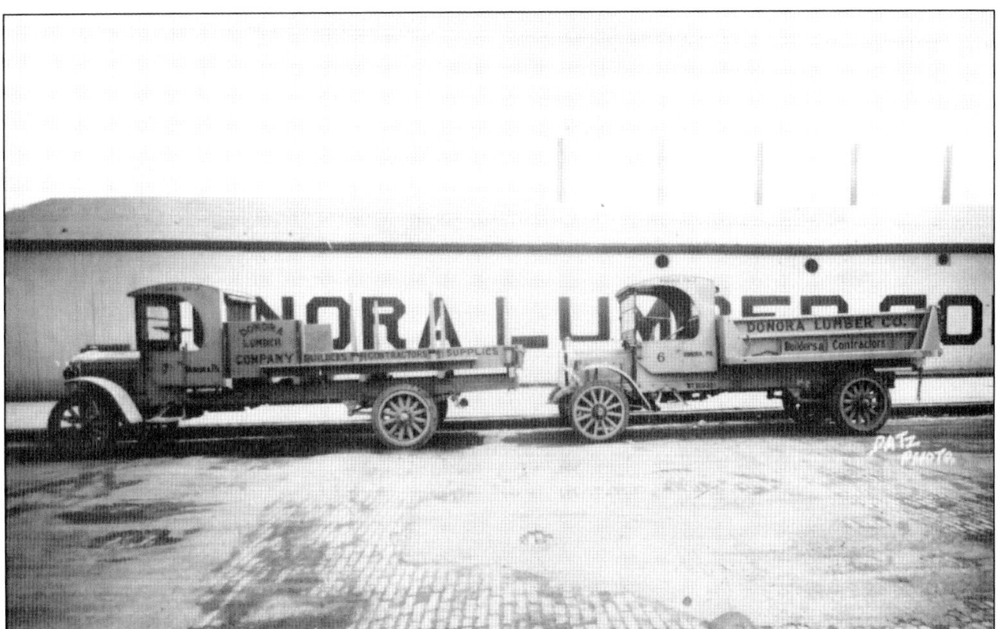

The Donora Lumber Company was one of the first businesses to open in the new town. After more than a century of providing building materials, it continues to serve the residents of the mid-Monongahela River Valley.

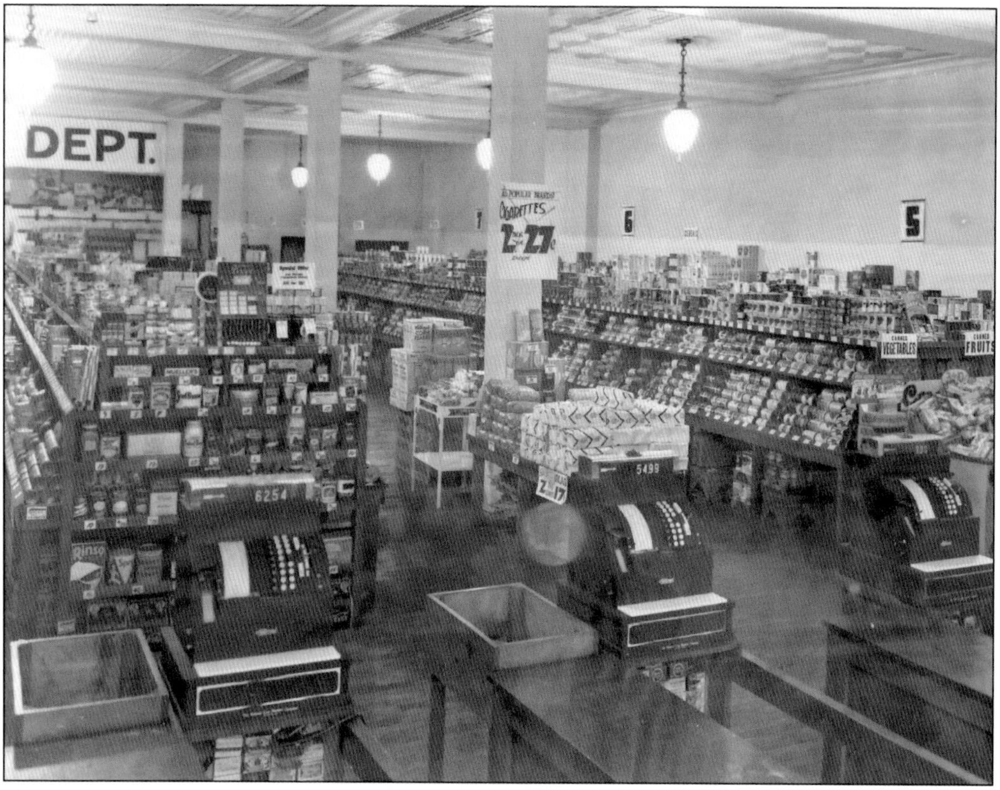

Before the age of shopping malls, the people of Donora did their grocery shopping in a number of family-owned neighborhood stores. This photograph shows one of those typical groceries in the early 1940s. Note the deal on cigarettes—two packs for 27¢.

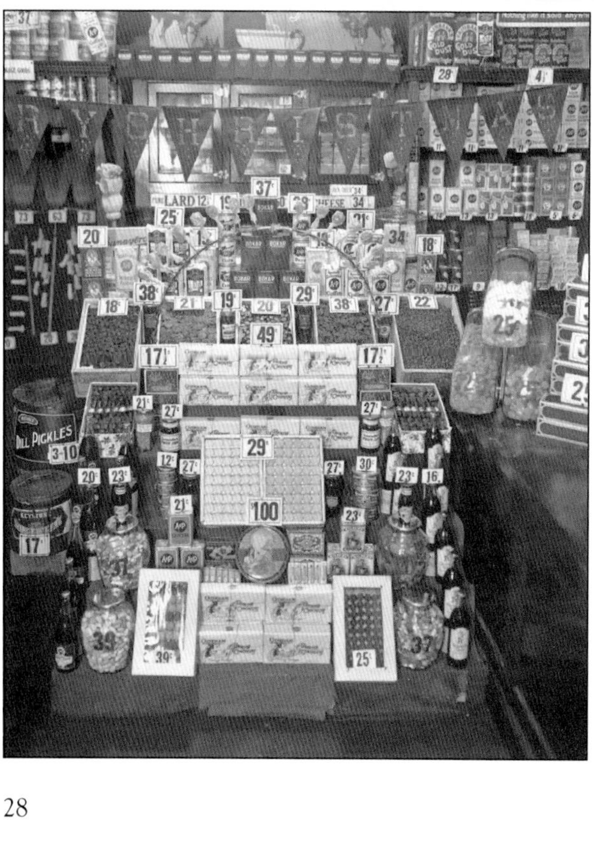

The A&P grocery, originally located between Ninth and Tenth Streets on McKean Avenue and operated by the Gamble family, was one of the first chain stores to come to Donora. The franchise was moved to the heart of the business district in the 500 block of McKean Avenue in the 1950s. Pictured here is a Christmas display of typical A&P goods around 1925.

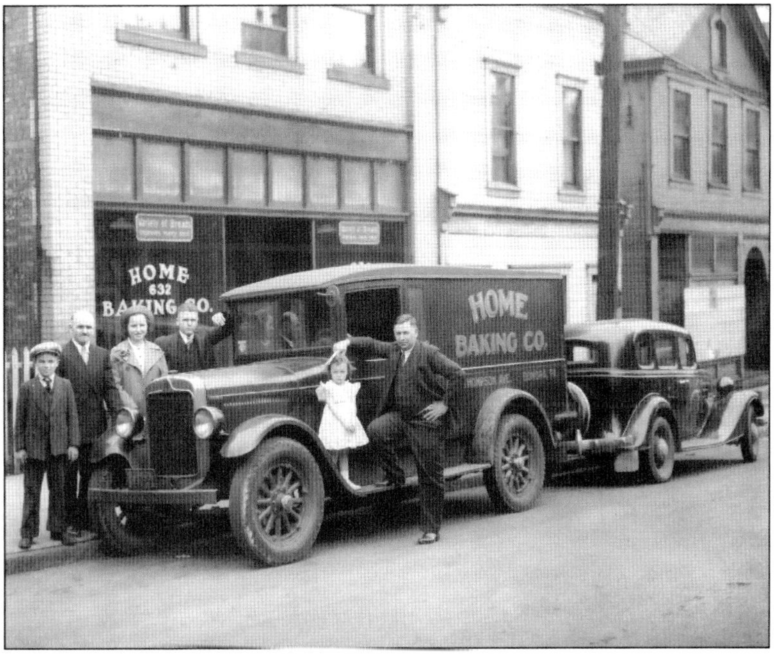

The Home Bakery Company, located on Thompson Avenue near Sixth Street, was owned and operated by Charles and Mary Guyker and Clyde and Helen Guyker Walsh. Bread, donuts, and other goods were sold on-site and also delivered. This photograph, taken around 1938, shows members of the Guyker and Walsh families in front of the store. (Courtesy Janet Walsh Olenik.)

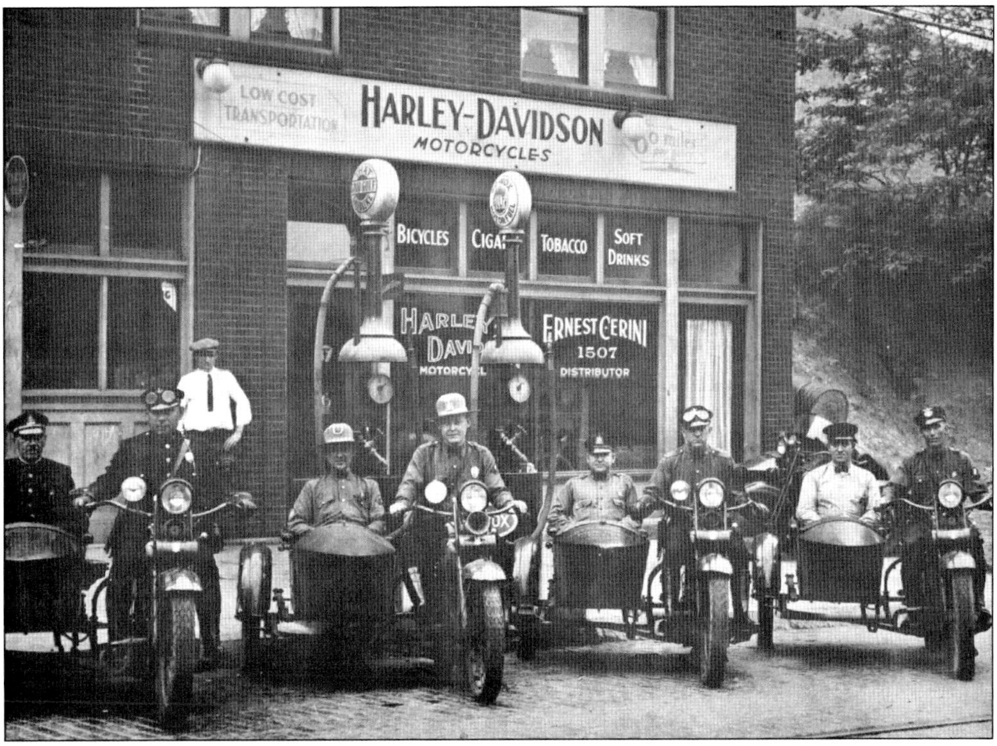

The motorcycle shop established by the Cerini family on Meldon Avenue at Fifteenth Street eventually became the oldest continuous Harley-Davidson franchise in the state. Pictured here are representatives of the Donora, Charleroi, Monessen, and Monongahela police departments, which all purchased motorcycles from the shop. After relocating to Rostraver Township, the family sold the business in 2009.

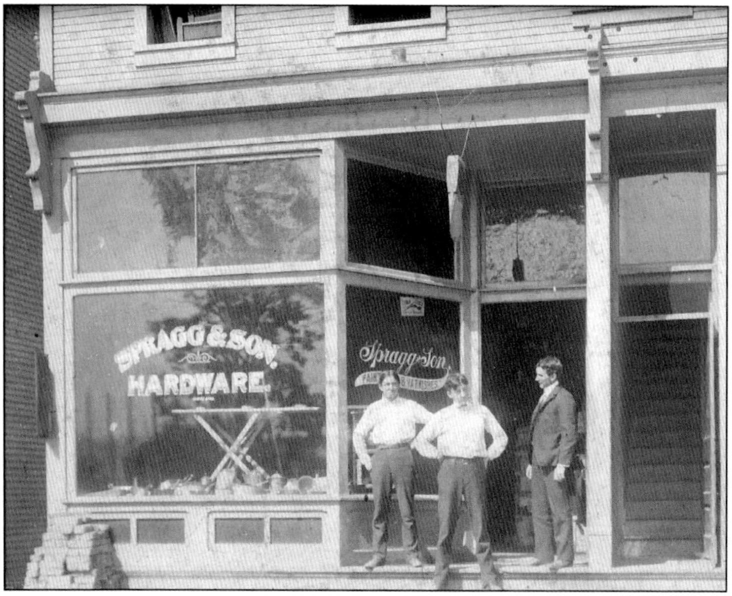

The Spragg and Son Hardware store, located at 732 McKean Avenue, was one of the first commercial structures in town when it opened in 1902. Owner Walter Spragg was active in community affairs. He organized the town's first baseball team, served as the first treasurer of the volunteer fire company, was an officer in the chamber of commerce, and lead the drive to build Donner Park.

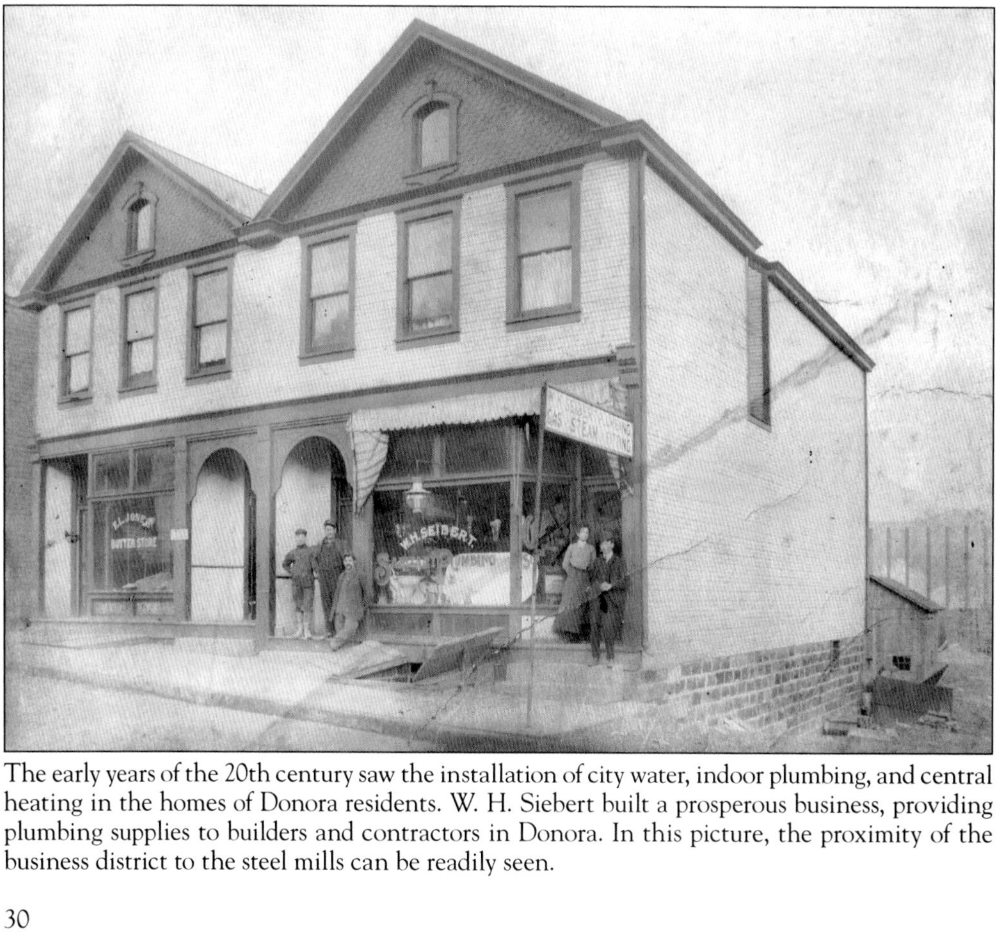

The early years of the 20th century saw the installation of city water, indoor plumbing, and central heating in the homes of Donora residents. W. H. Siebert built a prosperous business, providing plumbing supplies to builders and contractors in Donora. In this picture, the proximity of the business district to the steel mills can be readily seen.

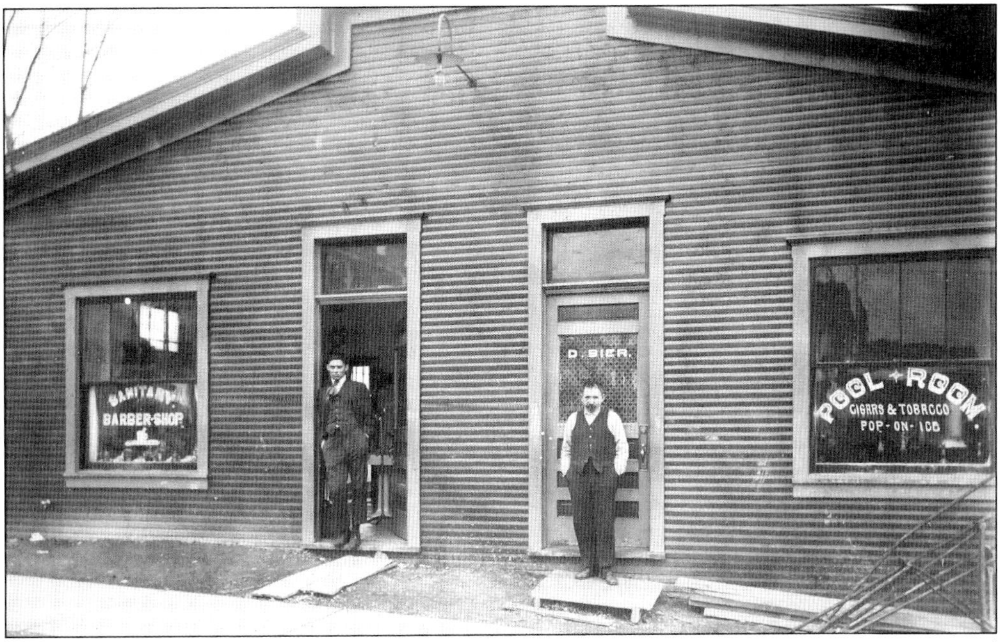

David Bier (right), a prominent member of Donora's Jewish community, was an energetic and creative businessman. In addition to the pool hall and barbershop operated in the building shown here, he also owned a grocery store.

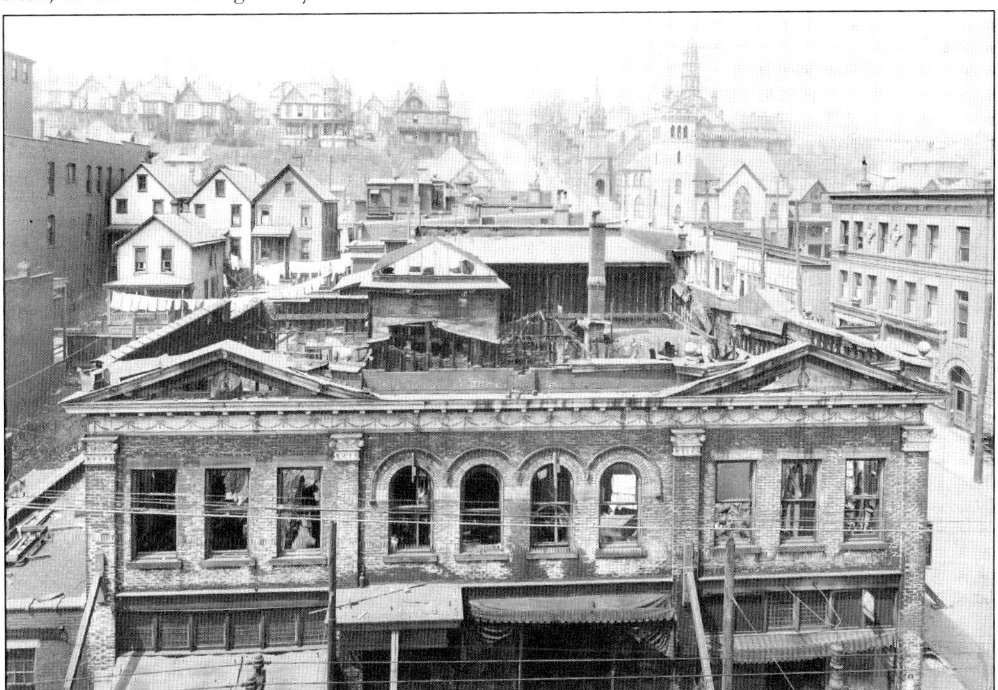
On April 17, 1917, the "worst fire in the history of Donora" did $60,000 in damage and destroyed the post office, six apartments, two doctors' offices, two law offices, a dentist office, and a postcard store. This view along Thompson Avenue shows the post office building in front as well as the St. Michael parish, the St. Joseph Roman Catholic Church, and the Methodist church.

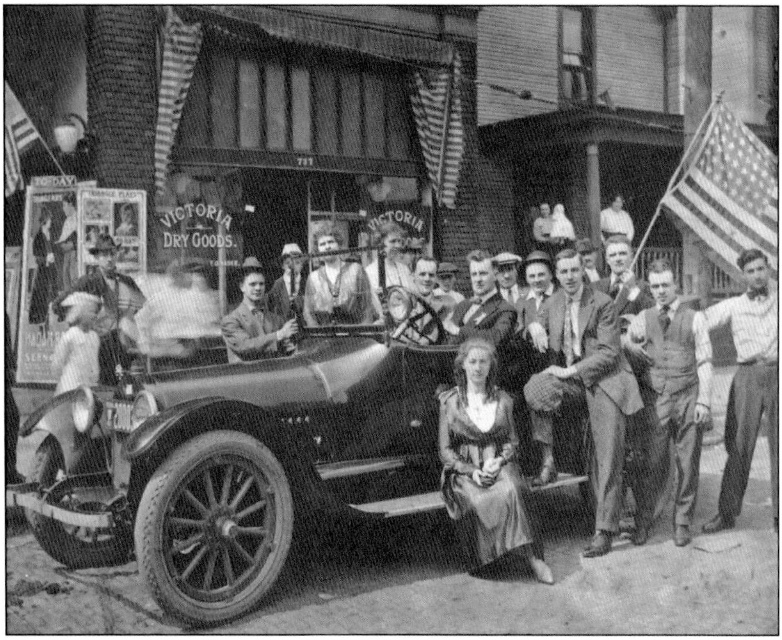

The Victoria Dry Goods Store in the background of this picture was located on McKean Avenue next to the Liberty Theater. The large car and formal dress of the people in the picture indicates this was a gathering of the town's more affluent residents.

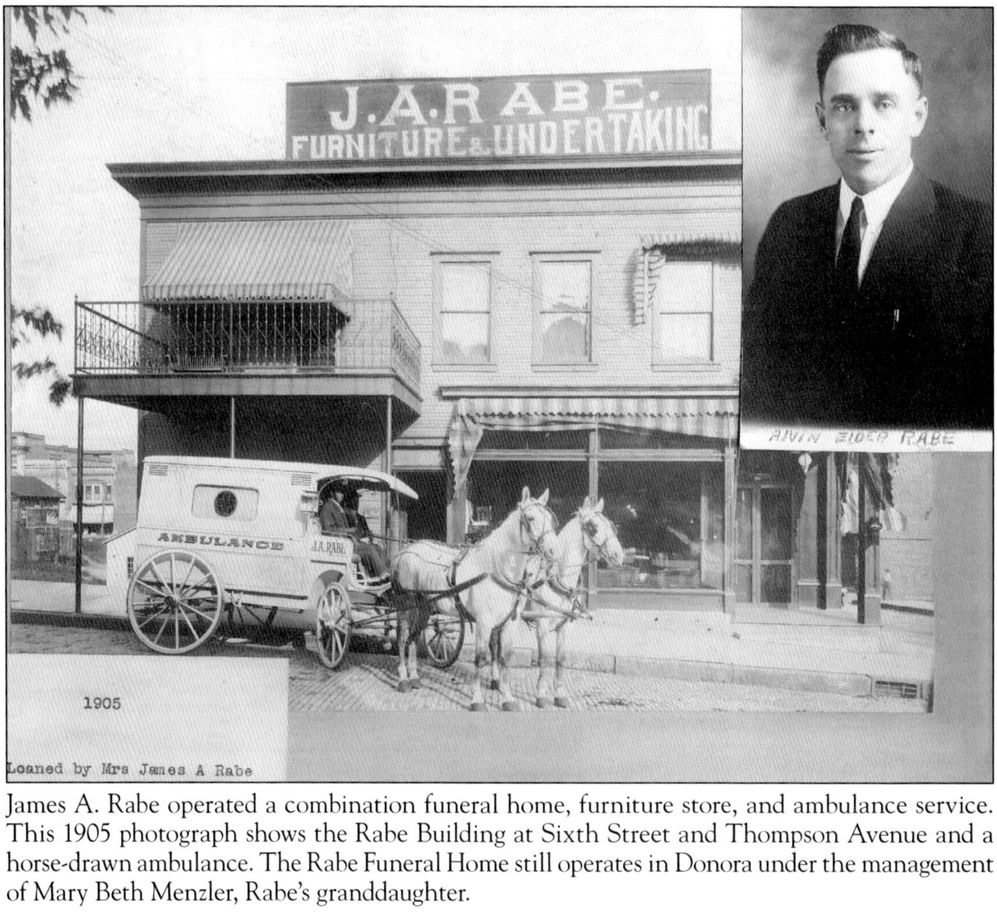

James A. Rabe operated a combination funeral home, furniture store, and ambulance service. This 1905 photograph shows the Rabe Building at Sixth Street and Thompson Avenue and a horse-drawn ambulance. The Rabe Funeral Home still operates in Donora under the management of Mary Beth Menzler, Rabe's granddaughter.

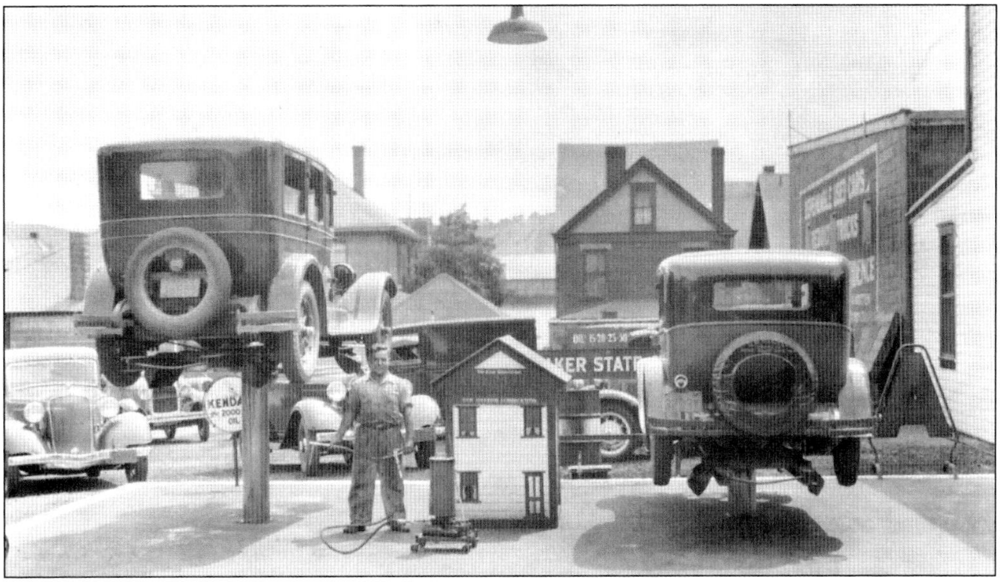

Ross Ridgely opened what is believed to be the first Dodge-Plymouth dealership in Pennsylvania on Ninth Street and McKean Avenue in 1923. Oil changes were performed in the service station next to the family home. Like many other businesses, it fell victim to the economic decline of the 1950s and 1960s.

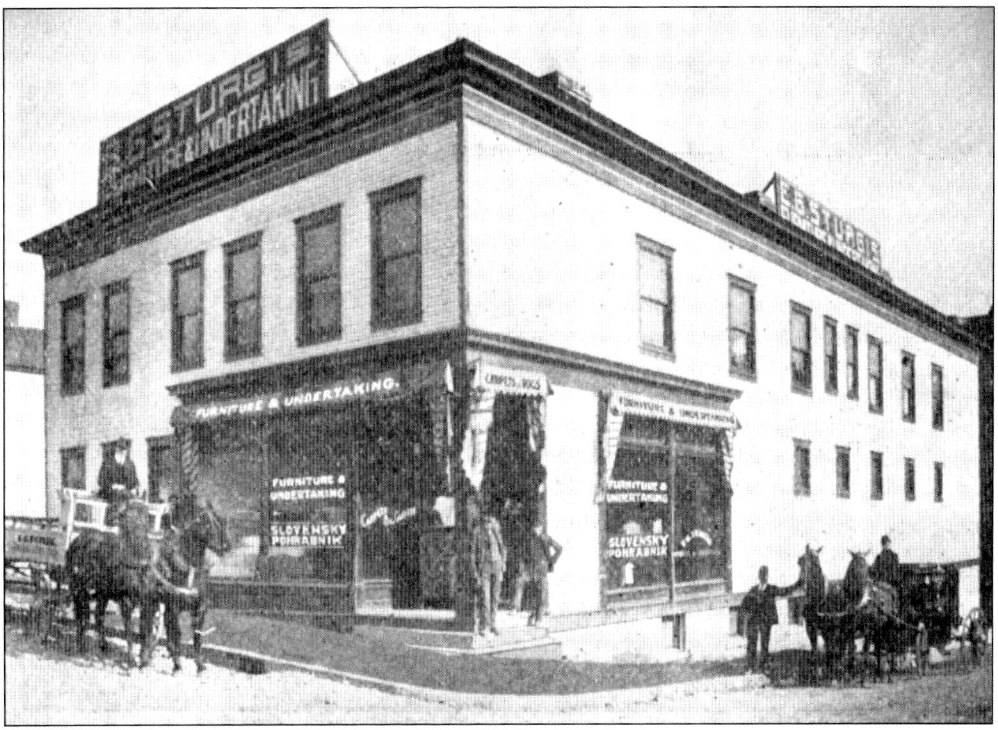

The strong ethnic identities of Donora residents were reflected in the choice of funeral parlors. Pictured here at Sixth Street and Thompson Avenue is the Sturgis Funeral Home and Furniture Store, a common combination of services at the dawn of the 20th century. The Sturgis clientele was largely Slovak, as evidenced by the sign, which translates to "Slovak undertaker."

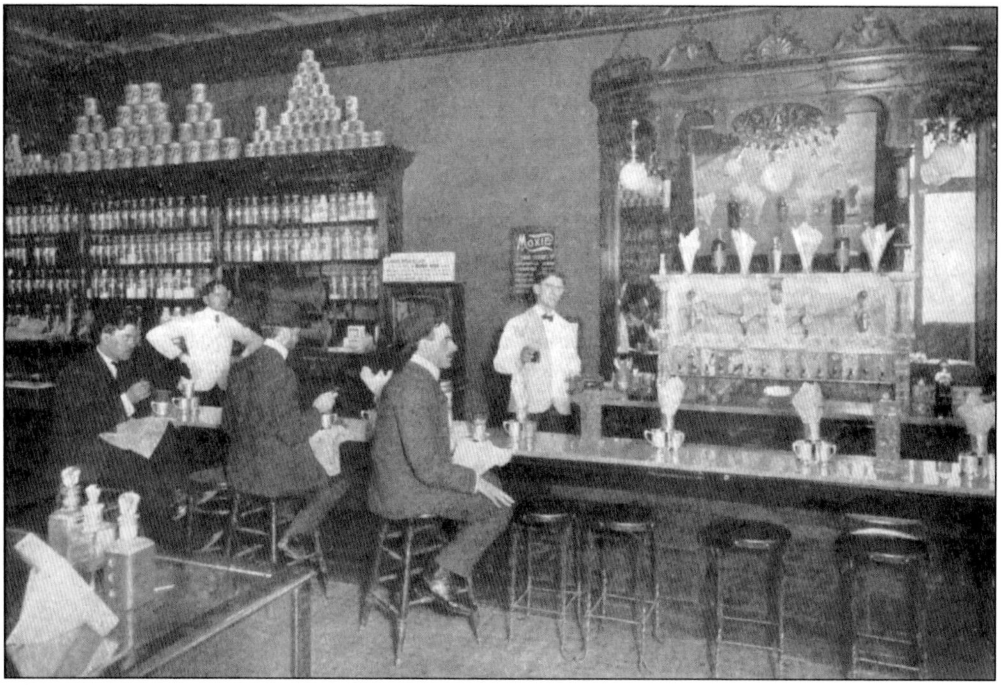

The Corner Drug Store was typical of such establishments in Donora, and was a combination pharmacy, lunchroom, and meeting place. F. W. Allison and Harry B. Wiley, graduates of the Medico-Chirurgical College of Philadelphia, were partners in the business.

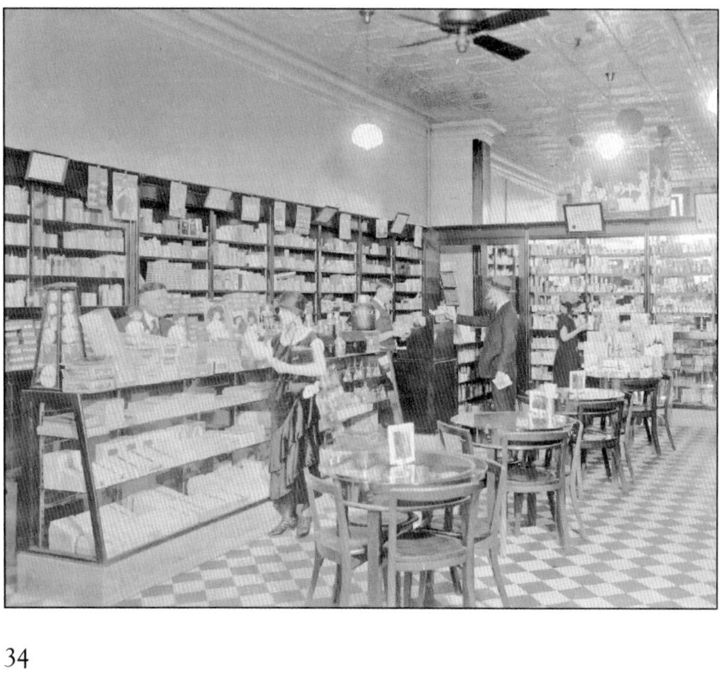

The Union Pharmacy, owned by James Carter, Lewis Tomer, and John Culbert, found a permanent home in the First National Bank Building at Sixth Street and McKean Avenue. The pharmacy filled prescriptions, sold over-the-counter drugs, handled a fine line of ladies toiletries and choice confections, and was the primary agent for Eastman Kodak products. The business was eventually sold and became Zubrick's Pharmacy.

Donora had an exceptional number of automobile dealerships. An unsubstantiated belief held by many residents was that the town had the highest per capita car ownership in the country. Bindi Brothers dealership and service station was located at Eighth Street and Meldon Avenue. Even in prosperous times, the business sold more Pontiacs than Cadillacs.

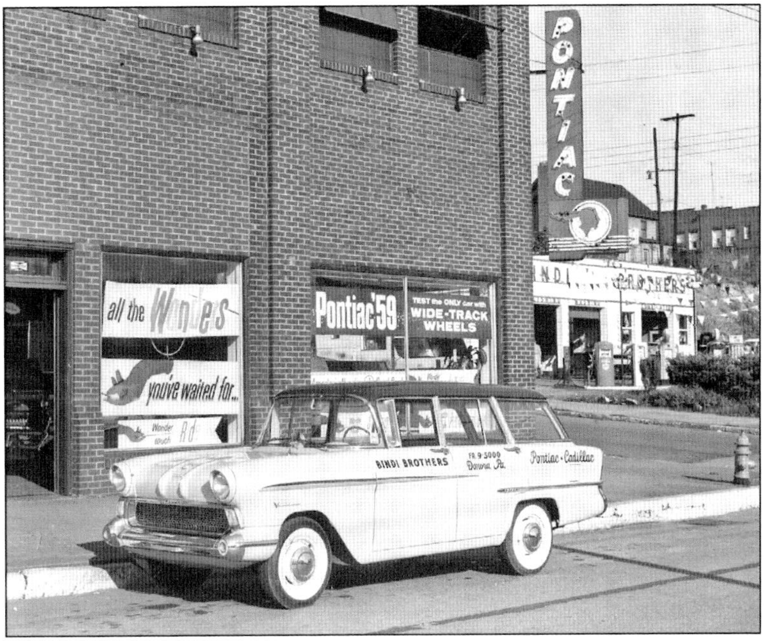

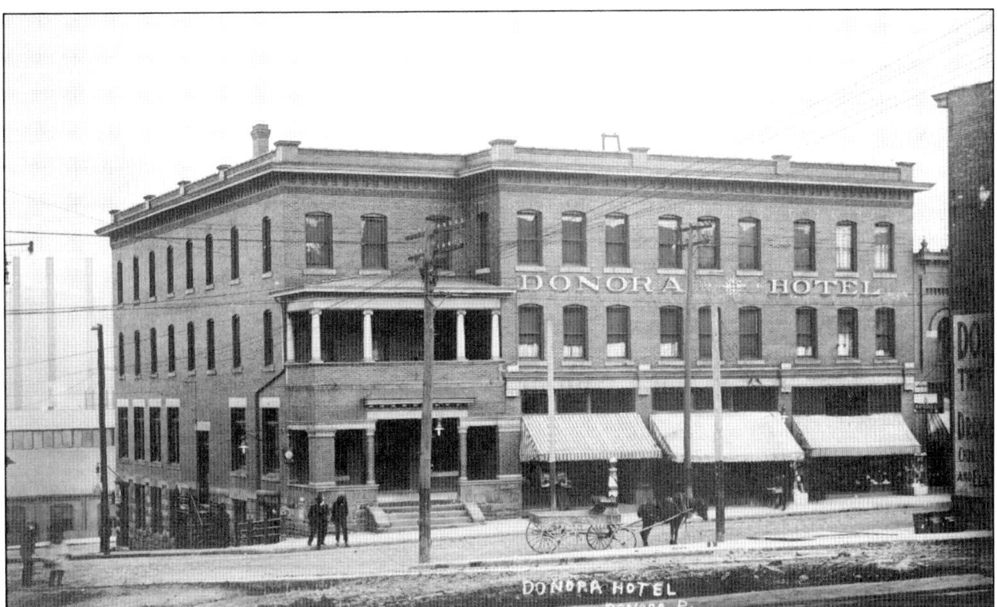

The Donora Hotel, located at the corner of Seventh Street and McKean Avenue, was one of several landmark hotels in early Donora. This photograph shows the close proximity of the hotel to the mill, making it convenient for workers caught in the housing shortage. Over the years, the hotel housed not only people but also the public library, the community center, and a temporary morgue during the 1948 smog disaster.

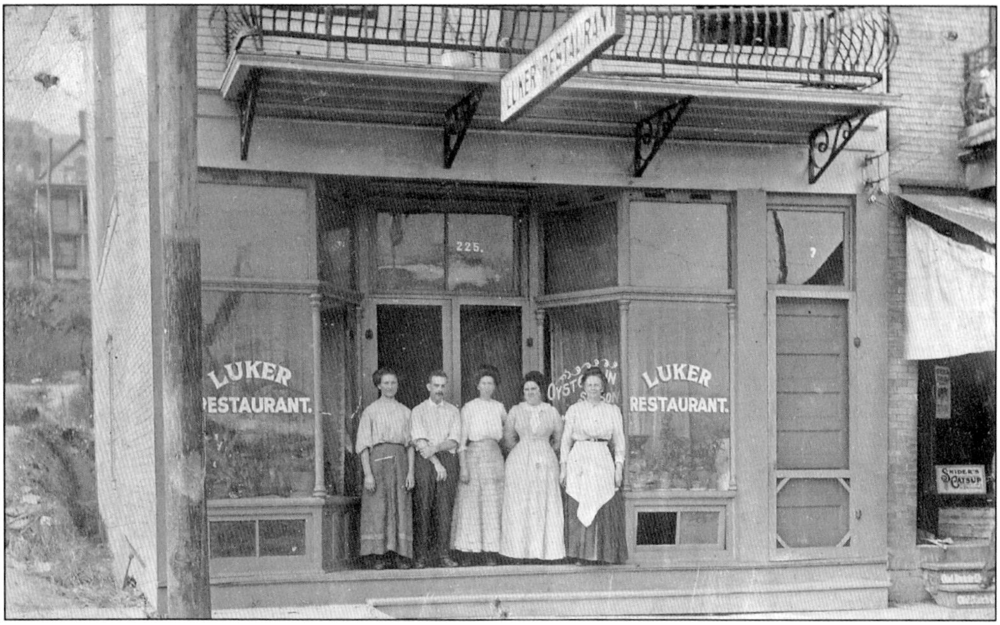

Restaurants proliferated in the town to serve the large number of bachelor steelworkers. The Luker Restaurant, pictured here, was one of Donora's many eating establishments. The interior view below shows the table seating and lunch counter. The linen tablecloths and aprons suggest an attempt to convey a sense of elegance. The establishment also sold baked goods, canned foods, and greeting cards. The exterior image above depicts the neatly attired Luker family and their restaurant staff standing at the entrance of the building.

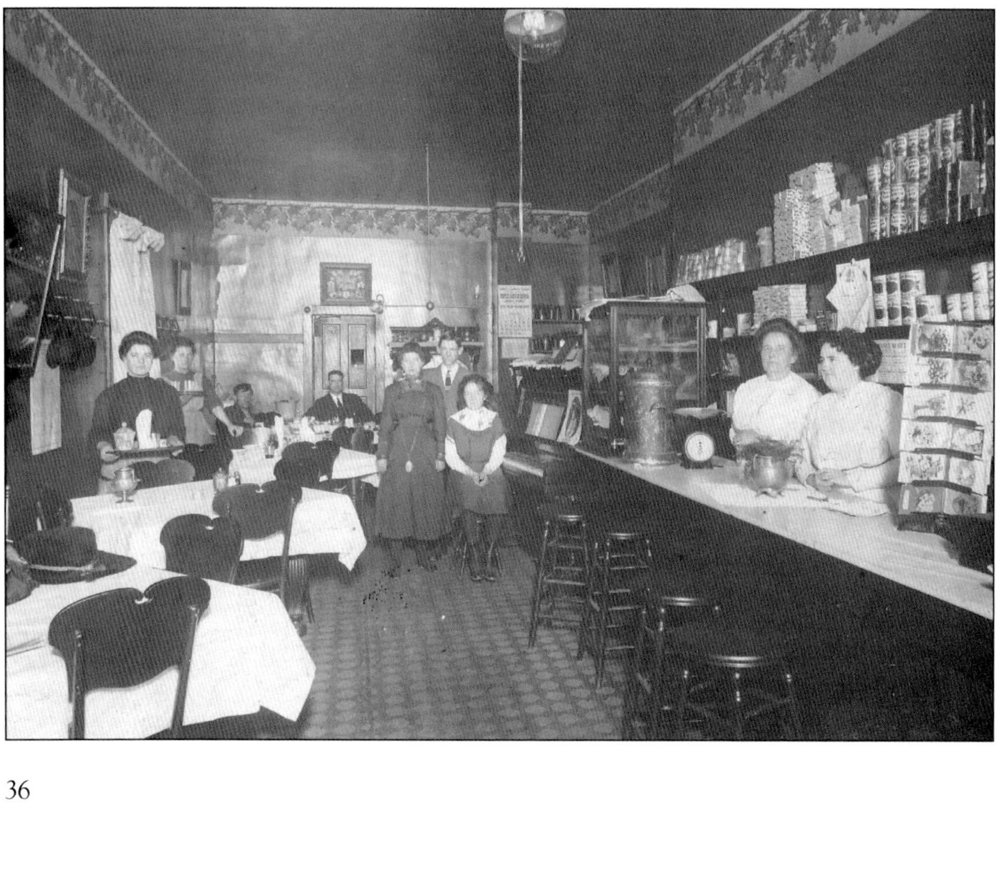

Three

Gathering Together

Donora's ethnic, racial, and religious diversity led to the creation of a considerable number of social clubs and service organizations. The population boom that followed the building of the steel mill and the incorporation of the borough brought a variety of new residents into the town. Many of these were European immigrants who tended to worship and socialize with people of similar backgrounds. As a result, a plethora of organizations affiliated with churches and dedicated to the preservation of ethnic identity were formed. Later, youth organizations that crossed ethnic and religious lines, such as the Boy Scouts, Girl Scouts, and the Boys Brigade, were created to enhance the physical and moral development of the town's young people. A few service organizations, usually made up of mill managers and businessmen, were founded to encourage community improvement.

Since the decline of the borough's economic and population base, many of these historic associations have ceased to exist. Nonetheless, Donora residents still enjoy the benefits of the work of a significant number of civic and social organizations.

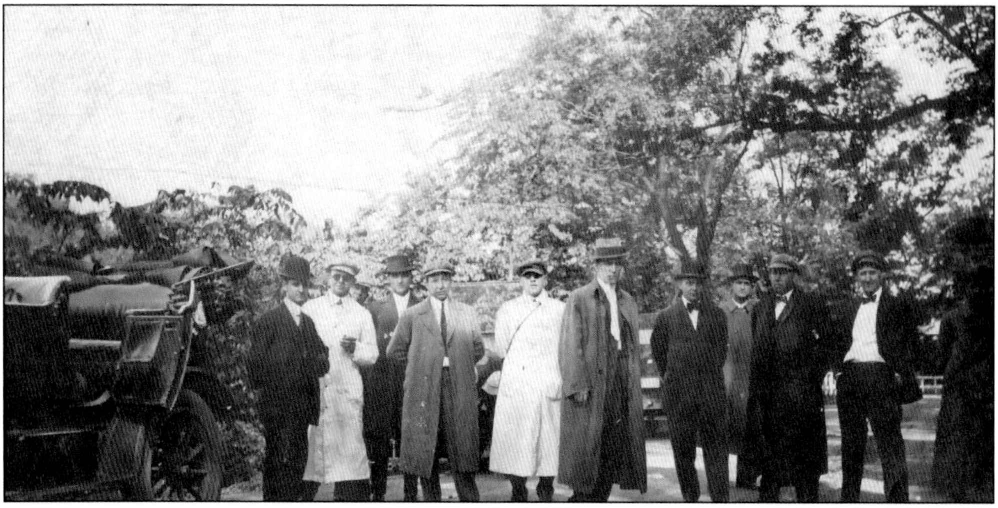

Some of Donora's more affluent citizens spent their Sunday afternoons enjoying an automobile tour. Several drivers formed a caravan and traveled throughout western Pennsylvania, admiring the scenery and visiting places of interest. The large roadster on the left illustrates the luxurious cars that often made up the caravans.

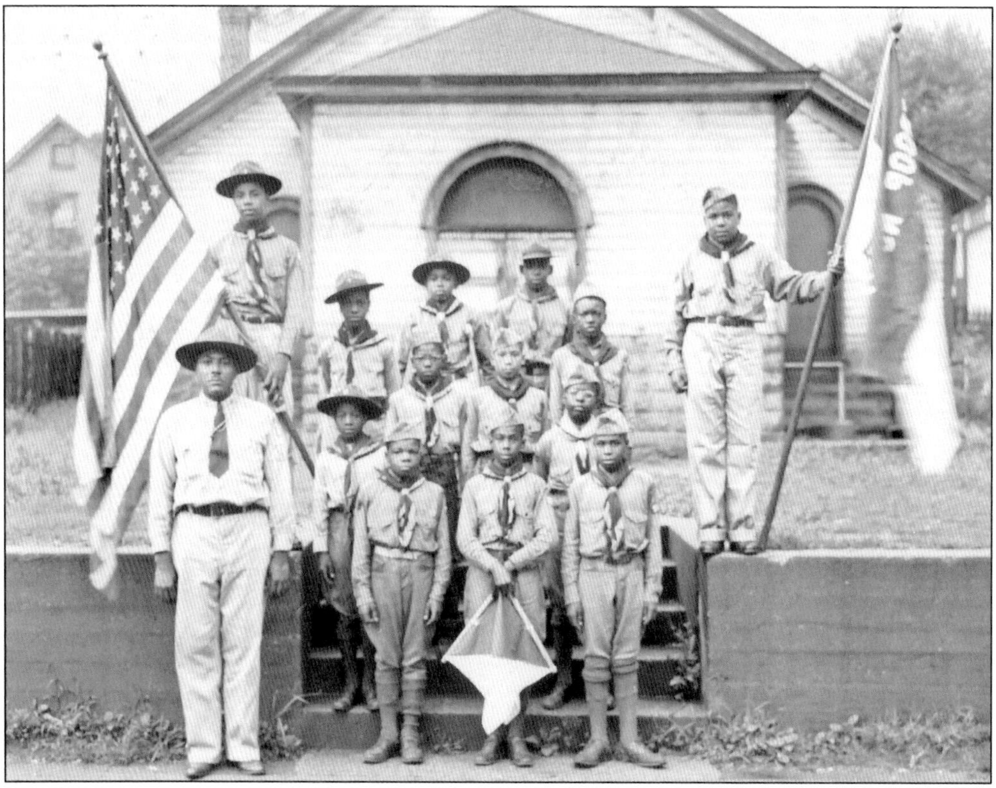

Boy Scout troops were among the more prominent youth groups in town and were affiliated with various churches of the community. Here is a 1940 picture of a group of African American Scouts proudly displaying the flags of their troop and their country in front of the "Colored" Baptist Church on Allen Avenue.

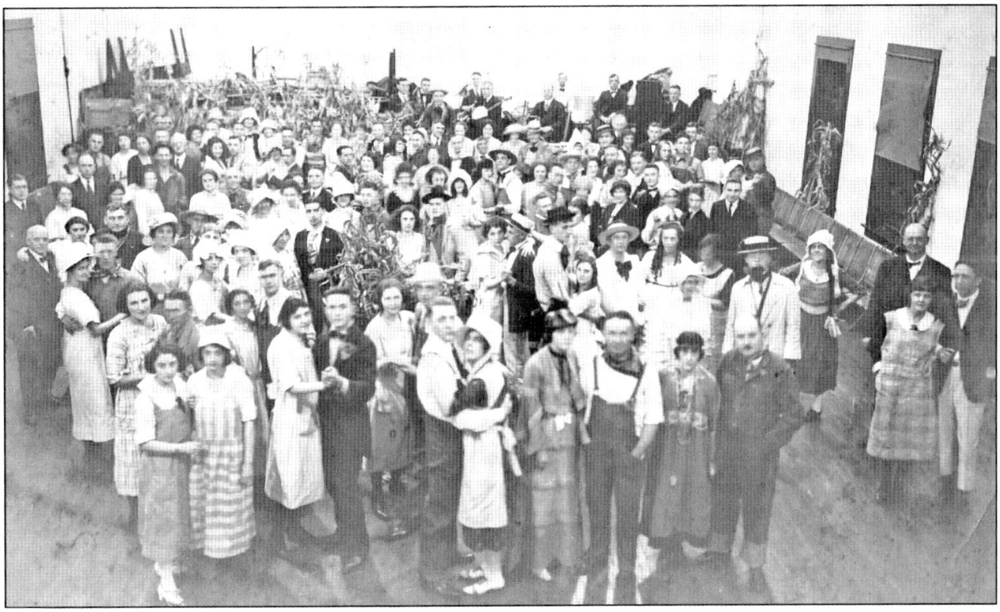

The Americo Club was an organization formed by the American Steel and Wire Company and was made up of higher-ranking mill employees. One of the yearly events of the club was known as the "Hick Dance," where attendees were encouraged to dress in rural costumes. Such events were precursors of the Sadie Hawkins Day dances. This is a photograph of a 1923 Hick Dance held in Donora.

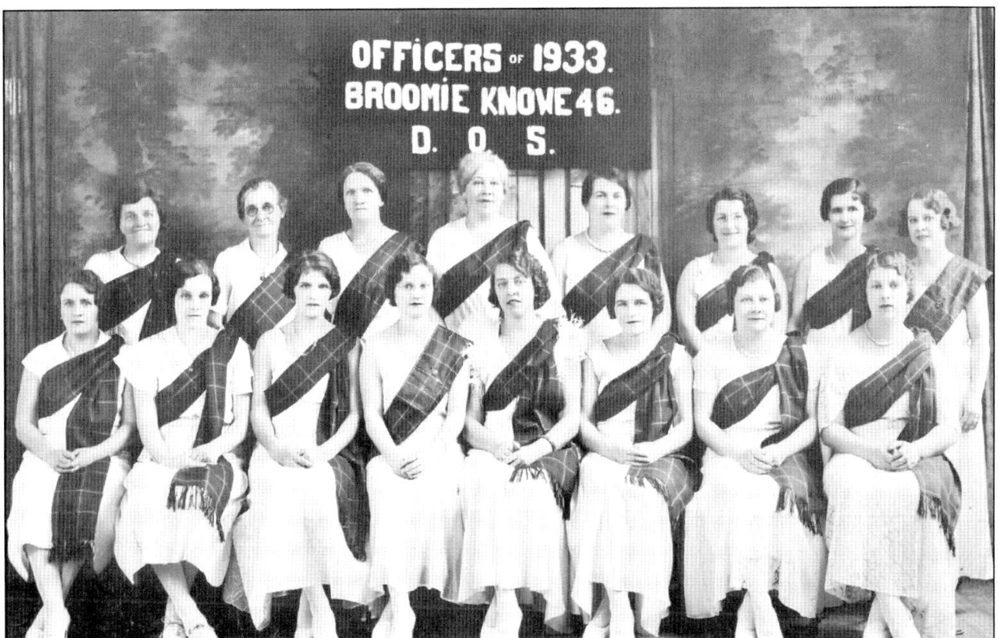

There were a large number of Scots in early Donora. The men had come to the area as coal miners and machinists in the steel mills. The men organized the Clan Grant, and the women formed the Broomie Knowe lodge of the Daughters of Scotia. In this 1933 photograph, the lassies pose proudly.

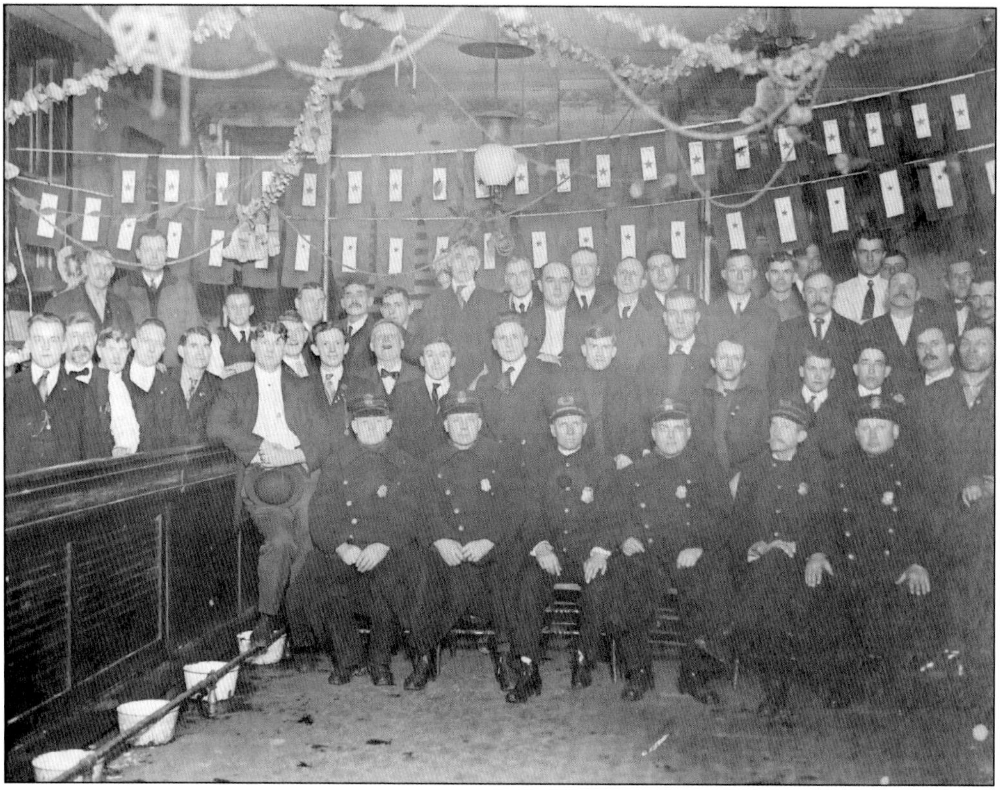

In this 1920 photograph, the German Political and Beneficial Union celebrates Christmas. Such clubs provided socialization opportunities as well as low-cost insurance to its members. Note the uniformed members that include borough and mill police and the spittoons on the floor. (Courtesy Adrian Huebner.)

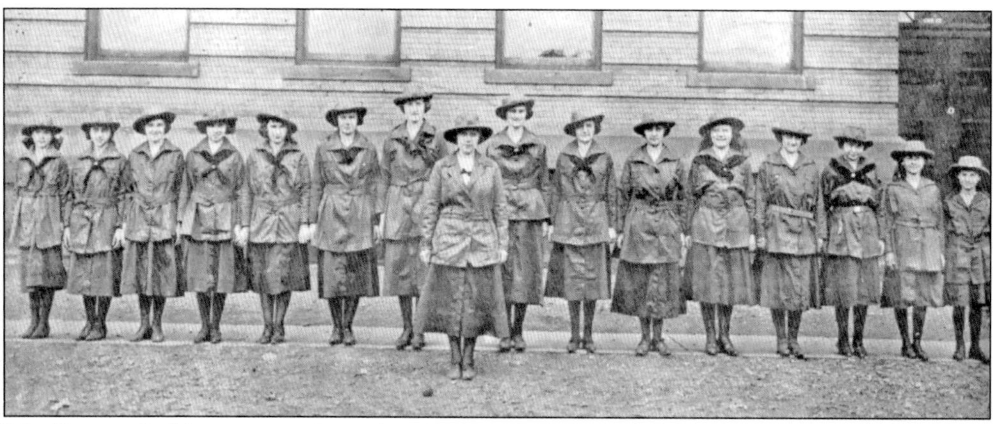

The Donora Girl Scouts were formed in 1920 in response to the success of the town's Boy Scout troops. Within a year, the Girl Scouts had eight troops and 160 members in town. Viola Cox (front, center) was a teacher in the Donora Public schools who resigned to take on the job of local director for the Girl Scouts.

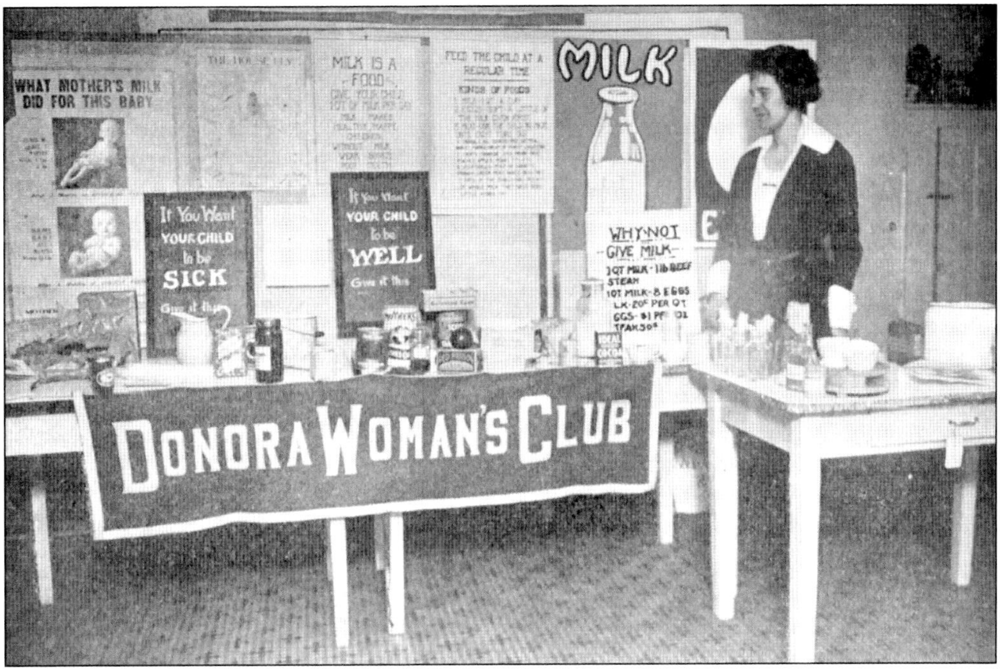

The Donora Woman's Club was originally founded to educate new mothers in the art of child rearing. Emphasis was placed on good nutrition, cleanliness, and vaccinations. The club members enlisted the aid of local nurses and doctors in their projects. These pictures were taken at the club's baby clinic in 1921.

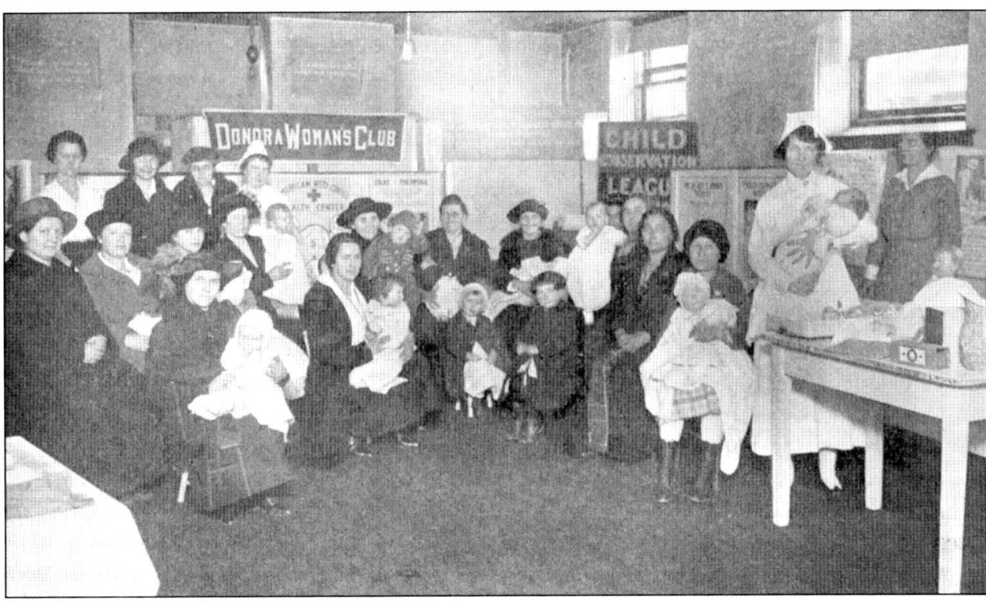

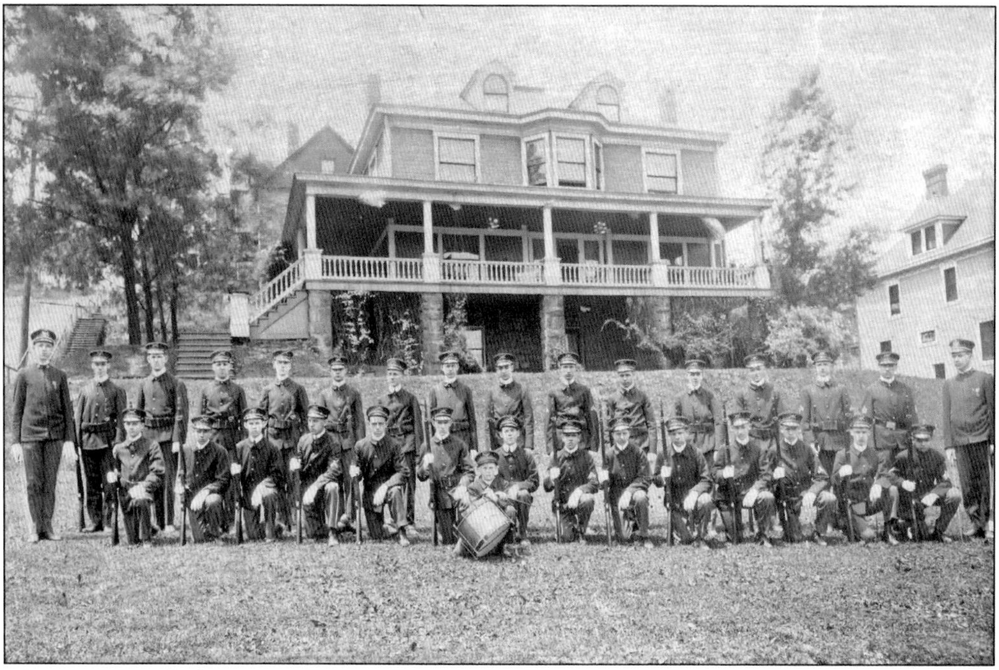

The Boys Brigade from St. John Episcopal Church is shown in this 1912 photograph taken from Thompson Avenue between Seventh and Eighth Streets. Harrison Iiams, who served with the Army Corps of Engineers in France during World War I, is third from the left in the second row.

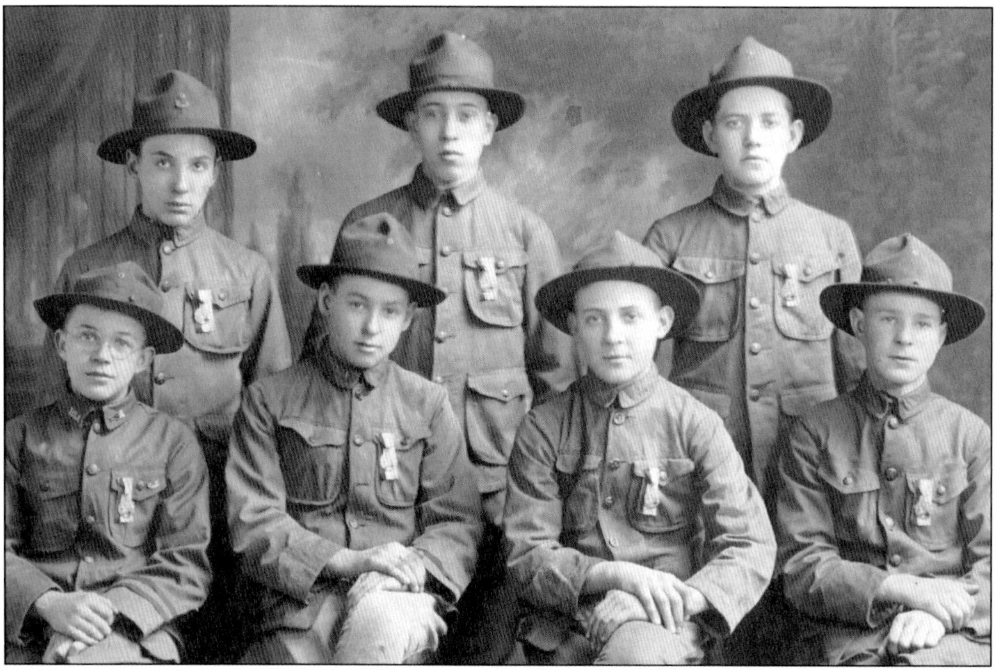

A devastating influenza epidemic impacted nearly every corner of the globe in the years following World War I. Pictured is the Donora Boy Scout Troop I with their medals for meritorious conduct during this crisis. Members are, from left to right, (first row) Sam Wichterman, J. Albert Watkins, Herbert Smith, and Wesley Cox; (second row) James Tierney, Harold Brown, and Fred Hartstein.

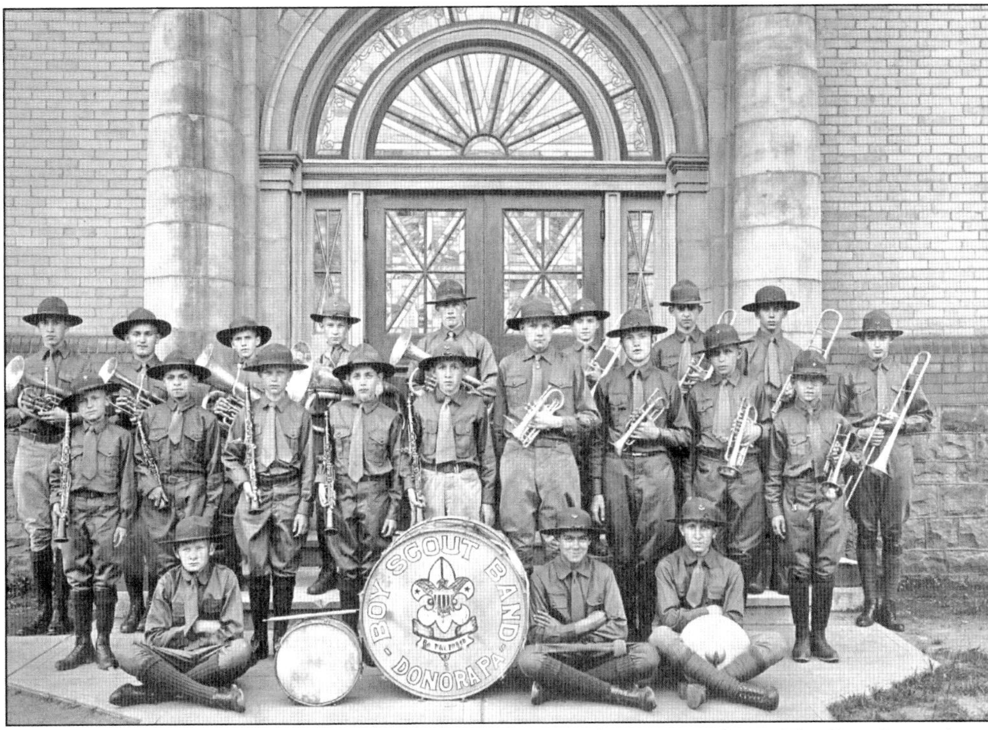

By 1920, Donora had seven Boy Scout troops with nearly 700 members. The Boy Scout band traveled to parades, jamborees, and conferences with other bands.

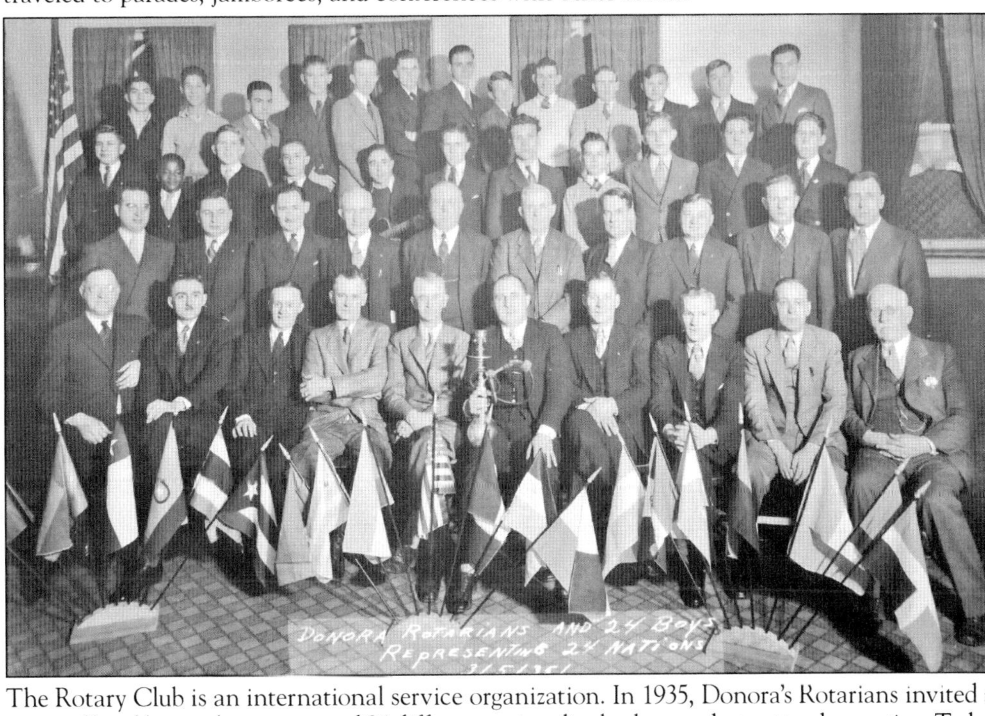

The Rotary Club is an international service organization. In 1935, Donora's Rotarians invited a group of local boys, who represented 24 different nationality backgrounds, to attend a meeting. Today Donora's Rotary Club is part of an international effort to eliminate polio from the world.

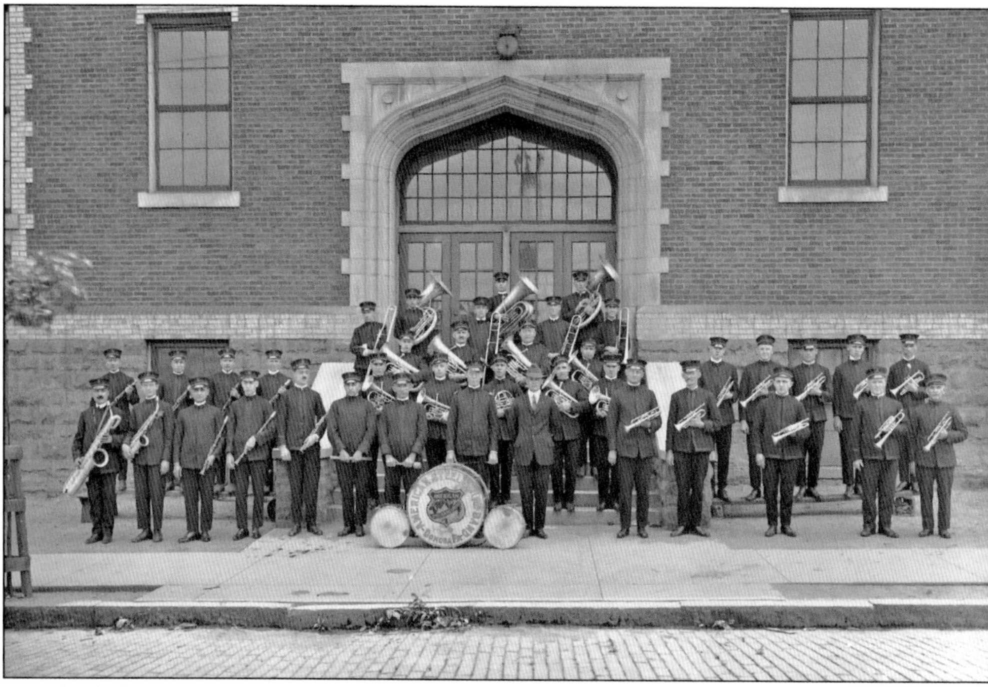

Everybody loves a parade. This is especially true of the people of Donora, who turn out in great numbers for parades on all occasions and holidays. In the community's early years, the American Steel and Wire Company sponsored a marching and concert band. Here is a picture of the group, instruments in hand, standing in front of the First Street School.

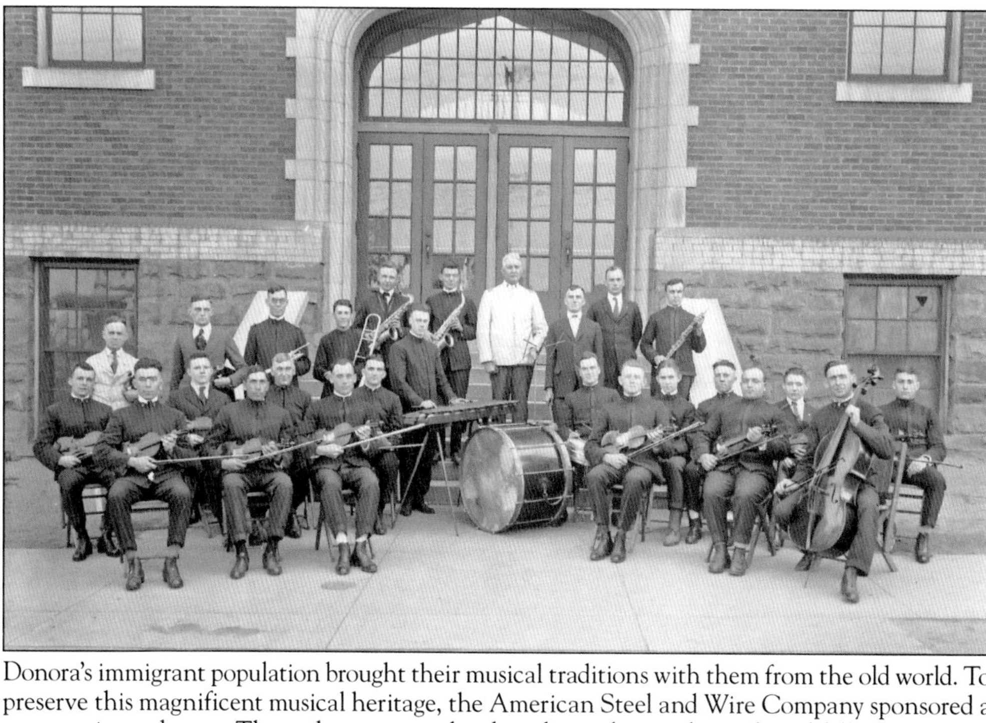

Donora's immigrant population brought their musical traditions with them from the old world. To preserve this magnificent musical heritage, the American Steel and Wire Company sponsored a community orchestra. The orchestra specialized in classical, semiclassical, and folk music.

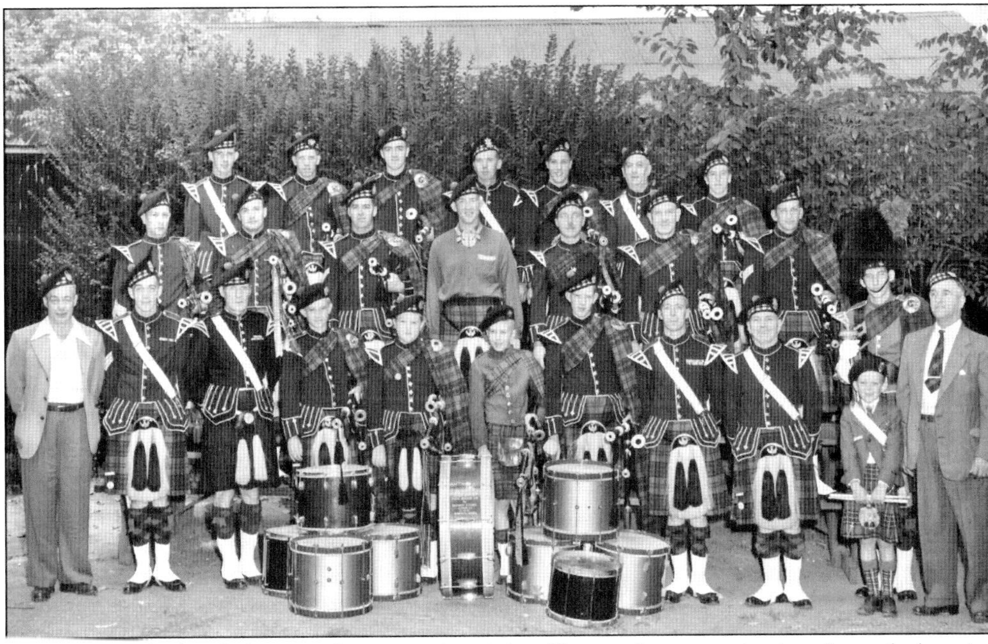

Clan Grant, the local chapter of a national social and benevolent organization, formed a bagpipe band in the years after World War II. The band played in concerts and parades throughout western Pennsylvania. The closing of the mills forced many band members to leave Donora to find employment. This led to the eventual demise of this unique community organization.

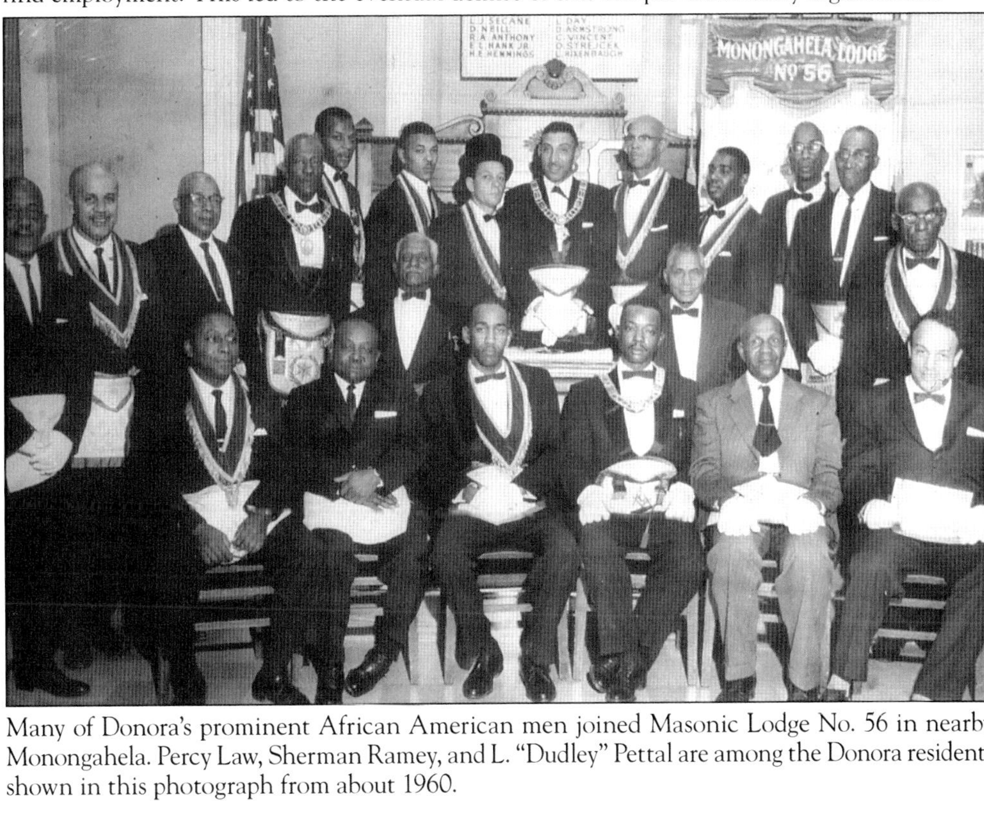

Many of Donora's prominent African American men joined Masonic Lodge No. 56 in nearby Monongahela. Percy Law, Sherman Ramey, and L. "Dudley" Pettal are among the Donora residents shown in this photograph from about 1960.

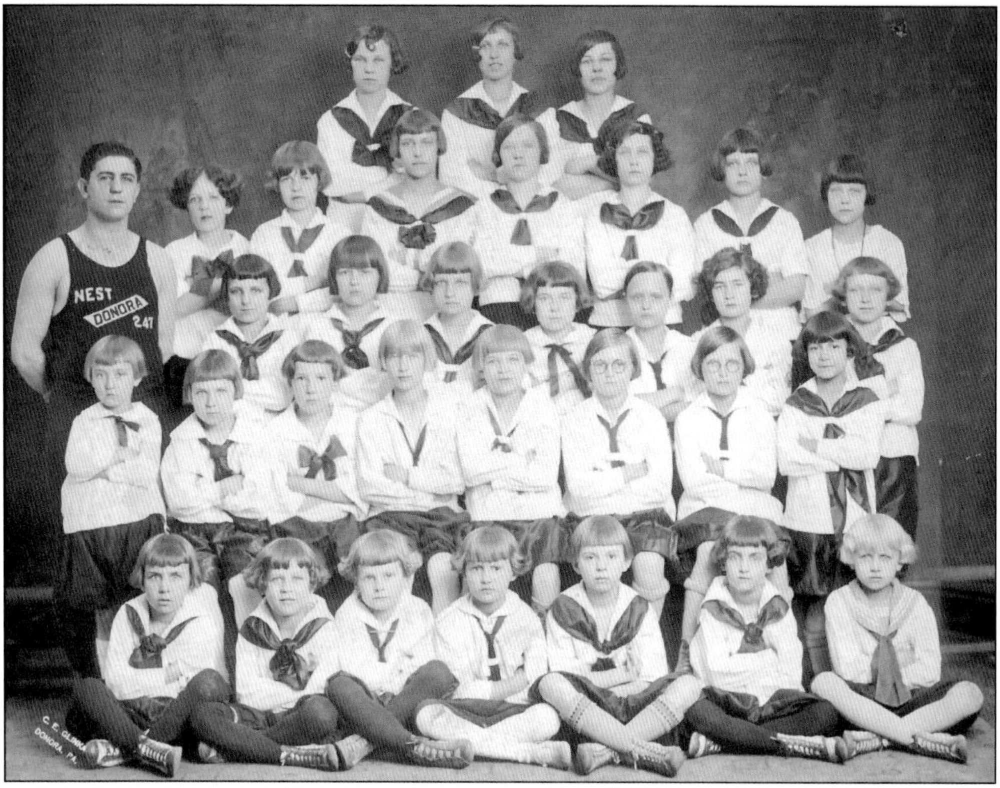

Gymnastics training was a historic part of the physical development regimen of young people in southern and eastern Europe. Many of Donora's ethnic clubs continued this tradition by providing boys and girls with the opportunity to train for and compete in gymnastic competitions. Pictured here is a girls' gymnastic team sponsored by Donora Polish Falcons Nest 247. The date of the photograph is unknown.

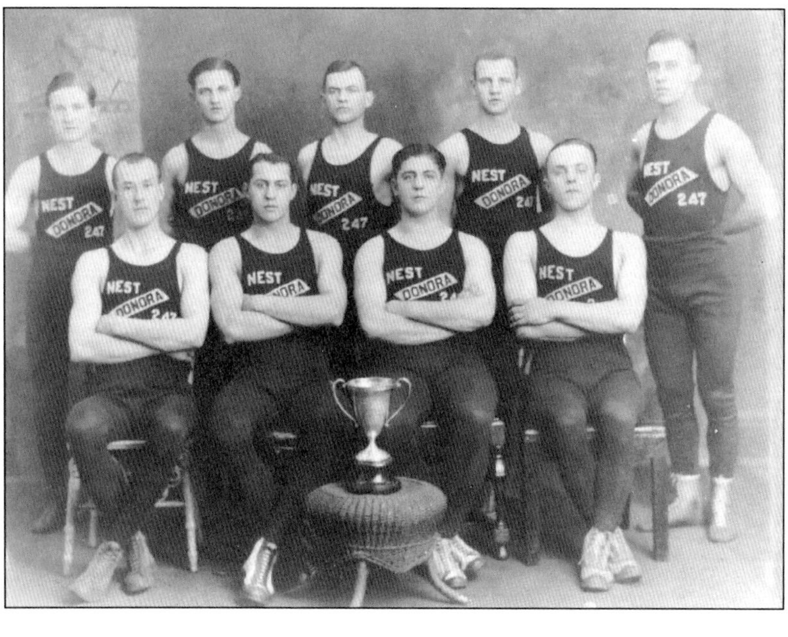

The cup in this picture was presented to Frank Musial (first row, second from right) after the Polish Falcons Alliance of America Nest 247 of Donora won the overall athletic championship at the Polish Falcons National Convention in 1926. (Courtesy Mark Pawelec.)

The premier event of the summer in Donora was the Spanish Fiesta. The afternoon program held in Palmer Park attracted thousands of people of different ethnic backgrounds. Spanish music, folk dances, and athletic contests were featured. The evening activities took place at the Spanish Club Building and involved a floor show and dancing.

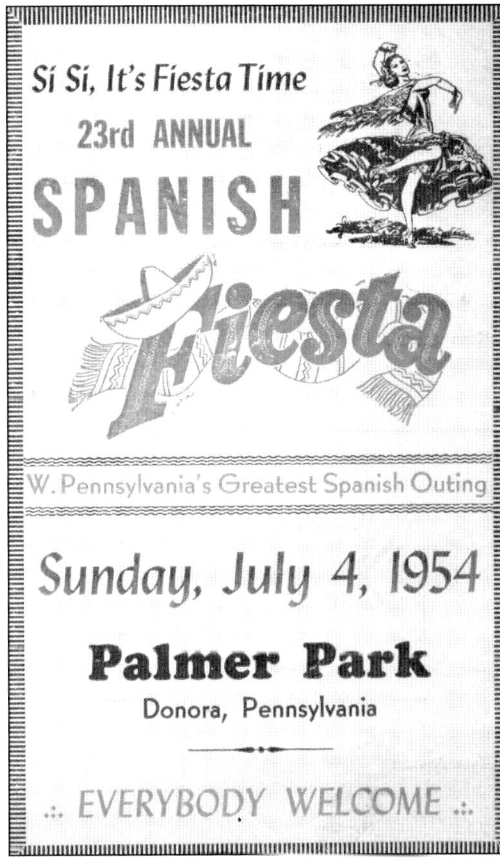

The Donora Lions Club membership was primarily drawn from the town's business and professional men. This summer picnic was held at the Kuma farm in nearby Rostraver Township. (Courtesy Glenn Howis.)

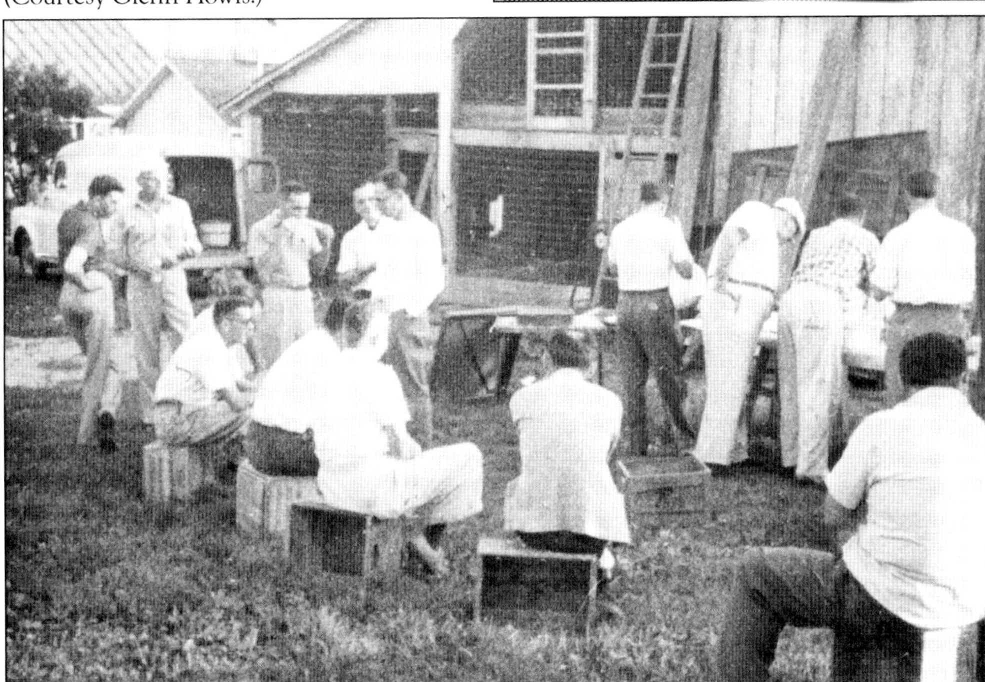

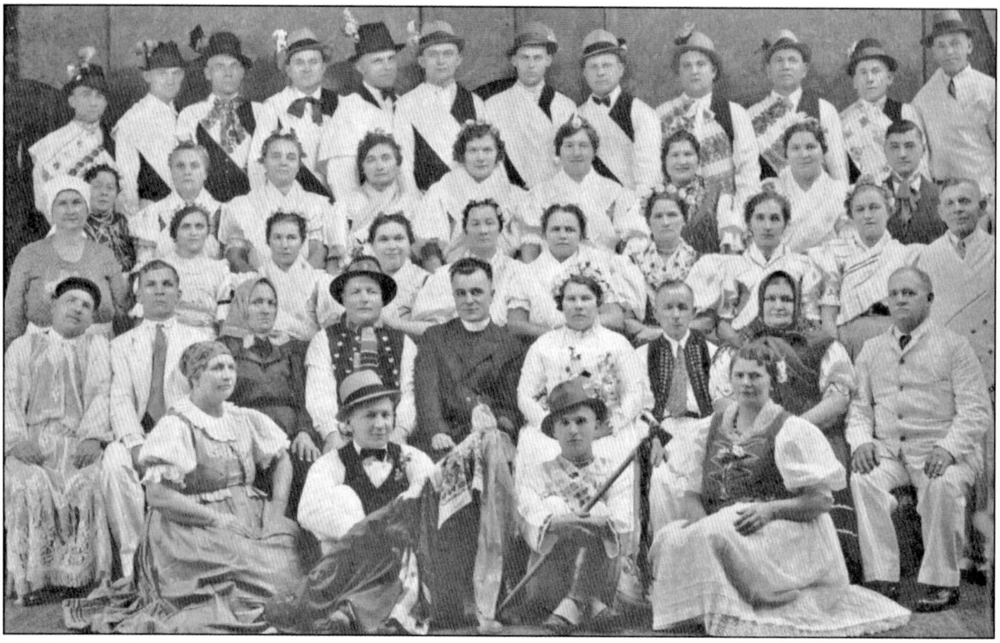

The Slovak Club was incorporated on August 15, 1915, shortly after it moved into a new building at 922 Meldon Avenue. This building had a large auditorium on the second floor that included a stage and balcony. Over the years, the room hosted everything from "donkey basketball" to wedding receptions and dances. This November 4, 1935, photograph shows the Slovaks of Donora embracing their heritage with a traditional wedding ceremony.

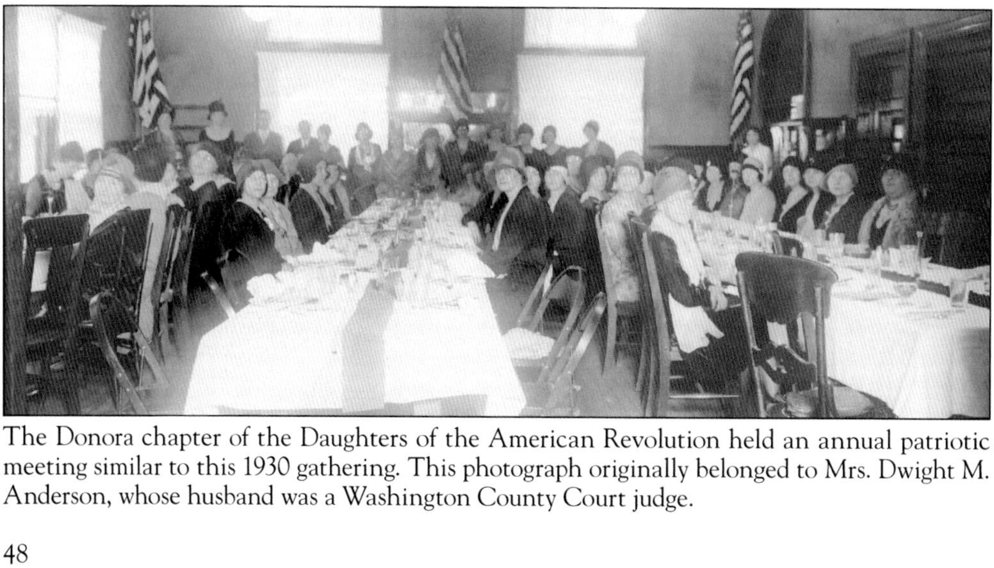

The Donora chapter of the Daughters of the American Revolution held an annual patriotic meeting similar to this 1930 gathering. This photograph originally belonged to Mrs. Dwight M. Anderson, whose husband was a Washington County Court judge.

Four

All Through the Town

Throughout much of Donora's history, its residents have had to cope with polluted air, dirt, and grime. However, people accepted these troublesome aspects of life as the price to be paid for the benefits of employment and economic security. Furthermore, few of the early townspeople could afford large plots of land and needed to live within walking distance of the mills. Therefore, large numbers of cheap frame houses were compacted together, creating an ongoing pattern of overcrowding in some sections of the borough.

Nonetheless, most residents truly believed Donora was a fine place work, live, and raise their families. The institutional growth of the community reflected this belief. Community residents supported a large number of churches, established excellent public and parochial school systems, and patronized numerous social and recreational facilities. The creation of police and fire departments enhanced feelings of safety and security in the borough's homes and streets.

In general, the people of the town are friendly and willing to help neighbors and strangers alike. The community's core value system has produced a disproportionate number of Donorans who have gone on to achieve success and fame in education, athletics, the arts, law, and government. Most of these achievers proudly proclaim that the foundation of their accomplishments can be traced to their roots in Donora.

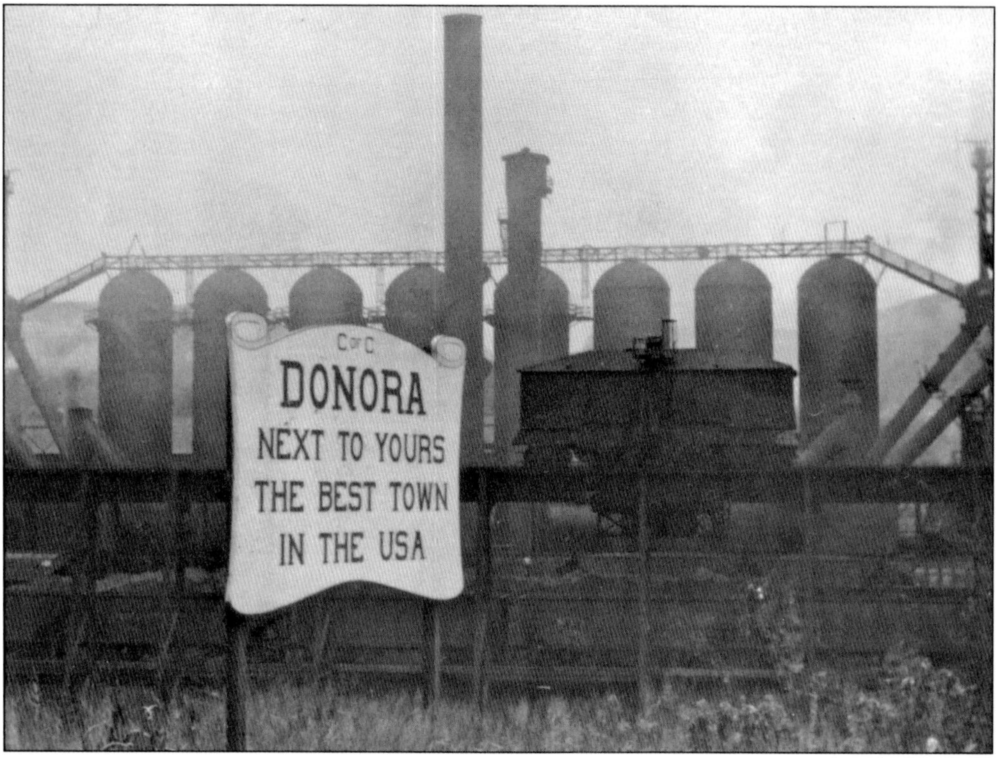

On McKean Avenue at the south end of town and on Pennsylvania Route 51 leading to Pittsburgh are two large identical signs that read, "Donora—Next To Yours, The Best Town In The USA." These unique signs received notice in several national magazines and newspapers. The sign that now greets visitors to the south end of the community near the Donora-Monessen Bridge proclaims, "Donora: The Home of Champions."

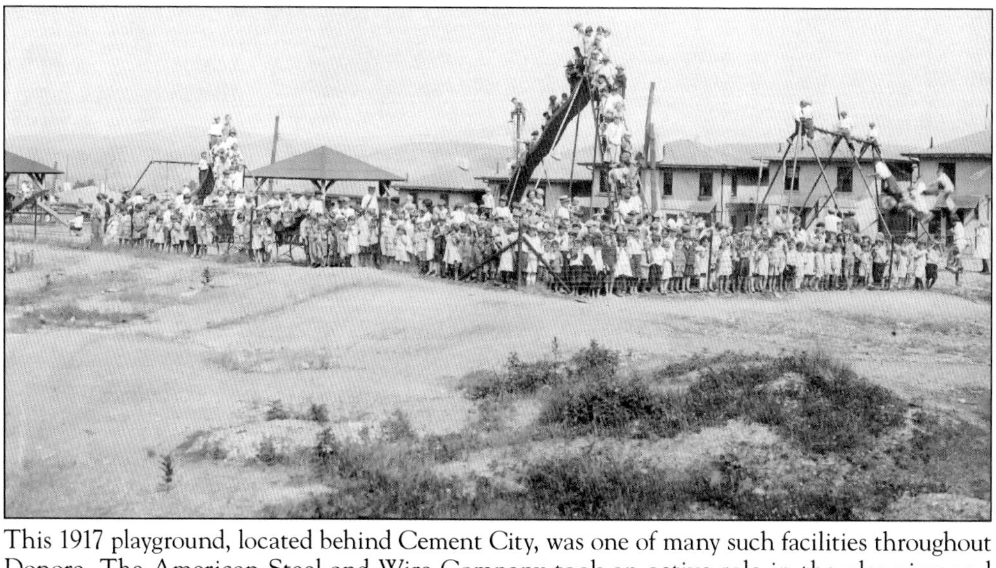

This 1917 playground, located behind Cement City, was one of many such facilities throughout Donora. The American Steel and Wire Company took an active role in the planning and construction of Cement City, whose homes were built to house mill foremen. The children in this picture are posing for mill photographer Bruce Driesbach. (Courtesy Robert Turnbull.)

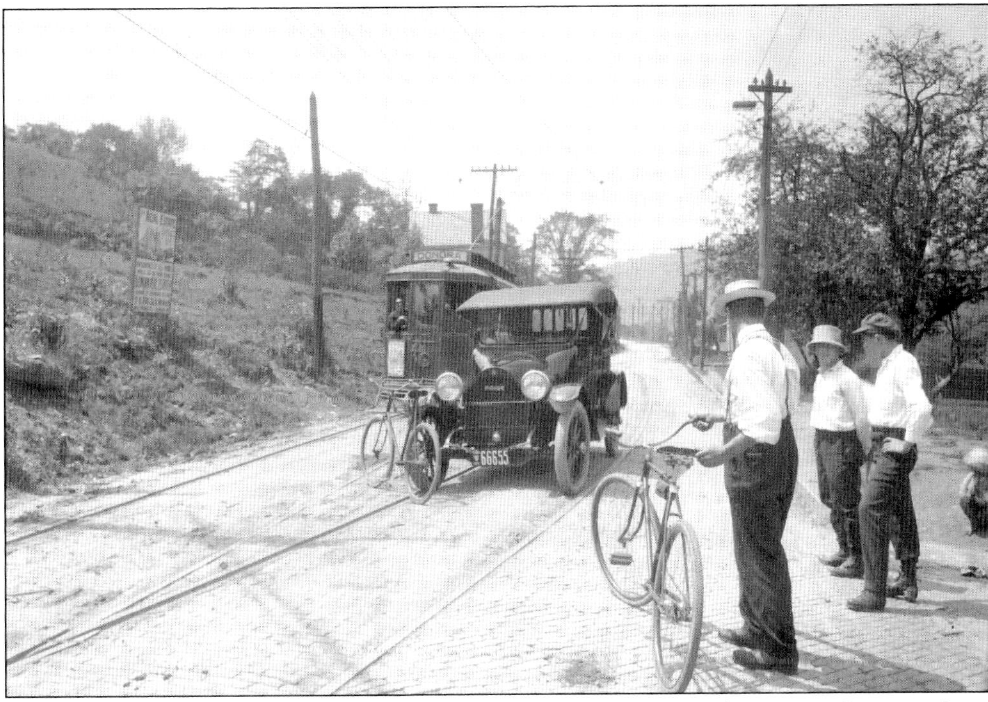

This photograph shows the evolution of transportation in the early years in Donora. Since automobiles were available only to the affluent, most Donora workers and their families used the trolley to get around town and to travel to neighboring communities and Pittsburgh. These men are standing near the intersection of Meldon Avenue and Fifteenth Street.

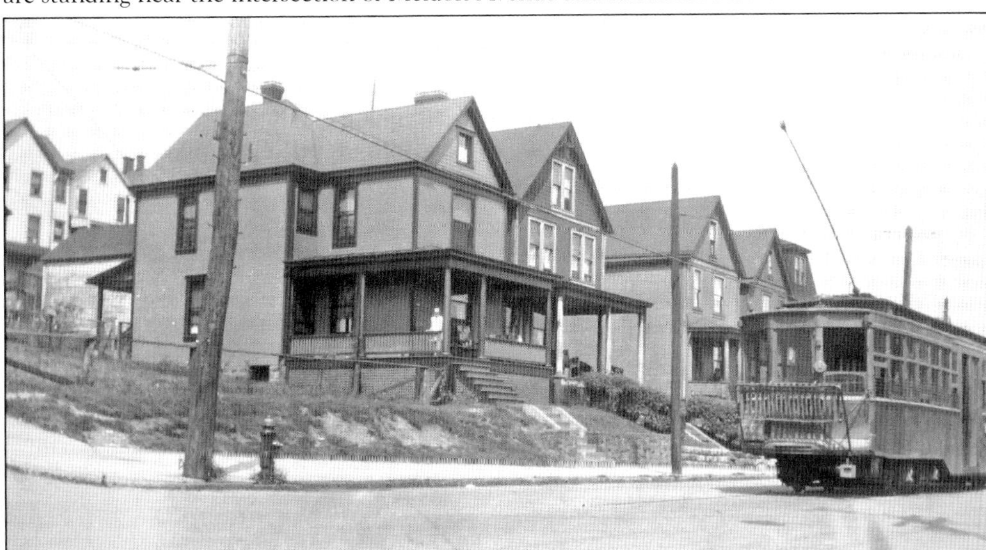

McKean Avenue, named for James McKean, vice president of the Union Improvement Company, is Donora's main street and extends for more than 2 miles, connecting the town's north and south borders. This is a picture of McKean Avenue at First Street that illustrates the pattern of compacting home construction. Electric power lines are visible, and the presence of the corner fire hydrant shows the availability of city water.

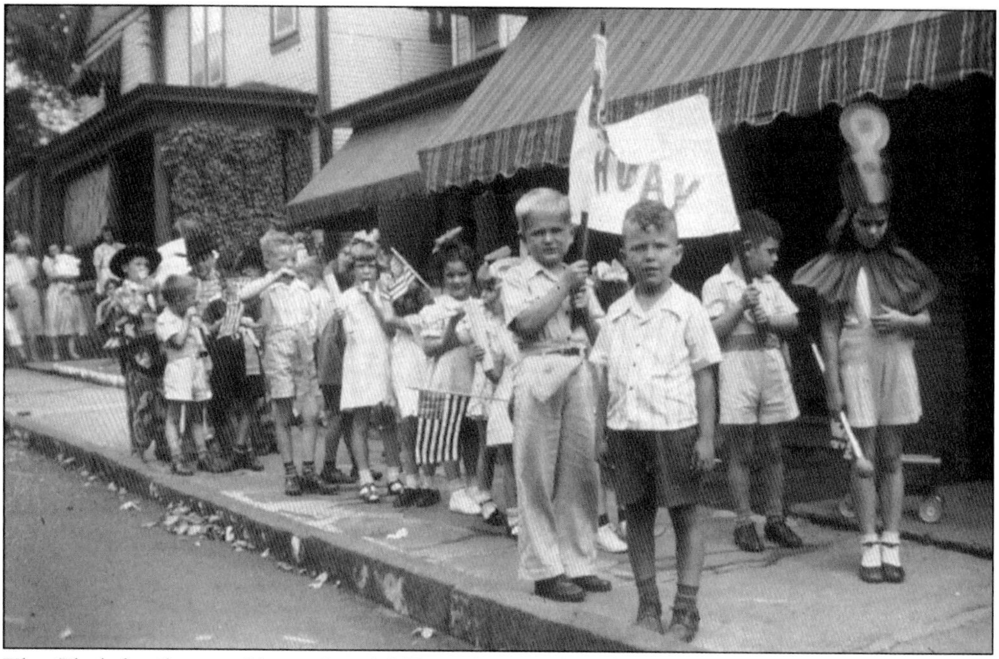

The Clark family was able to close McKean Avenue for a few minutes so their son Keith could have a parade for his fifth birthday in 1948. Keith and his friends marched from Ninth Street to Fifth Street, where they were treated to an Isaly's ice cream cone.

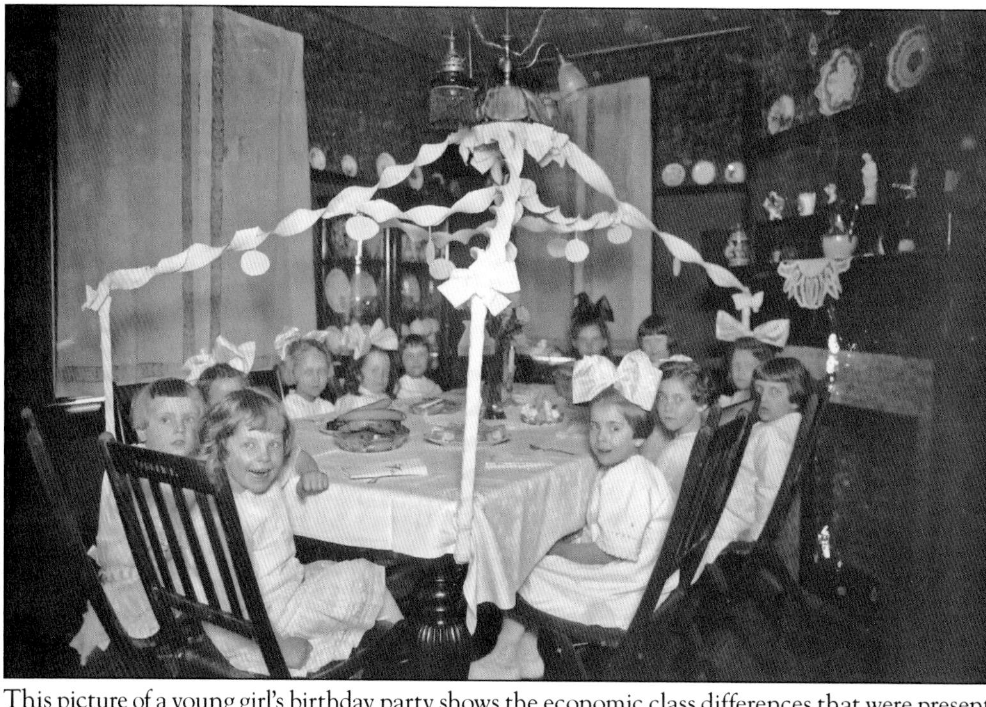

This picture of a young girl's birthday party shows the economic class differences that were present in early Donora. This family can afford an elaborate party held in a spacious, well-furnished home attended by well-dressed guests. Working-class children were not as fortunate. The name stamped on the back of the chairs indicates they were borrowed or rented for this special occasion.

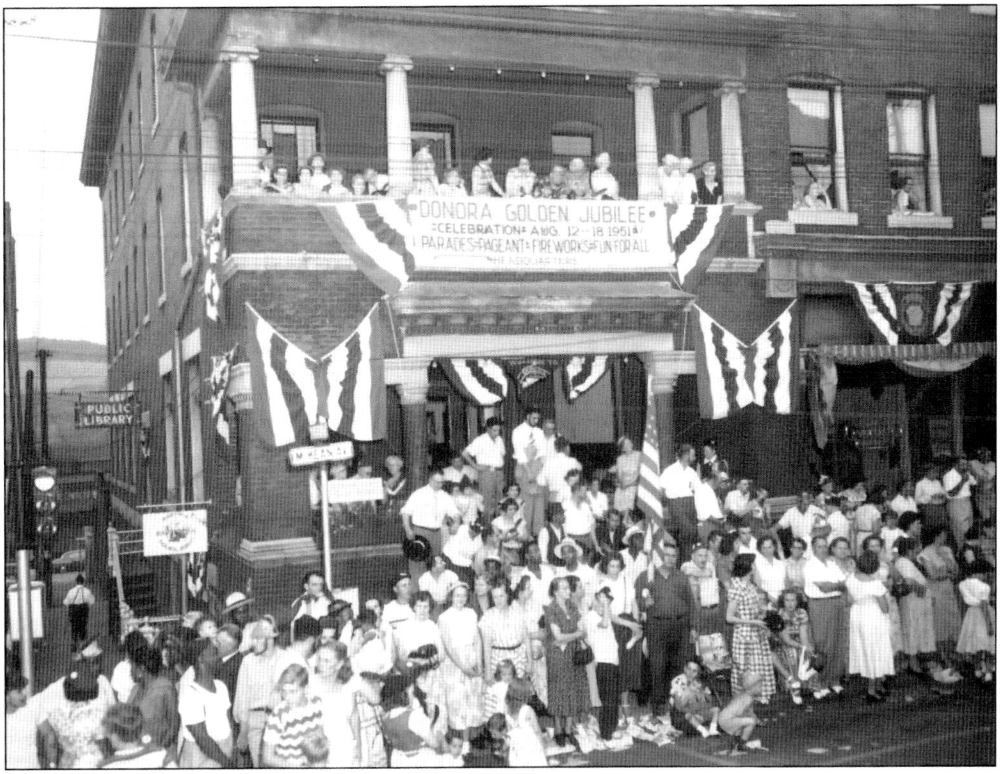

In August 1951, Donora celebrated the 50th anniversary of its incorporation as a borough. One of the highlights of this Golden Jubilee was a two-hour-long parade. Pictured here are people lining the streets eagerly awaiting the procession of parade units. The building in the background is the former Donora Hotel, which was purchased by the Donner family and donated to the community to house a library and meeting rooms. Within a decade of the Golden Jubilee, Donora's industry, population, and wealth were in decline.

This picture shows the Donora Lions Club float that participated in the 1951 Golden Jubilee parade. It was one of many sponsored floats in the lineup, and thousands of spectators crowded the streets to view the parade. The American Steel and Wire Company blast furnace can be seen in the background. The smoke rising from the stacks shows that the workers were on the job making steel in the midst of the community celebration.

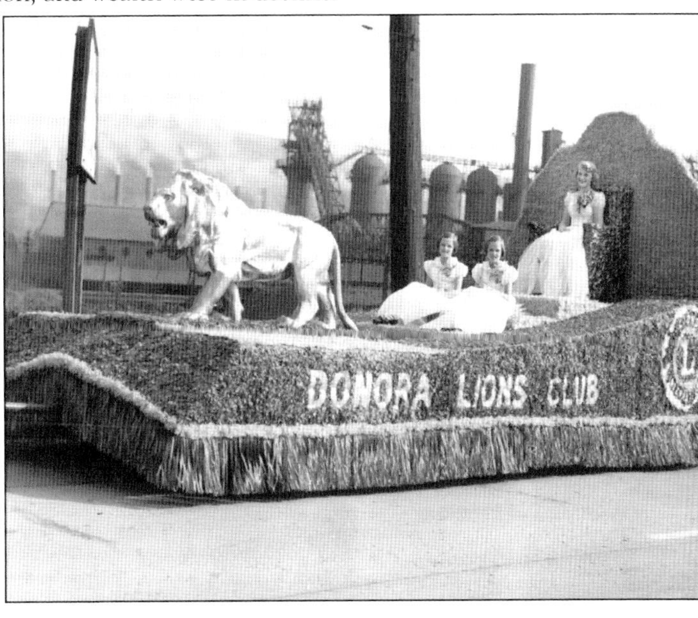

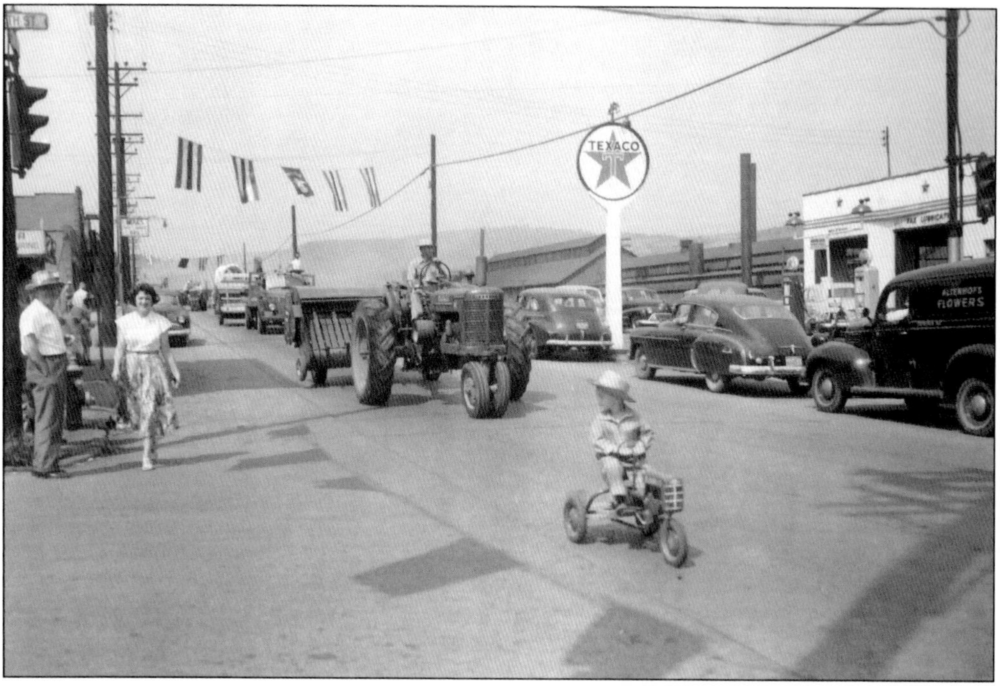

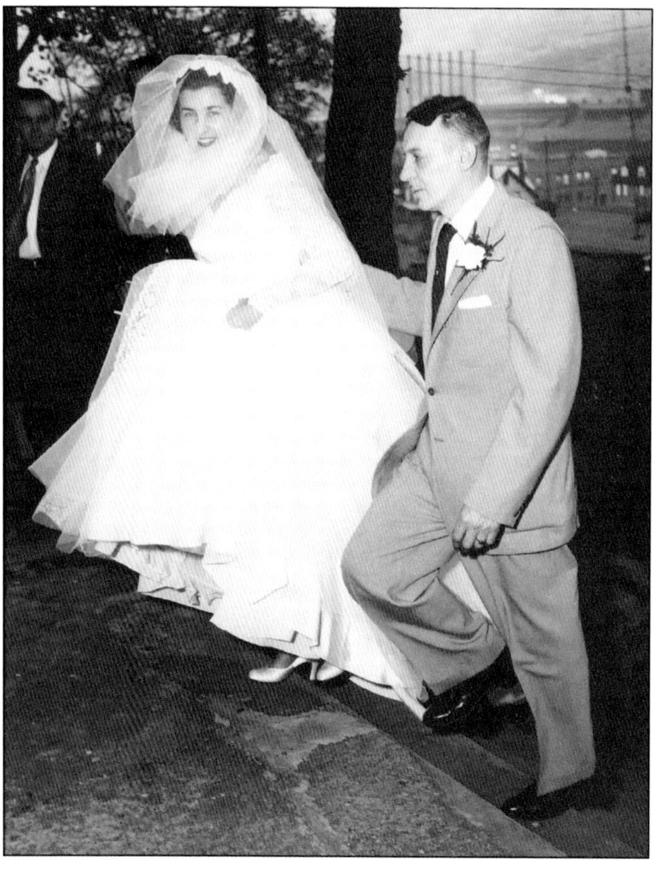

Tractors and other farm machinery participated in the 1951 Golden Jubilee parade. This young boy rides a toy pedal-powered tractor. In the background, the white acrid smoke and fumes from the zinc works are visible.

On October 9, 1954, Florence H. Musial married Raymond J. Pawelec at the Holy Name of the Blessed Virgin Mary Roman Catholic Church. In this picture, the bride is escorted in to the rear of the church by her father, Frank Musial. Note the mill in the background. (Courtesy Mark Pawelec.)

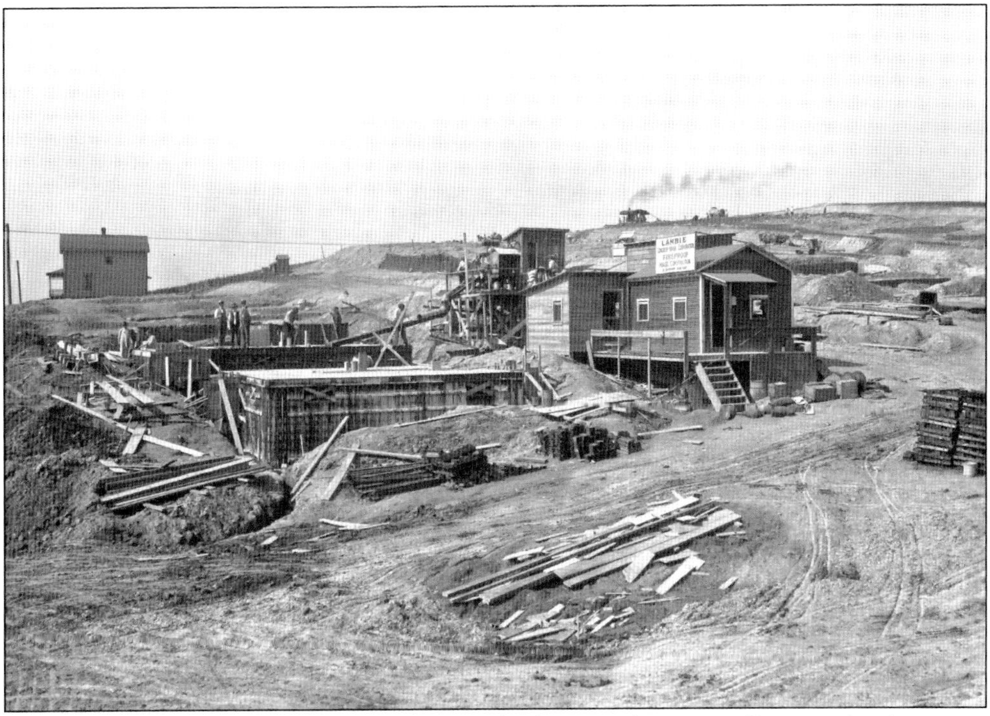

In an effort to stabilize its workforce and ease the housing shortage in Donora, the American Steel and Wire Company contracted Franklin Lambie to build 152 concrete homes of the type developed in the Thomas Edison laboratories. This photograph shows the Lambie Concrete House Corporation field-site office in 1916 at the corner of Modisette Avenue and Walnut Street.

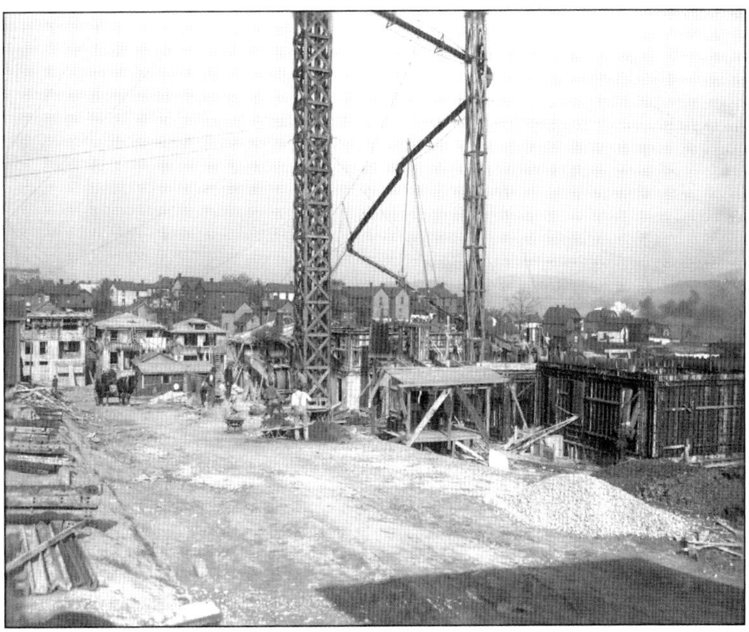

Lambie Concrete House Corporation workers used reusable mechanical panels called channels to create floor and wall forms. Using such light, strong innovations, each 10-man crew could complete one story of a house on each 10-hour shift.

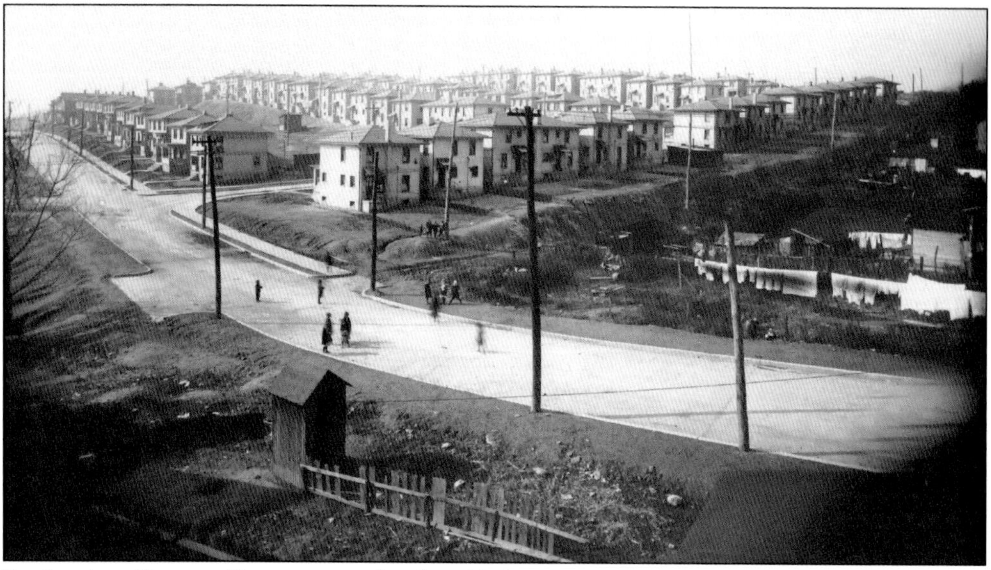

By the time Cement City was completed in 1916, it was apparent it was not as cost effective as hoped. A concrete home cost about $3,300, while a comparable frame house cost around $2,000. Eighty cement structures were erected in Donora.

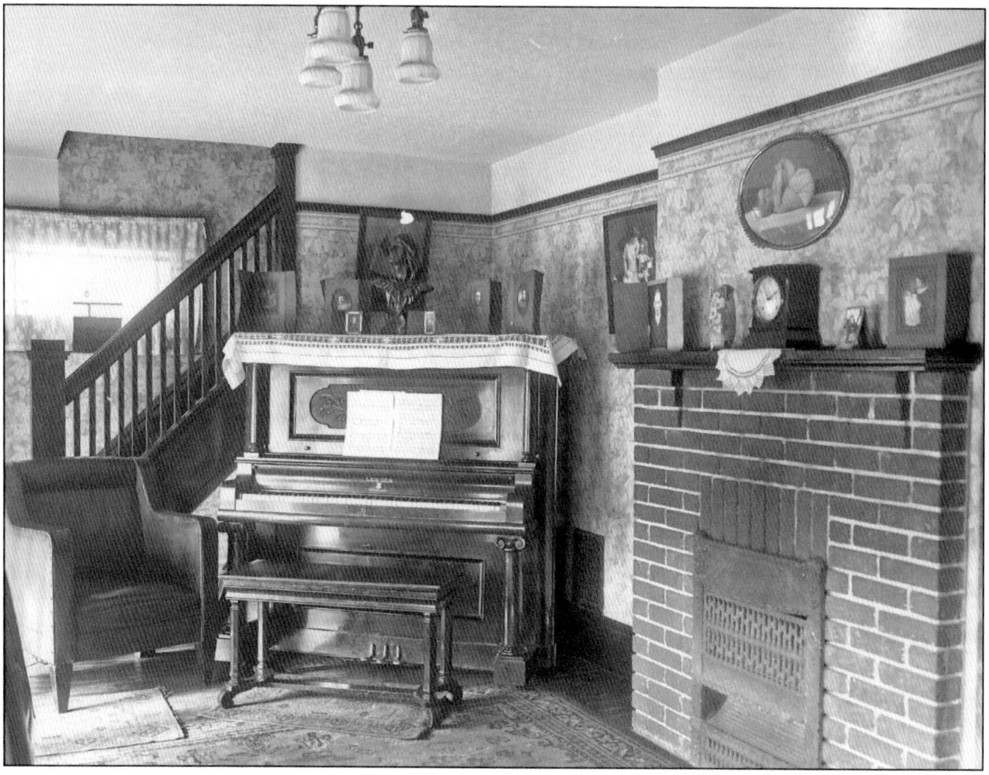

This parlor in a recently completed six-room Model 202 Cement City home reflects the affluence of the residents. The homes were equipped with natural-gas, hot-air heating systems and featured electric lights and outlets in every room. Notice the carpet, curtains, wallpaper, and the piano that enhanced this family's living conditions.

Palmer Park, in the northwest corner of the borough, contained picnic shelters, athletic fields, a bandstand, and walking paths. The land for the park was donated by the American Steel and Wire Company. For decades, church groups and service organizations held Sunday picnics in the park. In this picture, a group of young African American men and women enjoy an outing in this pleasant setting.

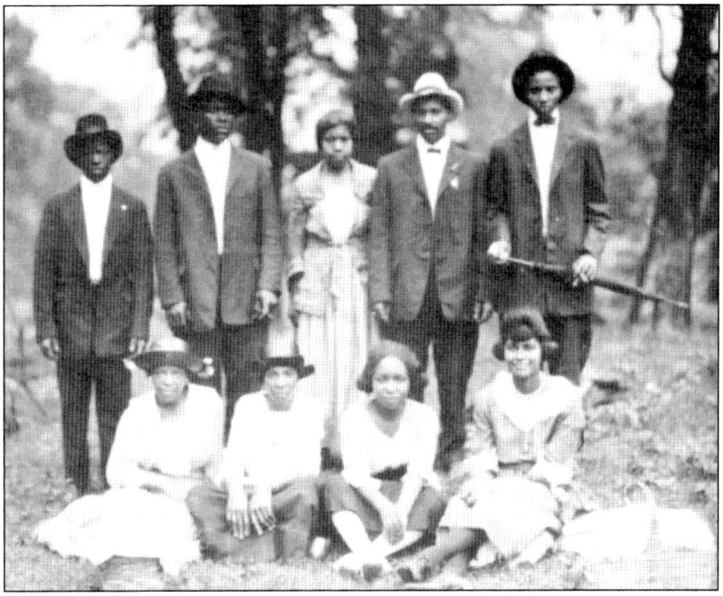

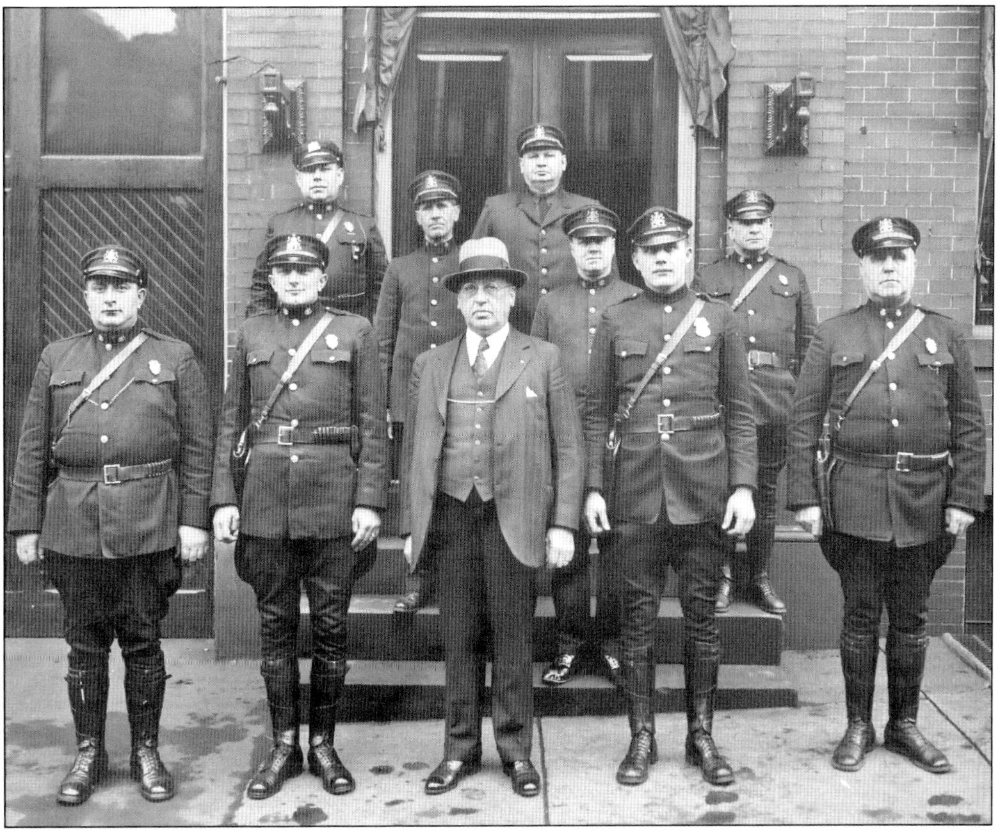

In spite of the presence of some rough characters who were common in steel mill towns, the Donora Police Department ensured a high degree of safety, law, and order. This 1935 picture shows the members of the department standing in front of the borough building, which also housed the town's jail. The man in the middle of the front row is thought to be Chief William Smedley.

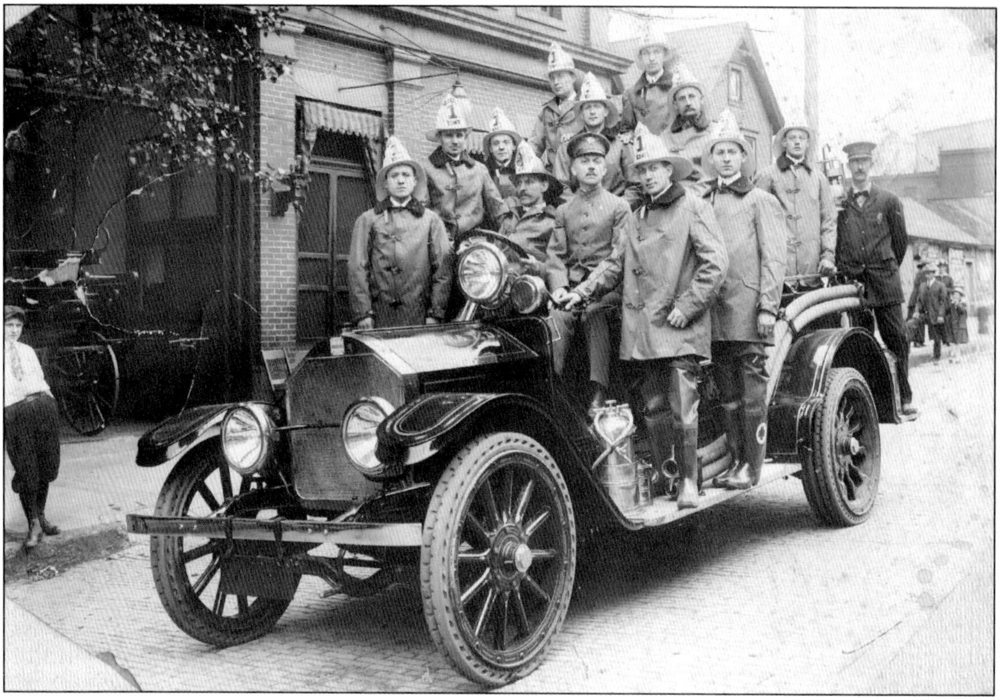

Gustave Schaaf was an army captain during the Spanish-American War and home guard company commander during World War I. He also served for many years as the chief of Donora's volunteer fire department. Because of their competency, dedication, and professionalism, Schaaf and the volunteer firefighters were honored by the state and designated as a model for other community fire departments.

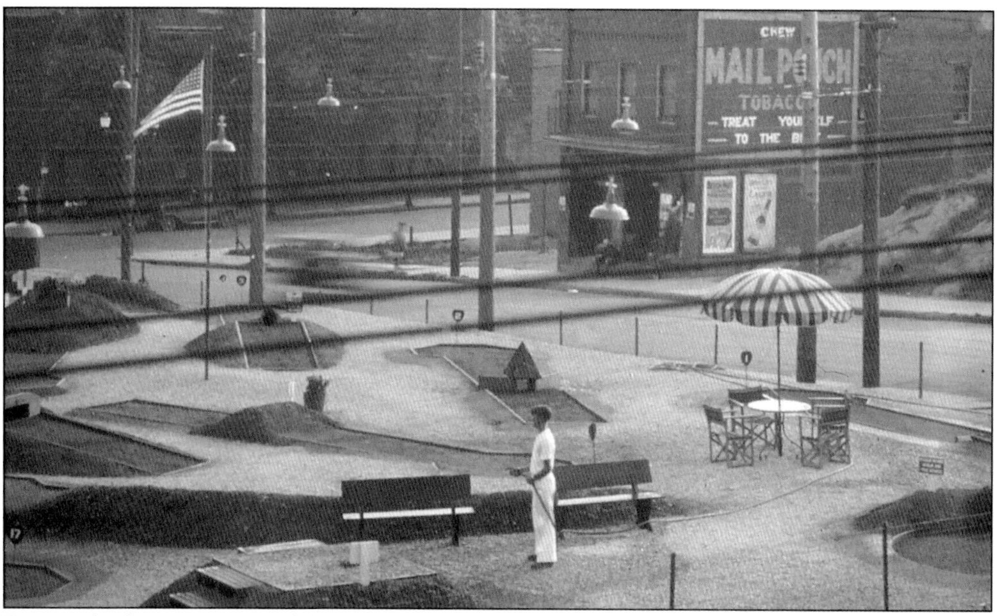

Donora had a miniature golf course long before the sport became a pastime for the working classes. This photograph, taken around 1920, shows the well-kept course that was located in the heart of town at Seventh Street and McKean Avenue.

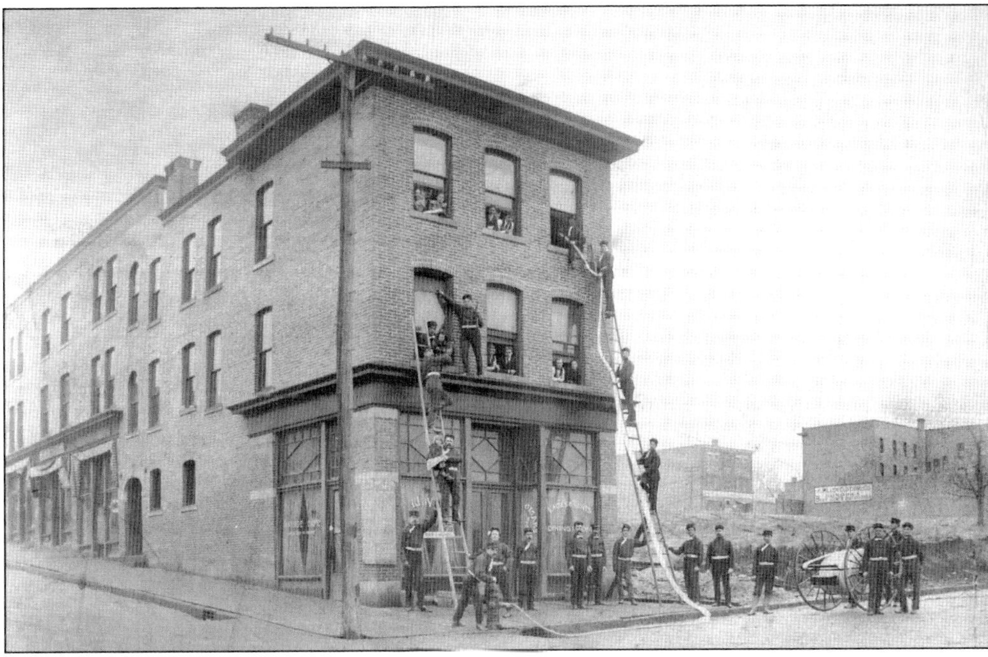

Like most small communities, Donora relied on a volunteer fire company, whose members donated their time and talent for both firefighting and training. This picture shows a fire drill at a three-story building on Meldon Avenue in 1902. The apartment residents seem to appreciate the ladder-climbing efforts of the firemen.

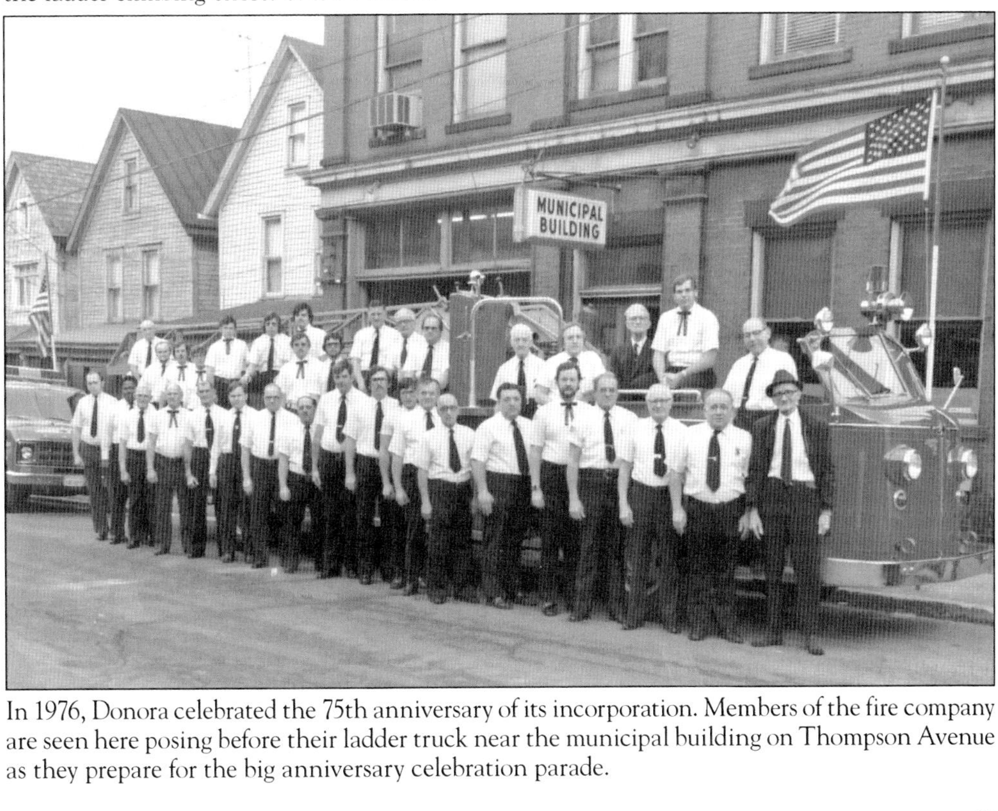

In 1976, Donora celebrated the 75th anniversary of its incorporation. Members of the fire company are seen here posing before their ladder truck near the municipal building on Thompson Avenue as they prepare for the big anniversary celebration parade.

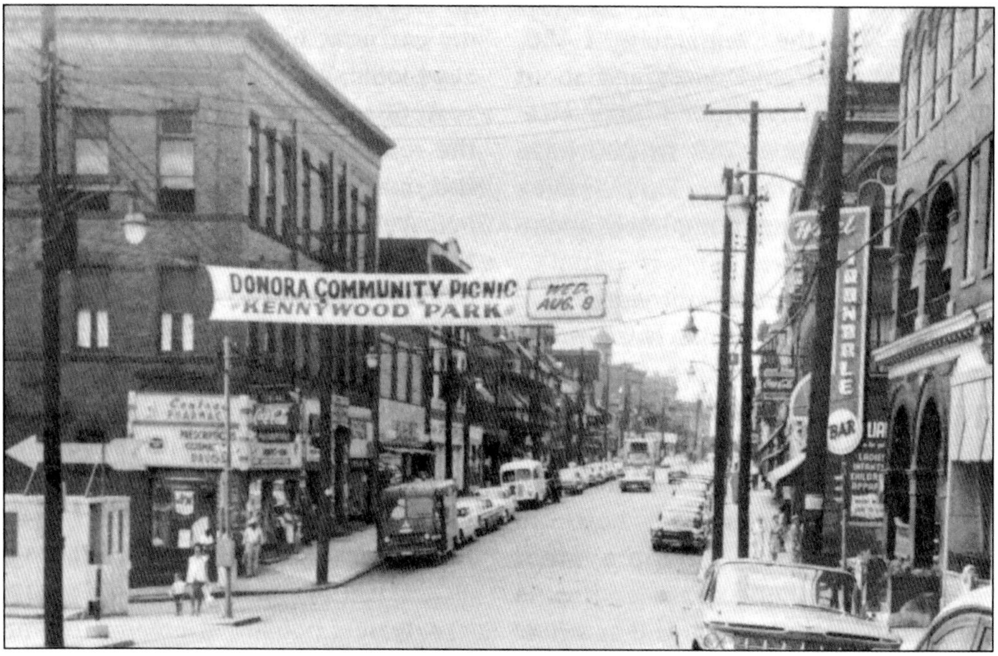

The second Wednesday in August is set aside for Donora's Community Picnic Day, sponsored by the local American Legion. Young people line up early to board the transportation that takes them to Kennywood Park for a day of rides, food, and fun. Thousands attend, and by the afternoon the town's streets are virtually deserted. This street banner across McKean Avenue announces the 1962 picnic.

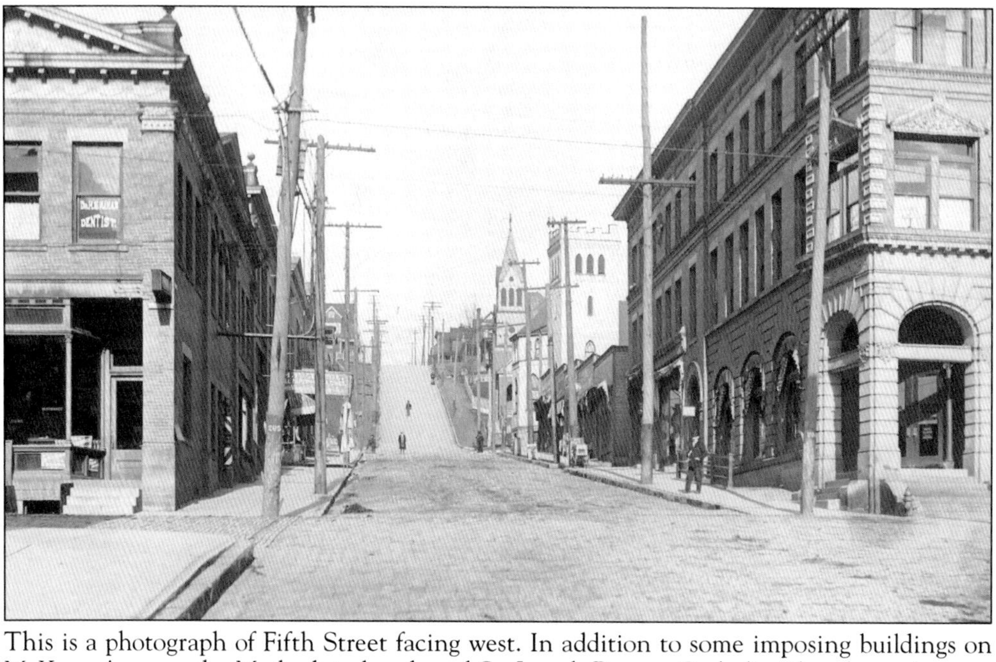

This is a photograph of Fifth Street facing west. In addition to some imposing buildings on McKean Avenue, the Methodist church and St. Joseph Roman Catholic Church can be seen near the corner of Fifth Street. Eventually the steep slope was closed to vehicles, and two sets of steps were built to help pedestrians climb the hill.

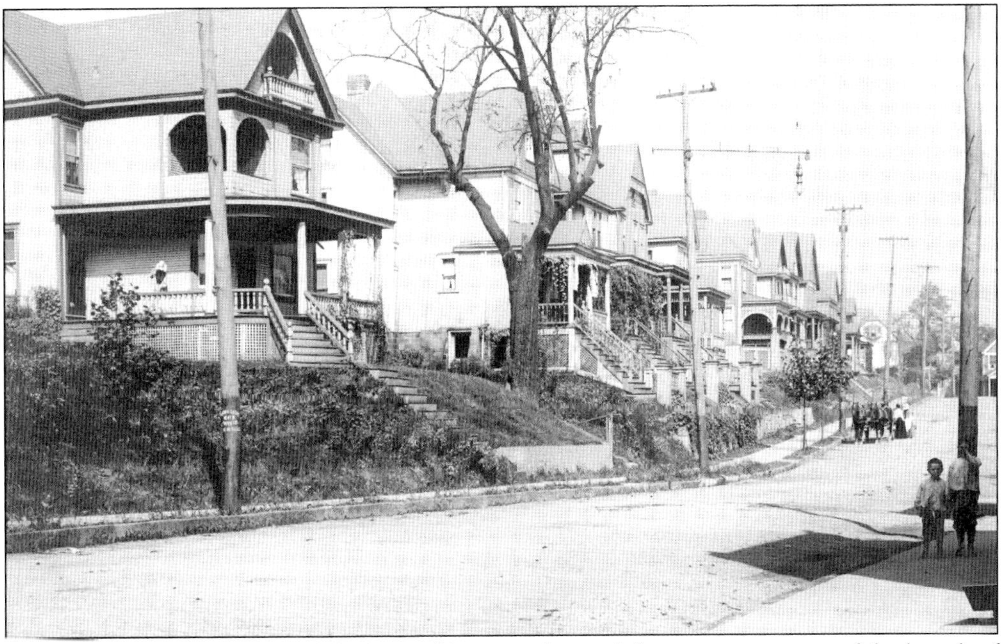

Thompson Avenue was one of the borough's major thoroughfares, running most of the length of the town. It was two streets up from the riverside mill property and one street above the McKean Avenue business district. Some of the mill managers and professionals built large homes along Thompson Avenue. Visible in the distance is the area considered to be "the other side of the tracks" by the community's social elite.

Prior to the coming of television and home videos, the citizens of Donora patronized the town's three movie theaters in large numbers. Youngsters were especially drawn in by the weekend serial features, which took up to 15 weeks to reach their ultimate conclusion. This picture shows a long line of children waiting outside the Harris Theater to purchase admission tickets on a Saturday afternoon.

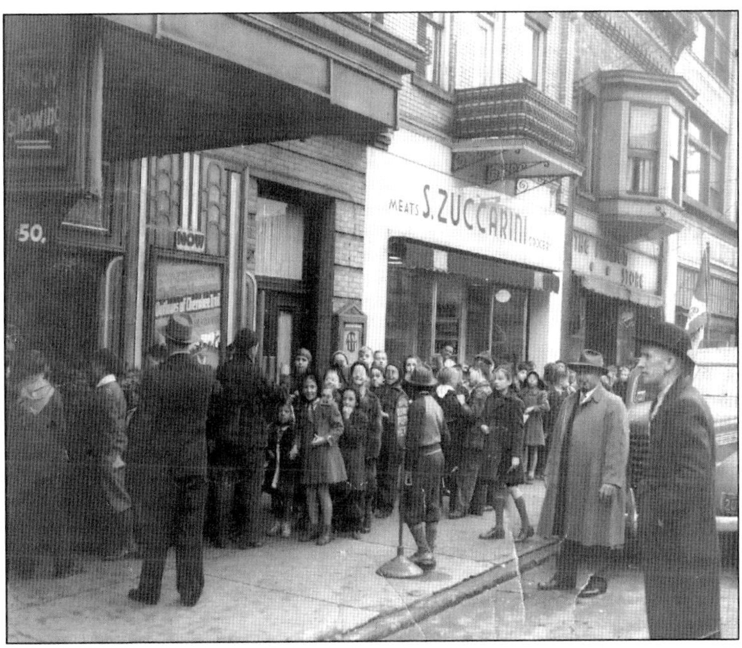

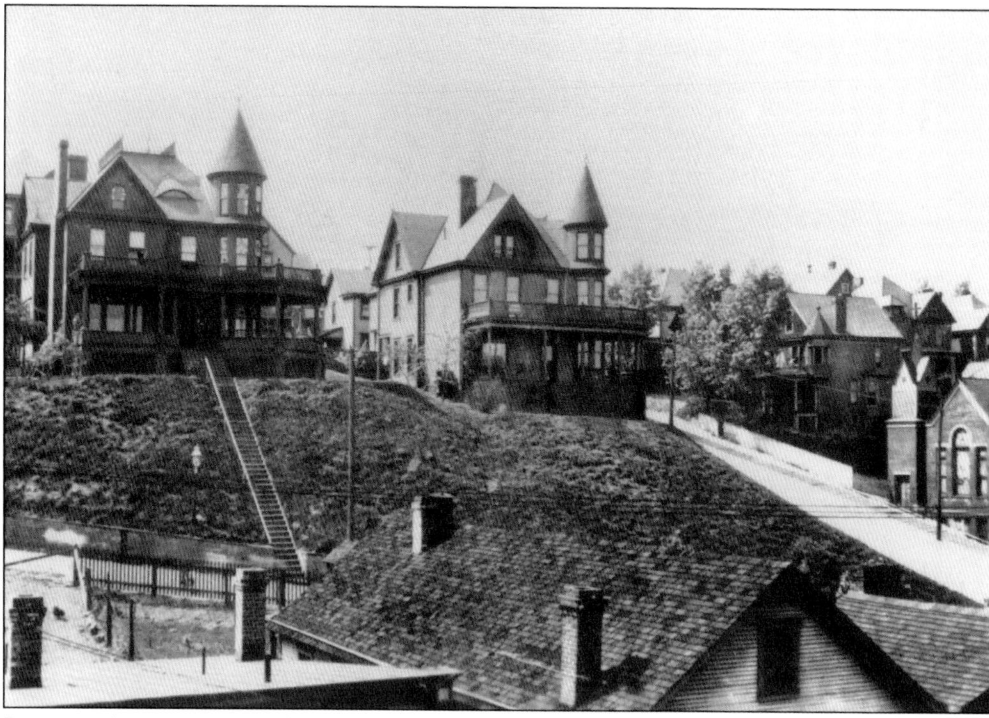

Prospect Avenue is one of Donora's unique streets. It begins at Fifth Street and Thompson Avenue and makes a circle up and around the steep hillside. Shown here are two of the elaborate homes built on the Fifth Street hillside. In order to enter the home at 427 Prospect Avenue, it was necessary to traverse a long flight of wooden steps. To the right is a building that serves as the Cumberland Presbyterian Church.

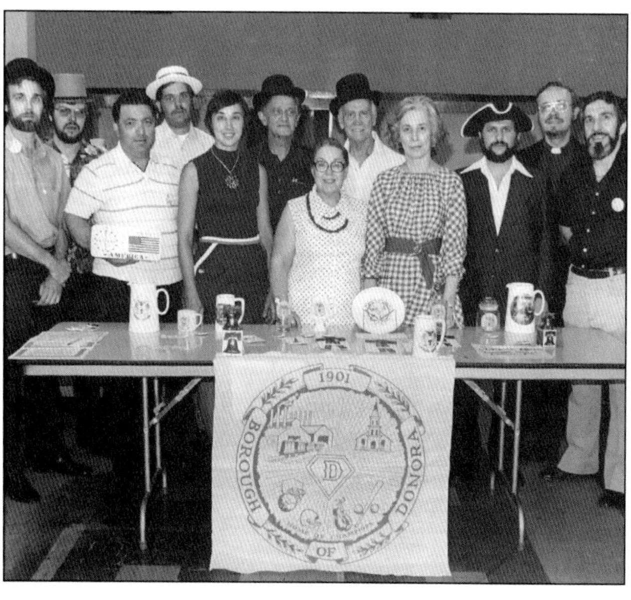

In 1976, Donora celebrated both the bicentennial of the United States and the 75th anniversary of the borough's incorporation. The town celebrated with street fairs, parades, dramatic productions, and numerous other activities. The community leaders pictured here planned and coordinated the festivities. From left to right they are (first row) Dave Lonich, John Lignelli, Joan Sento, Ruth Miller, Rozelle Roth, Bill DuVall, and Chuck Muia; (second row) John Conger, Fred Berestecky, Dallas Compton, John "Moon" Clark, and Fr. Albert Koser.

Five

People of Faith

Donora's many houses of worship feature some of the most distinctive architecture of the town. The numerous churches also reflect the ethnic and racial variety of the community, as well as the willingness of the residents to donate money, time, and labor to the proclamation of their faith. The power structure of early Donora was overwhelmingly Protestant, but the majority of people who came from southern and eastern Europe to labor in the mill were Roman and Greek Catholics or Eastern Orthodox. Early settlers congregated and socialized with their own nationality groups, and worship centers were a part of this tendency.

By mid-century, there were 23 churches and a synagogue within the town. However, the ending mill era and the declining population led to consolidations and closings of churches. Despite this, Donora remains a community of faith and religious fervor.

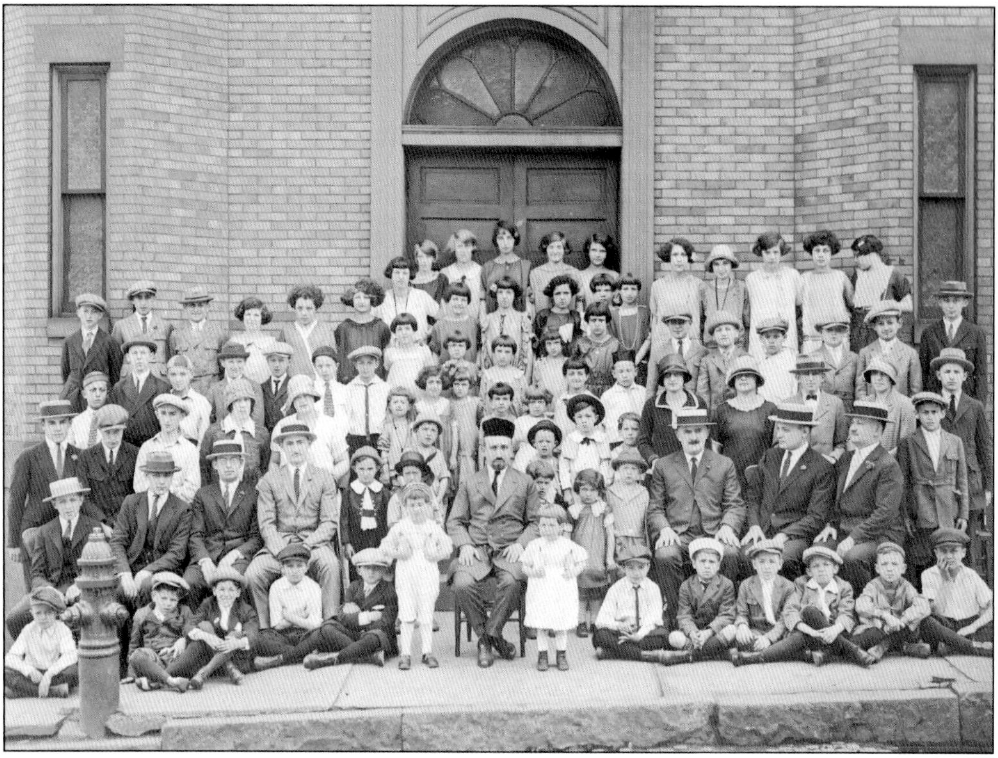

The Donora Hebrew Congregation was incorporated as Ohab Shalom in 1903 and renamed Ohav Shalom in 1964. This picture, taken around 1925, shows Rabbi Gilbert Elefant and students and teachers from the Hebrew school outside the orthodox synagogue, built at the corner of Second Street and Thompson Avenue in 1911. The congregation was disbanded in 1995, and the building now houses the Mon Valley Youth and Teen organization and the Donora Food Bank.

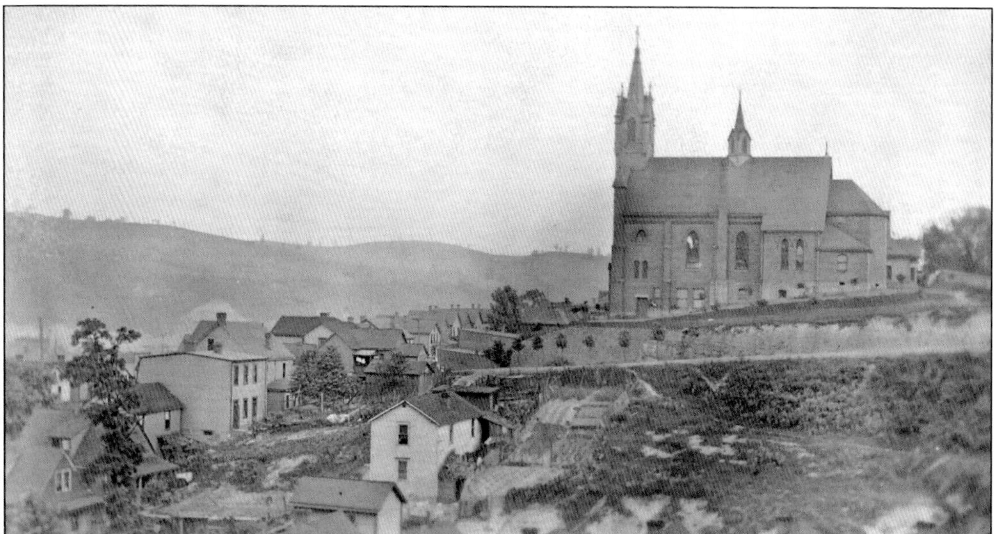

This early photograph of St. Mary Church on Second Street shows its Gothic-style architecture. The steeple towers over the frame houses of the workers. Donora's Polish Catholics viewed this structure as the symbol of their faith.

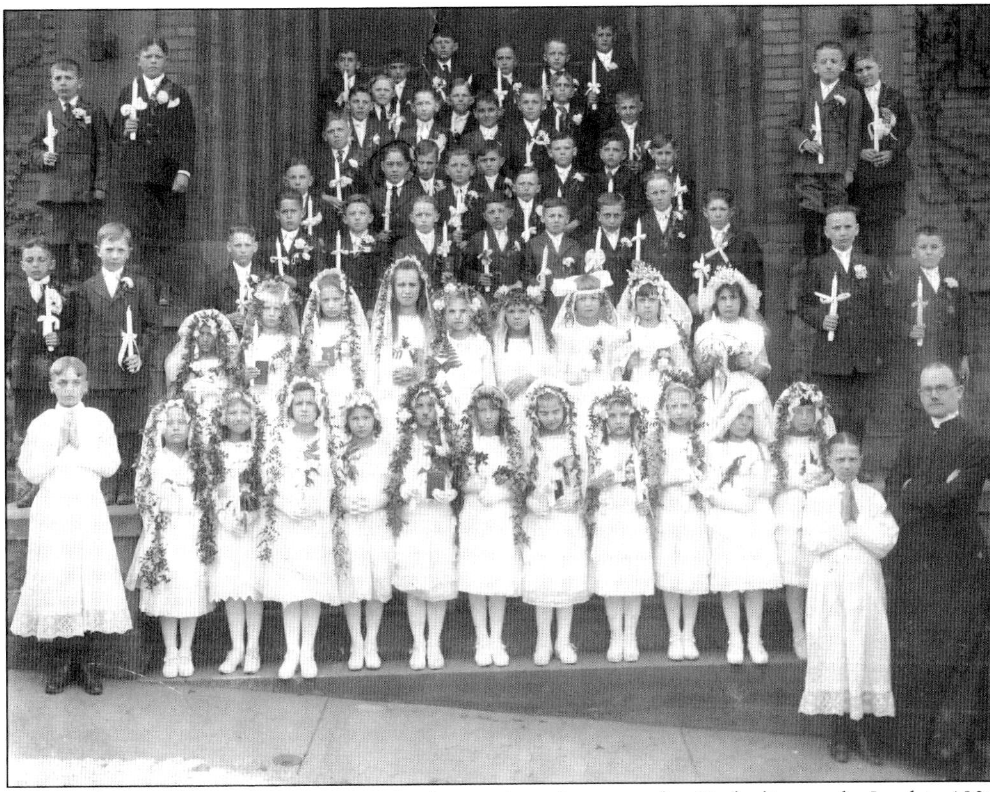

First Holy Communion remains a significant rite of passage for Catholic youth. In this 1920 photograph, a group of boys and girls in traditional attire stand in front of St. Michael Greek Catholic Church Byzantine Rite on Murray Avenue. Thomas Bell wrote about this particular church in his novel *Out of This Furnace*.

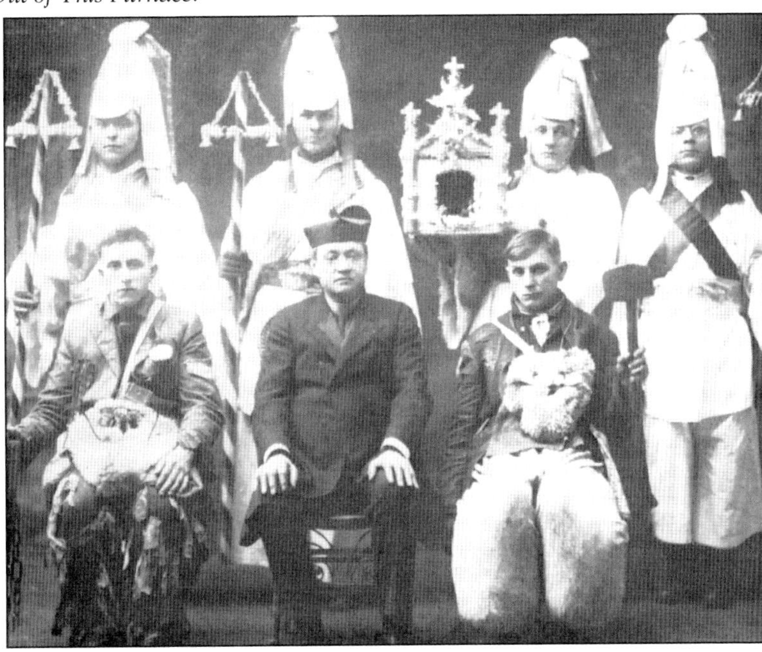

In the early years of the town, the ethnic and religious diversity of Donora was reflected in various holiday celebrations. Here is a group of male Christmas carolers of Slovak ethnicity from St. Dominic Roman Catholic Church. The priest in this 1921 photograph is Fr. E. E. Gellhof.

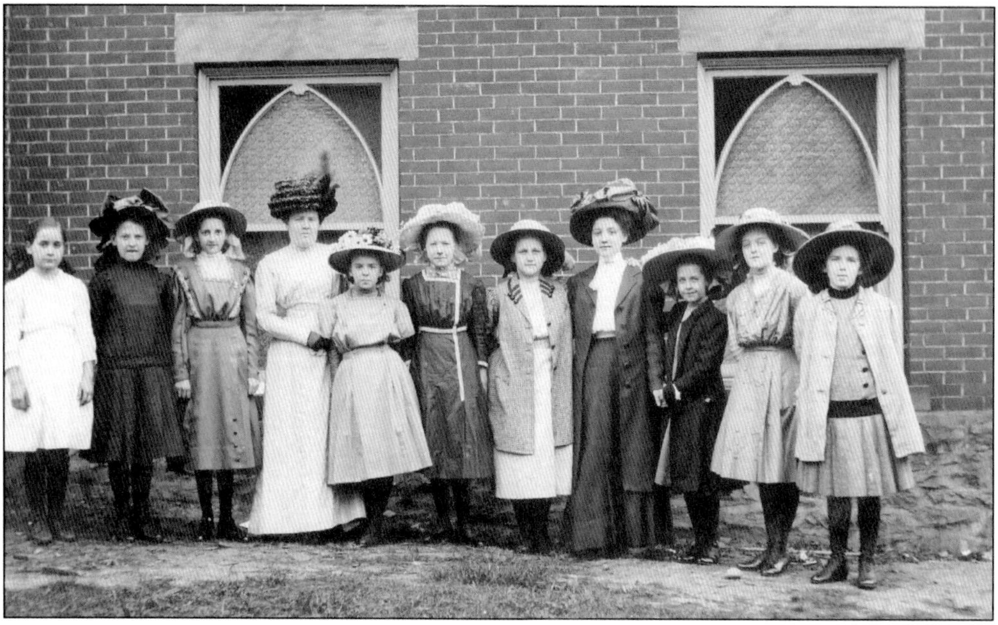

At one time, going to church was an occasion to dress up. In this picture, young ladies from the Sunday school of the First Presbyterian Church display their dress shoes and hats.

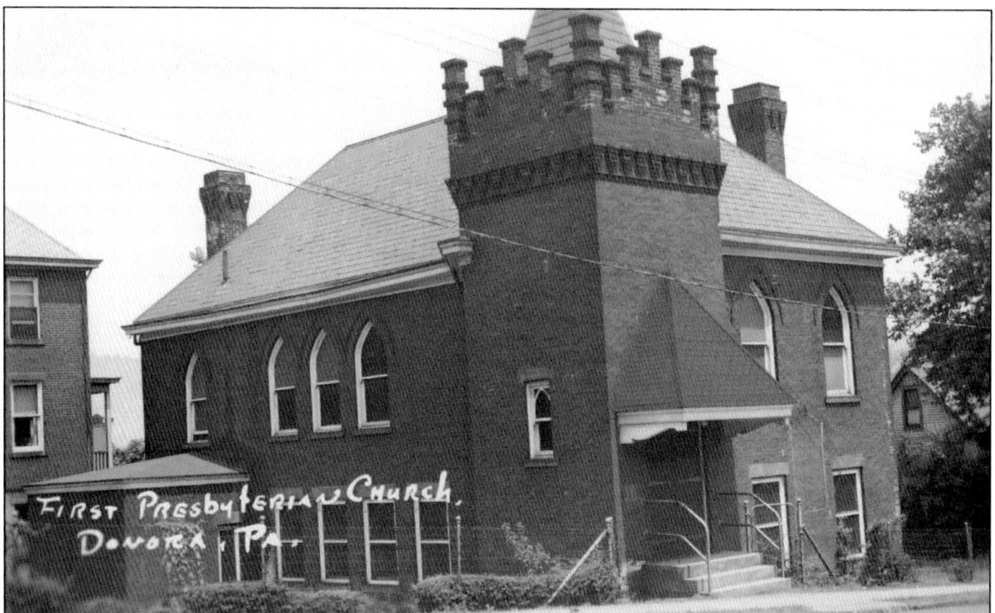

Donora once had three Presbyterian churches. In 1906, the First Presbyterian Church merged with the Cumberland Presbyterian Church. Eventually the Calvary Presbyterian Church was created by the merger of the First Presbyterian Church and United Presbyterian Church in 1960. The congregation continues to hold services in the building pictured.

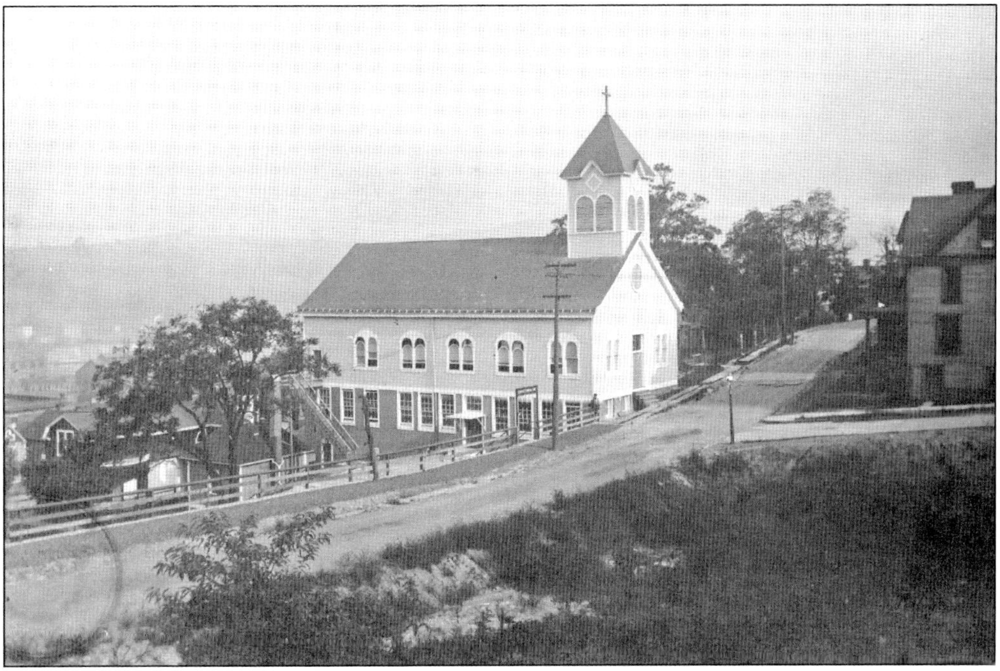

St. Charles was the first Roman Catholic congregation in Donora. It was formed in 1901 by a group of predominately Irish residents. The building seen here was constructed in 1903 on Heslep Avenue. The parish also operated a parochial school for a number of years.

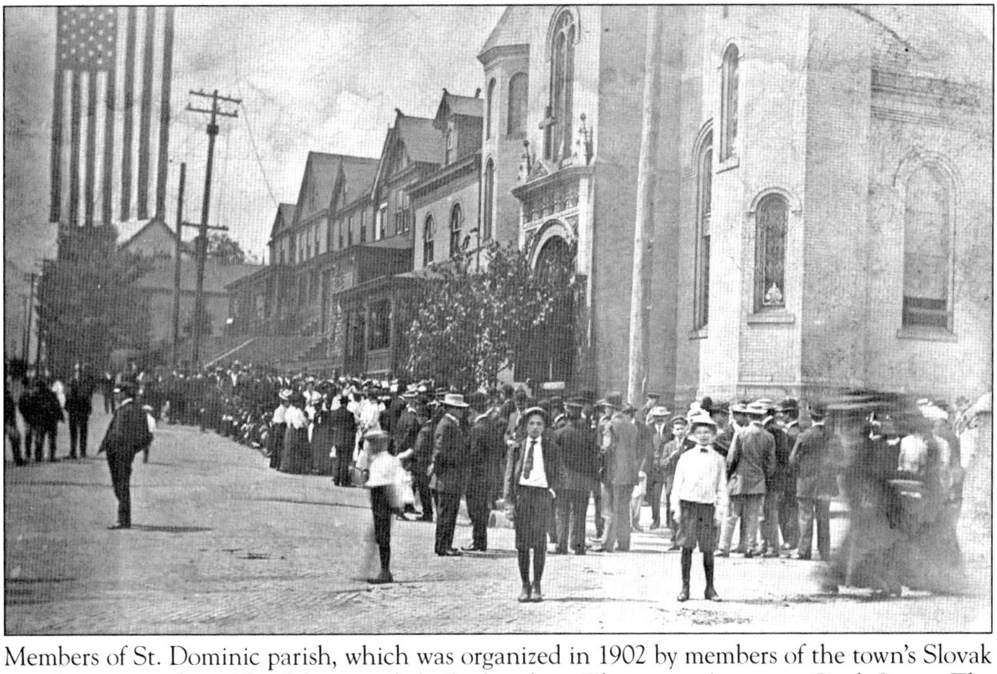

Members of St. Dominic parish, which was organized in 1902 by members of the town's Slovak population, stand outside of their newly built church on Thompson Avenue at Sixth Street. The first mass was celebrated by Fr. Edward Kitz on Easter Sunday, April 15, 1906. The church, with its distinctive yellow bricks and magnificent steeple, is now part of the consolidated Our Lady of the Valley Parish, which was formed in 1992.

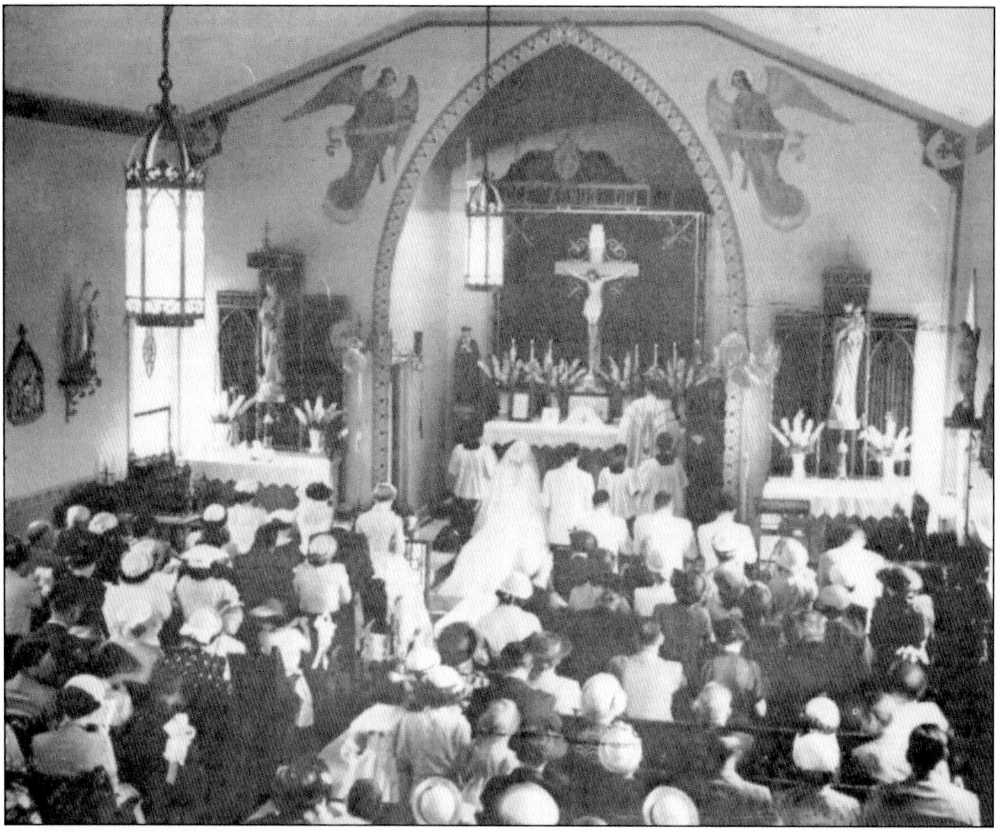

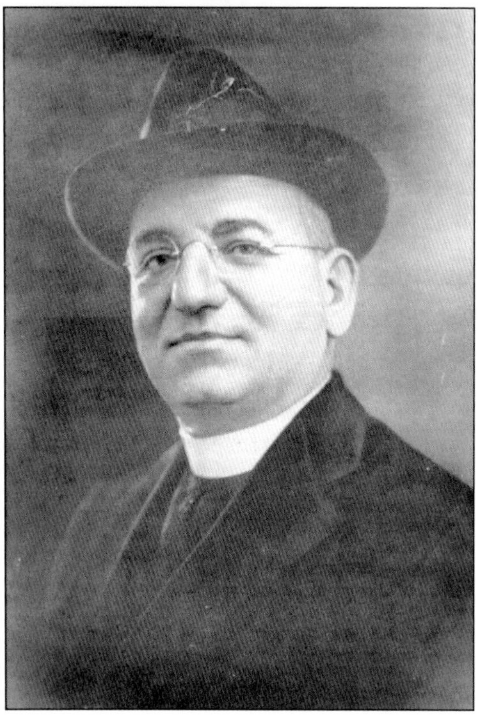

St. Philip Neri was founded in 1923 under the direction of Fr. Joseph Ranconi, an immigrant from Italy. The congregation built a beautiful stone church on Norma Avenue, where it worshiped until a larger facility with an extensive parking lot was constructed along Second Street Extension. The old church was converted to a coffin-storage facility by a local mortician.

Father Ranconi served as pastor of St. Philip Neri from 1923 to 1940. He engaged in charitable efforts toward the entire community. During the Great Depression, he established a soup kitchen that served adults and children of all creeds.

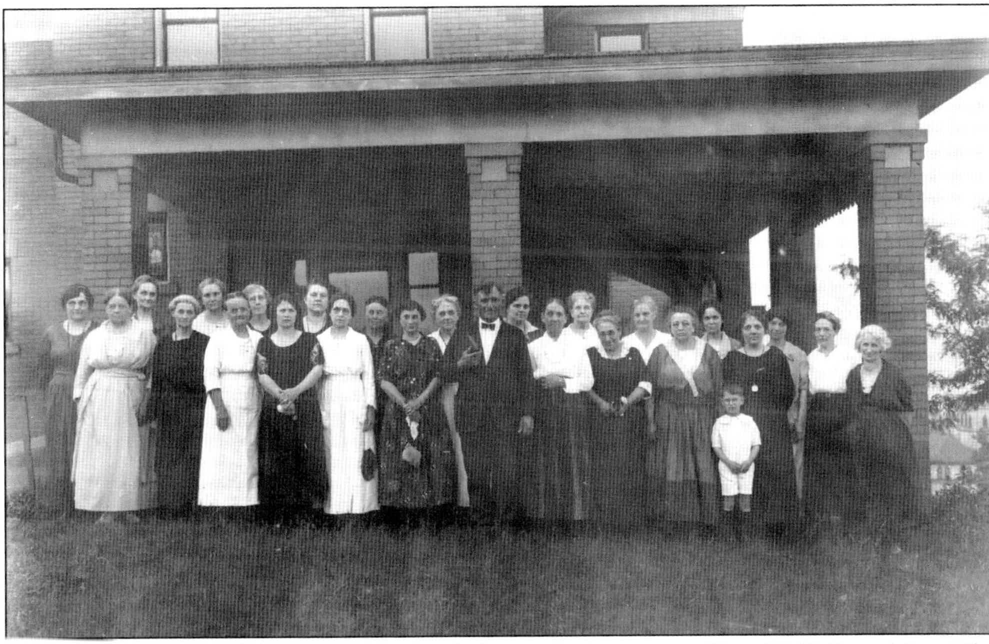

This is a group of well-dressed Methodist ladies with their pastor Rev. W. E. Boettichar. The building in the background is the spacious church parsonage. The church itself can be seen in the far right of the photograph.

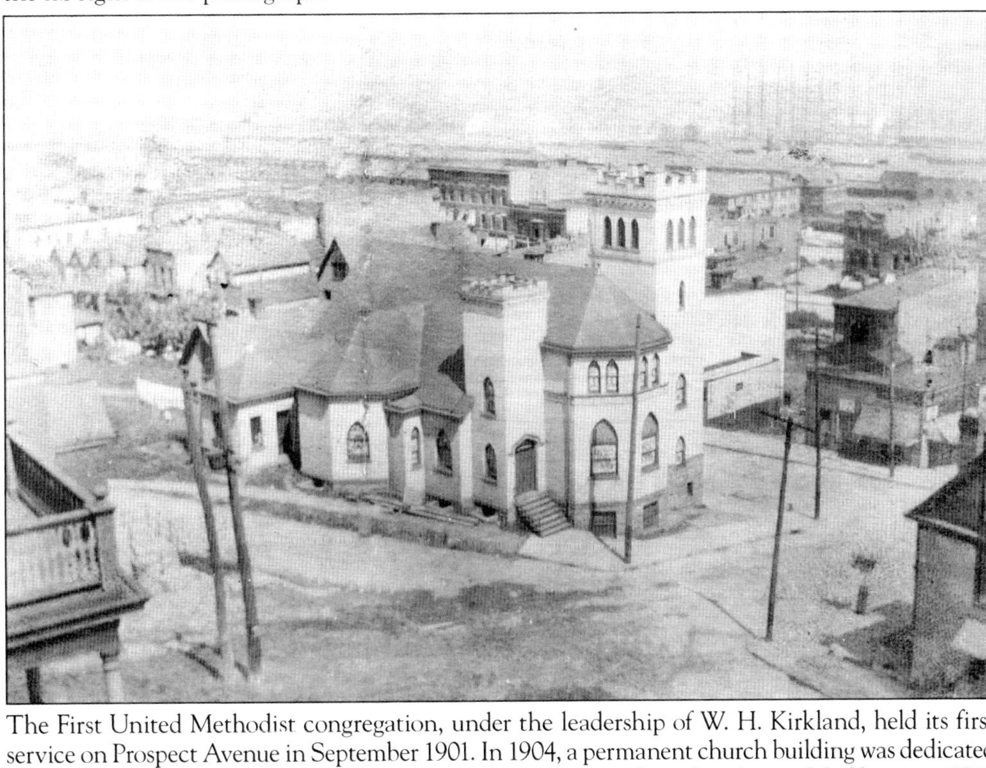

The First United Methodist congregation, under the leadership of W. H. Kirkland, held its first service on Prospect Avenue in September 1901. In 1904, a permanent church building was dedicated on the corner of Fifth Street and Thompson Avenue. It was enlarged and remodeled between 1919 and 1925. The church was eventually dissolved, and the building was given to the borough.

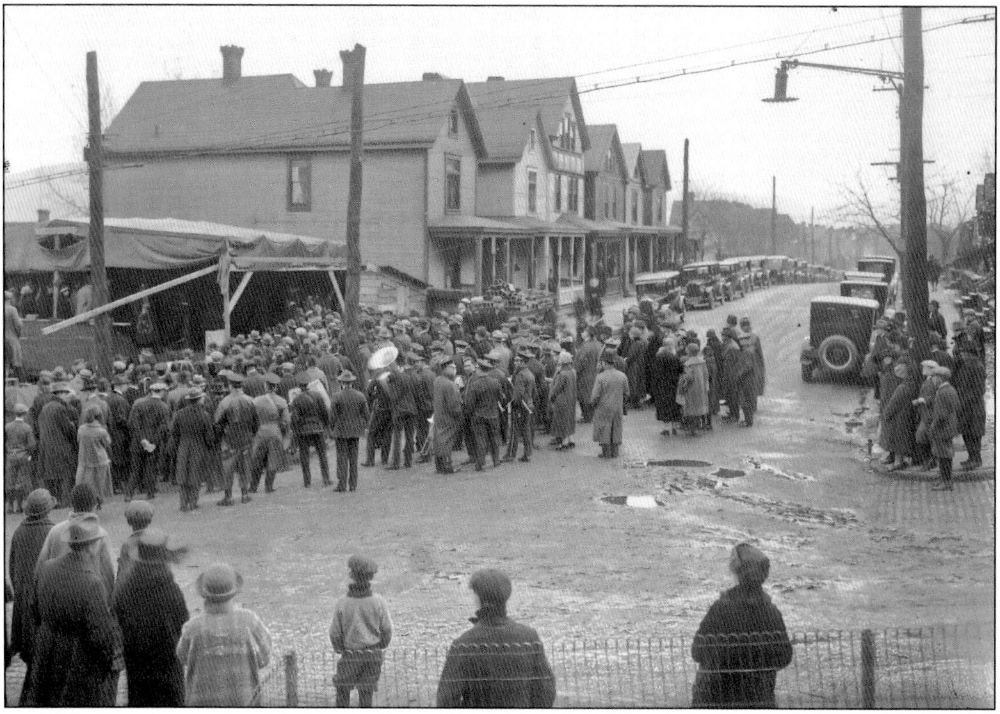

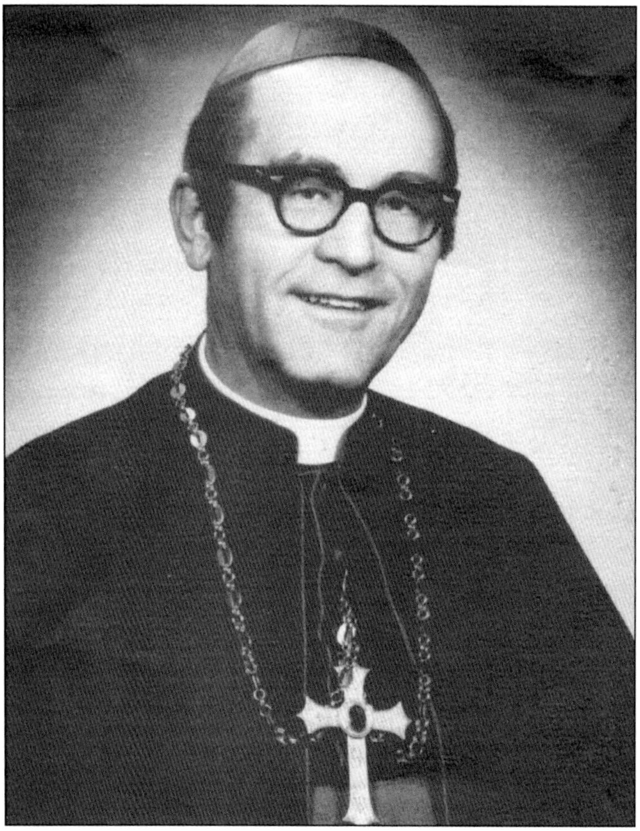

Although the Episcopal Church in Donora can trace its beginning to 1905, it was not until 1924 that a building was constructed. M. M. Neale, the superintendent of the zinc works, initiated the project. This September 5, 1924, photograph shows a crowd gathered at the corner of Tenth Street and Thompson Avenue to witness the laying of the cornerstone for the new church.

One of Donora's most distinguished clergymen was Archbishop Nicholas T. Elko. He was born and raised in Donora before he was ordained a priest in the Byzantine Rite of the Catholic Church. He was eventually elevated to the post of Archbishop of Cincinnati.

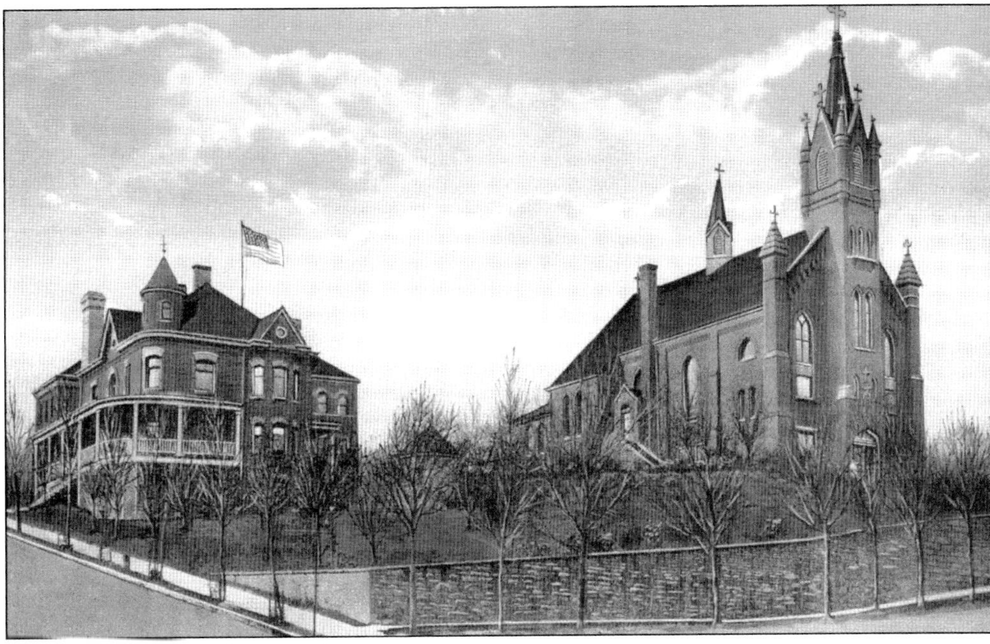

The Holy Name of Mary Parish was organized by a group of Donora families who had emigrated from Poland. In 1904, the church and large parish house were built on Second Street. The parish operated a parochial school staffed by the Holy Ghost Order.

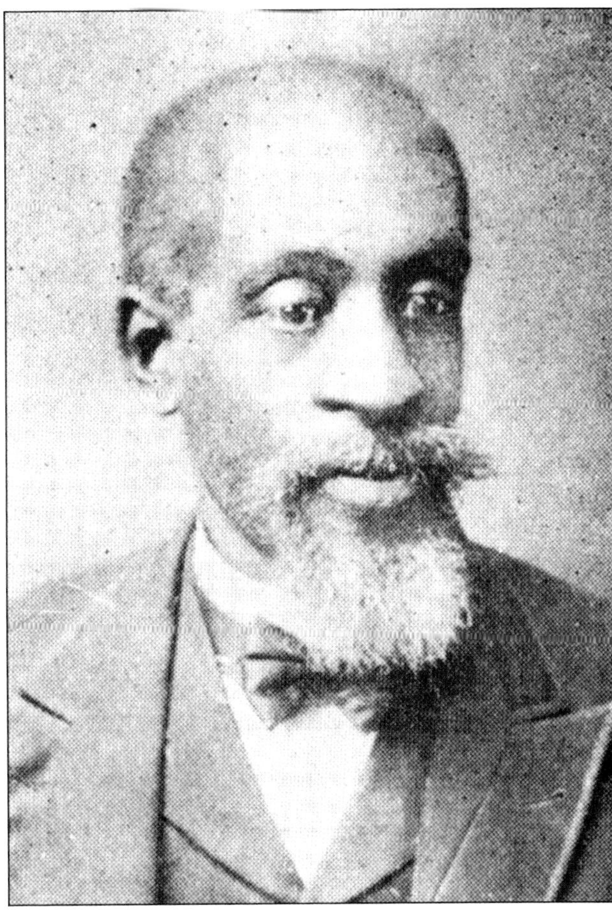

The first church in Donora was Quinn Chapel African Methodist Episcopal, built in 1901 by members of the town's African American community. The Reverend O. T. Davis, first pastor of Quinn Chapel, is pictured here. A year later, the First Baptist Church became the second African American church in town.

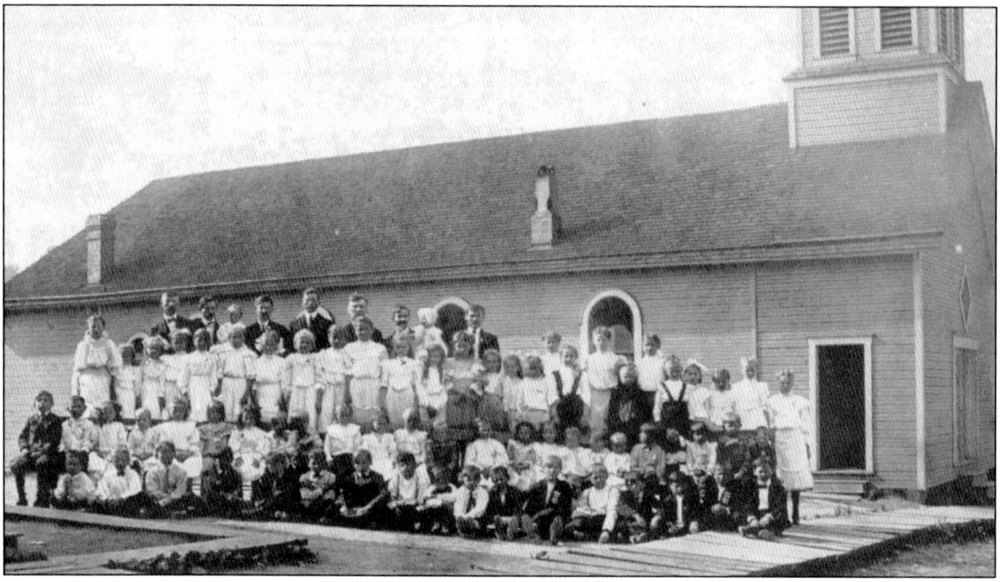

The first St. Michael Greek Catholic Church Byzantine Rite church was a small, wooden structure. This photograph shows unpaved streets with wooden sidewalks and the congregation proudly posing on the side of the structure. This building was replaced by a large, beautiful structure on Murray Avenue in 1912.

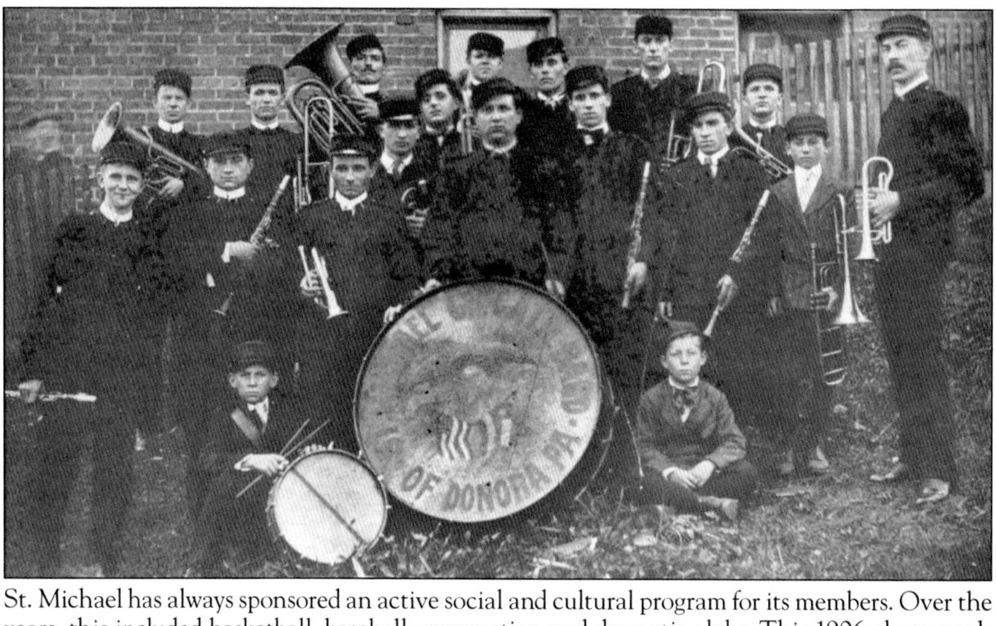

St. Michael has always sponsored an active social and cultural program for its members. Over the years, this included basketball, baseball, gymnastics, and dramatic clubs. This 1906 photograph shows the parish marching band.

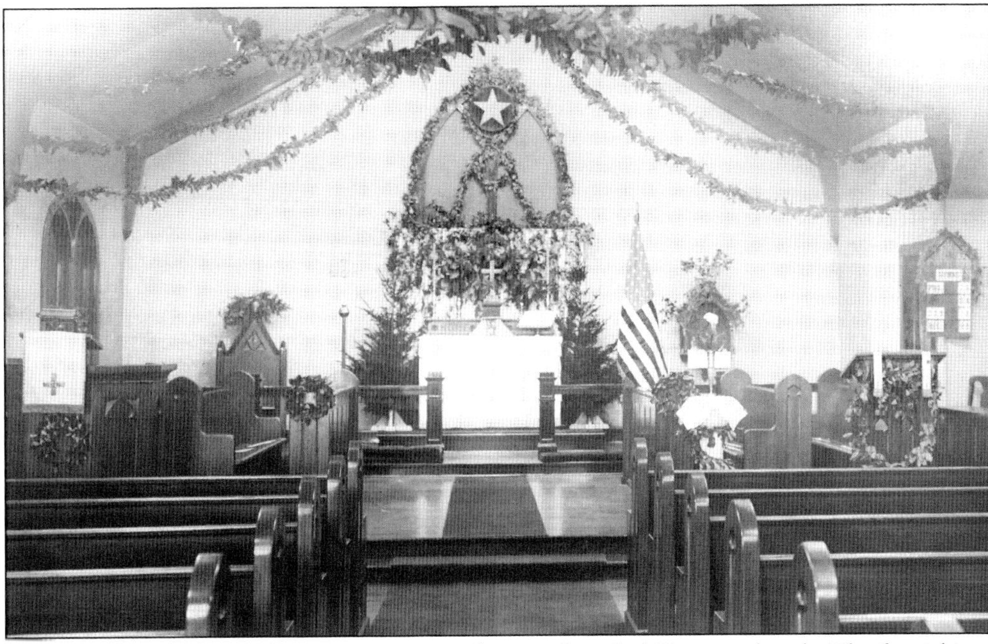

This photograph shows the ornate interior of an unidentified Donora church. The furnishings suggest a Catholic or Episcopal house of worship.

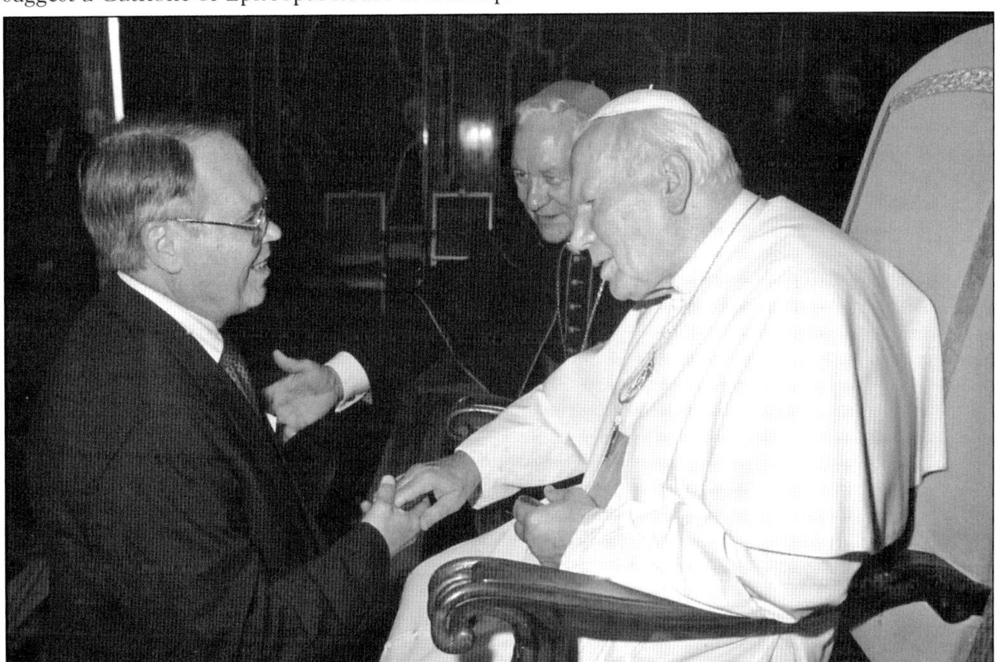

The Polish Falcons of America is one of Donora's fraternal organizations dedicated to preserving ethnic culture and providing information and educational benefits to its members. Town resident Wallace Zielenski served as national president of the association. While representing the Falcons, Zielenski traveled abroad and met prominent international figures of Polish heritage. In this photograph, he is seen in Rome during an audience with Pope John Paul II. He also met with Nobel Peace Prize winner Lech Walesa. (Courtesy Wallace Zielenski.)

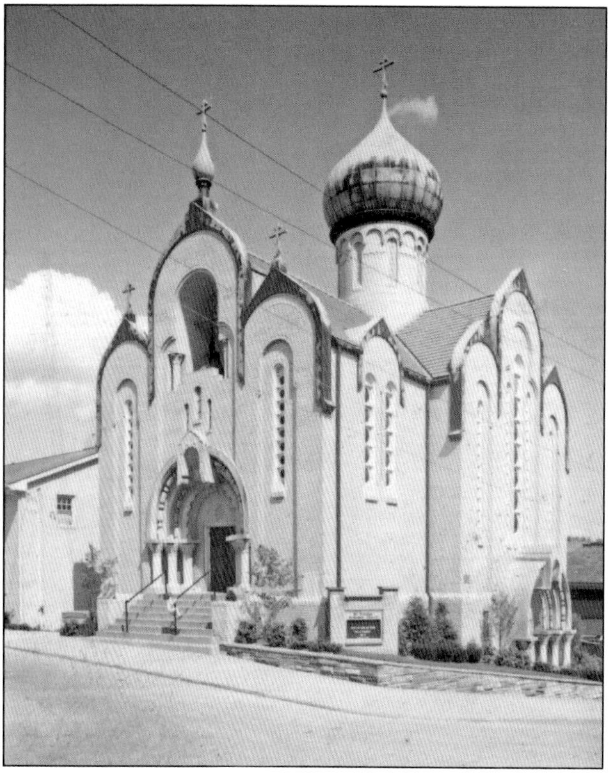

In 1916, a group of 15 families with roots to the Carpathian Mountain region organized St. Nicholas Russian Orthodox Church. In 1937, the congregation built an impressive church with a distinctive onion-shaped dome common to the Russian Orthodox style of architecture.

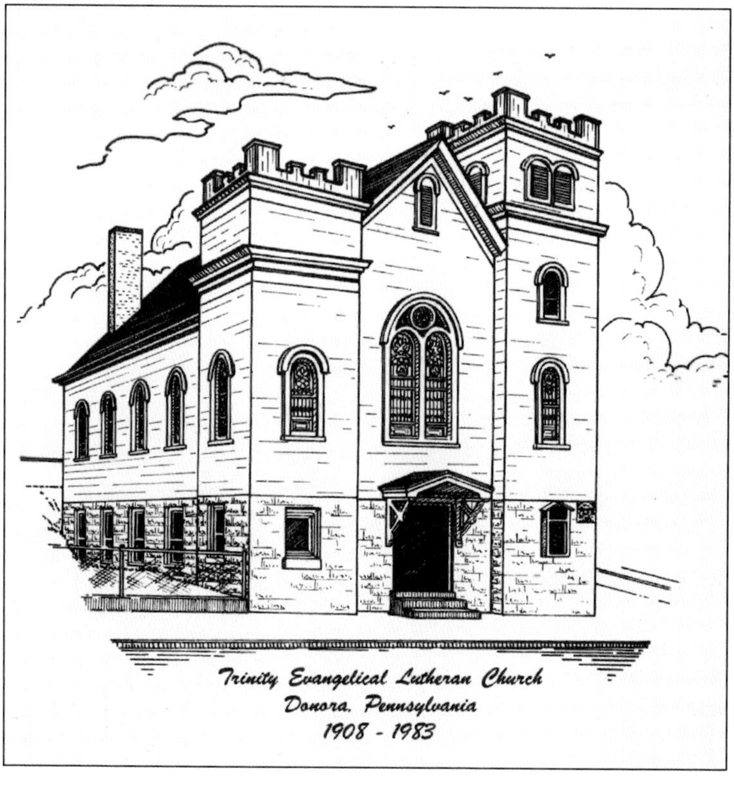

The Trinity Lutheran Church was organized in 1903. Architect C. C. Compton designed a church for the congregation that was built on the corner of Tenth Street and McKean Avenue in 1913. The church was closed in 2005 because of declining membership.

Six

Home of Champions

Few communities of any size can rival Donora's record of producing both outstanding scholastic sports teams as well as individual athletes who excelled in collegiate and professional competition. Over the years, two Donora natives have been named to Major League Baseball's All-Century Team. Two were named baseball player of the decade. Three Donorans have played in the Major League Baseball All-Star Game, and two were named the All-Star Game's Most Valuable Player. A Donora football player led the National Football League in rushing and was a Pro Bowl Most Valuable Player. The record for the most athletic letters earned at the United States Military Academy is held by a Donoran, and the first African American to become president of a professional baseball organization is from the borough.

Many people believe the success of Donora's athletes can be attributed to the work ethic that is part of the community's industrial heritage. From their youth, the citizens of the town have learned the value of physical and mental toughness, hard work, and persistence. These important characteristics were nurtured by the presence of admirable role models. The combination of these factors earned Donora its nickname, the "Home of Champions."

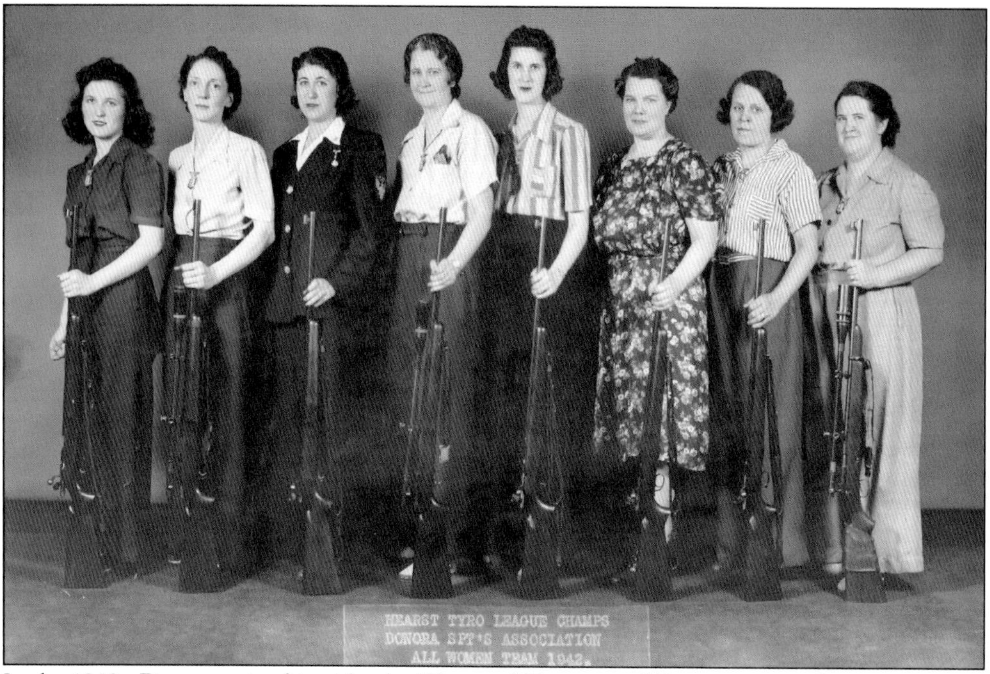

In the 1940s, Donora gained its title, the "Home of Champions." During a time when competition opportunities for female athletes were limited, the first championship won in that decade was done so by girls. In 1942, a ladies rifle team claimed the title trophy in the tri-state tournament sponsored by the *Pittsburgh Sun Telegraph*. Competitive shooting ended in Donora during World War II.

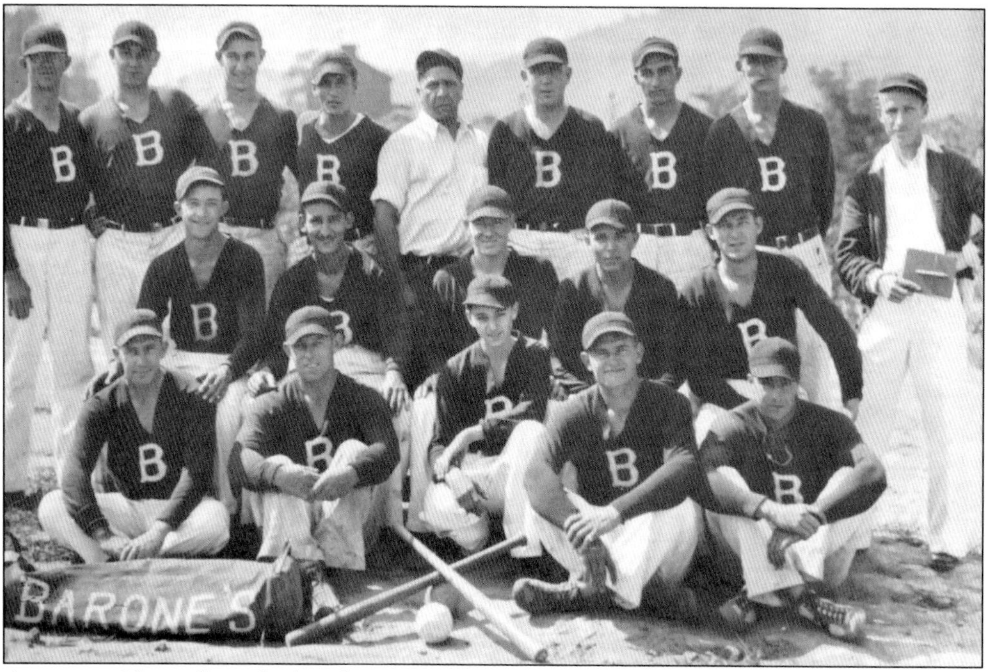

Amateur athletics flourished in the town in the years before television. Donorans turned out by the thousands to watch the highly competitive fast-pitch and slo-pitch softball games played at Palmer Park. Barone's Shoe Store sponsored the team shown in this picture.

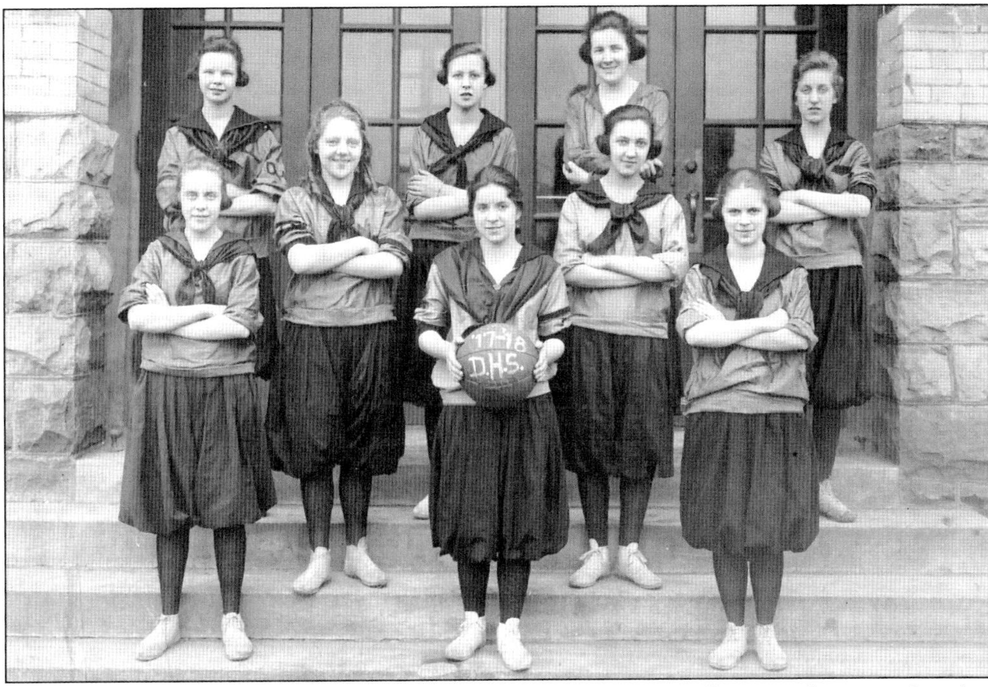

Pictured here is the 1917–1918 Donora High School girls' basketball team. The team played its home games in the small gym in the Fifth Street School, which at the time was a combination junior-senior high school. The girls are wearing typical uniforms, which were designed to allow free movement while maintaining feminine modesty.

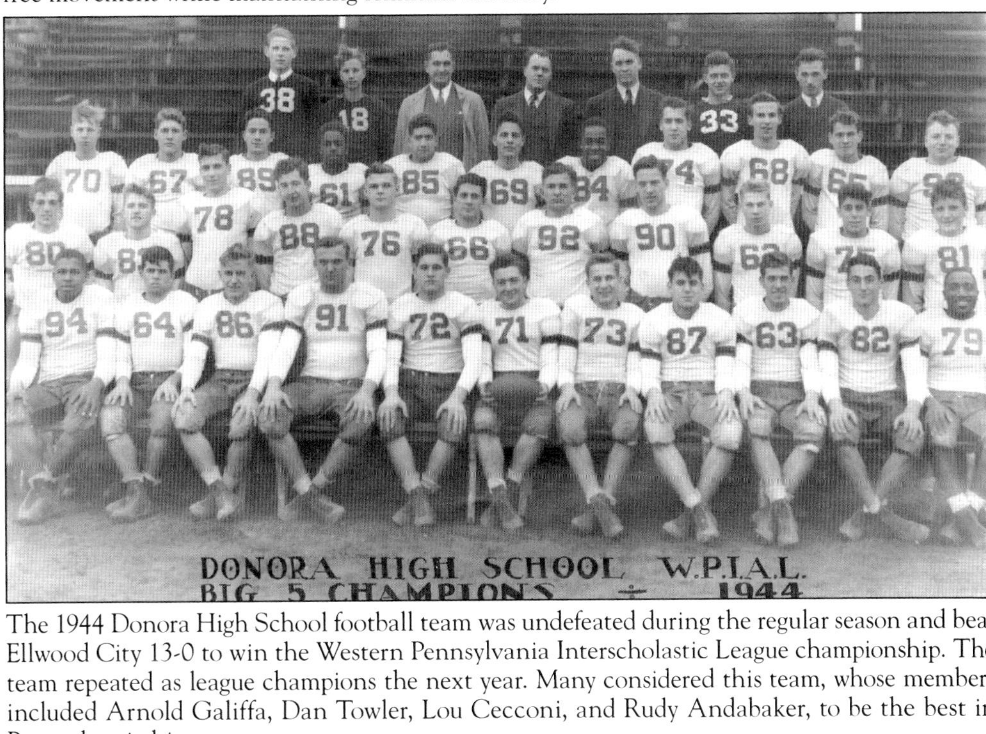

The 1944 Donora High School football team was undefeated during the regular season and beat Ellwood City 13-0 to win the Western Pennsylvania Interscholastic League championship. The team repeated as league champions the next year. Many considered this team, whose members included Arnold Galiffa, Dan Towler, Lou Cecconi, and Rudy Andabaker, to be the best in Pennsylvania history.

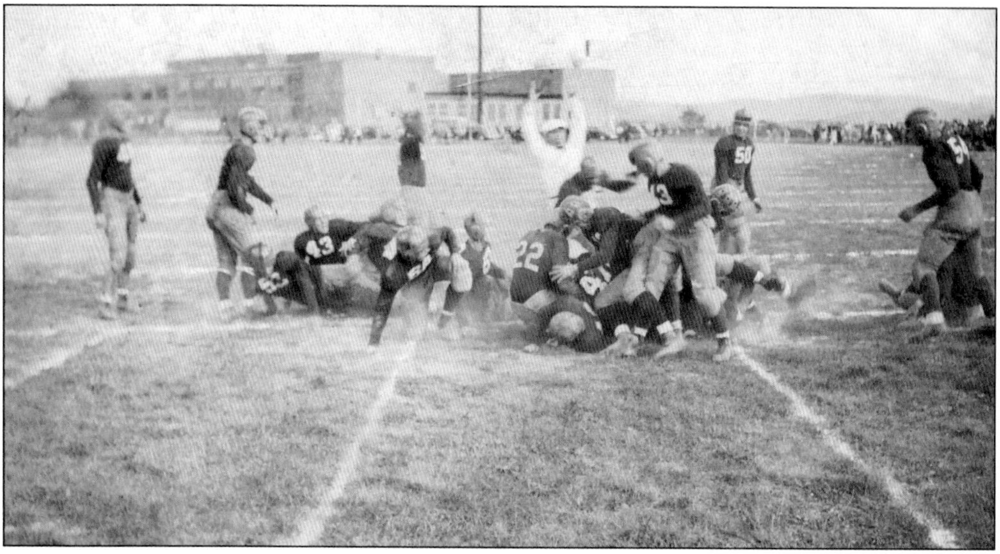

In 1931, the construction of the senior high school was completed, and the school's football and baseball teams moved their home fields from Palmer Park to the American Legion field adjacent to the school. This picture shows one of the first football games played at the new venue. The new school can be seen in the background. The standing fans indicate no bleachers had yet been built. (Courtesy Sally Hurha Phillips.)

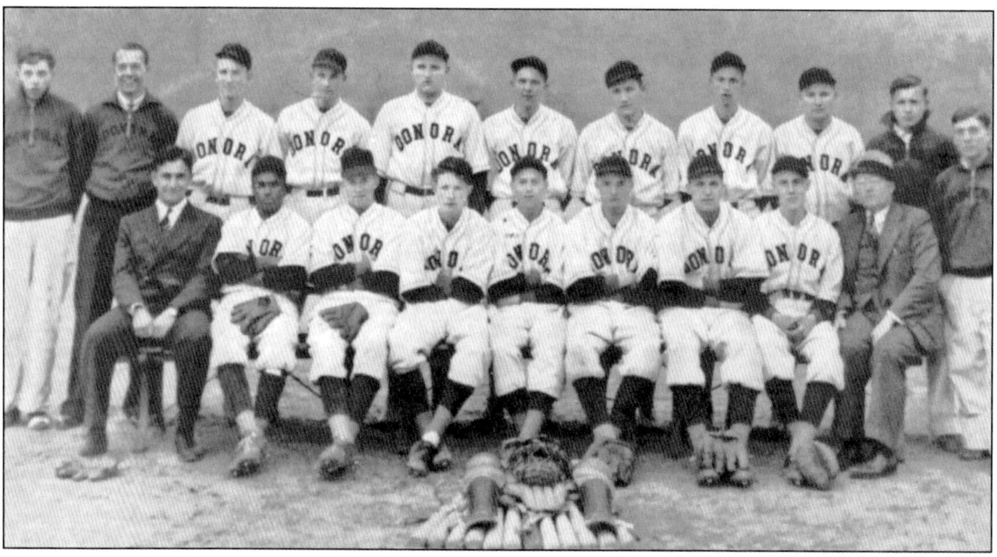

Members of the 1939 Donora High School baseball team are pictured here. In the second row, fourth from the left, is future hall of famer Stan Musial. Second from the left in the first row is Joseph "Buddy" Griffey, father of Major League Baseball All-Star Ken Griffey and grandfather of All-Star Ken Griffey Jr. The coach of the team is Dr. Michael "Ki" Duda, who later became president of California University of Pennsylvania.

Stan Musial is arguably Donora's most prominent athlete. "Stan the Man" always credited Donora and its people for much of his success. He frequently returned home to visit family and friends, often signing autographs and posing for pictures. This photograph shows Musial in town for the 1951 Golden Jubilee celebration.

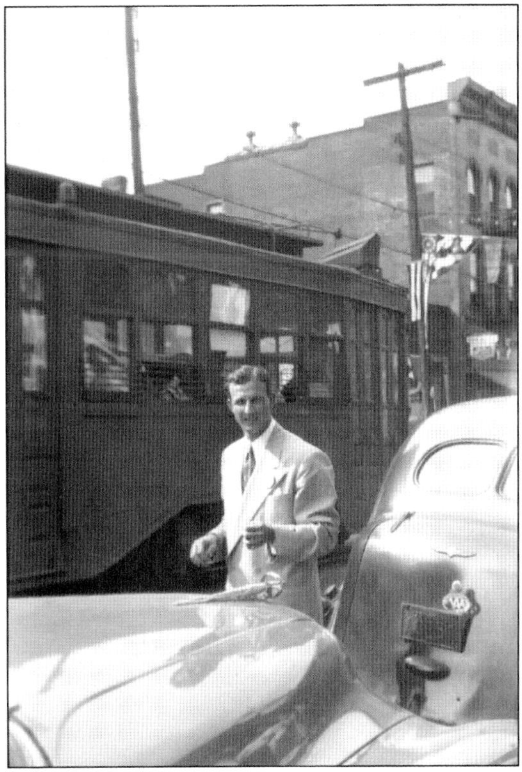

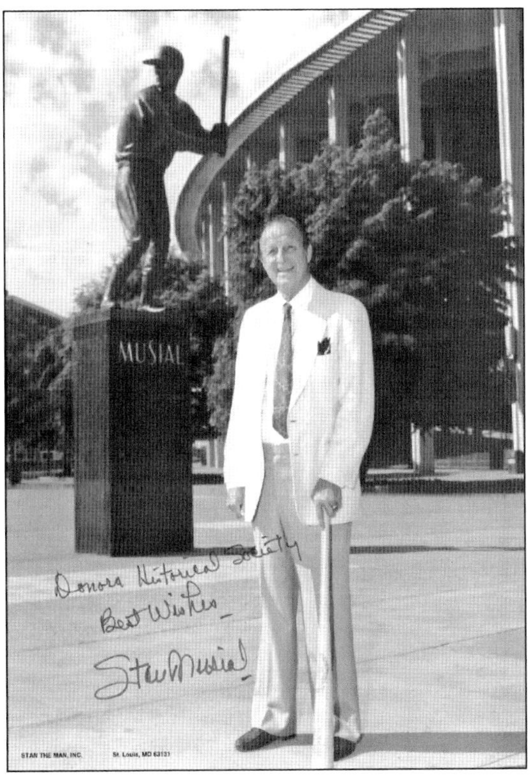

Before his exceptional career with the St. Louis Cardinals, Musial lived and worked in Donora. He retired from baseball in 1963 with a .331 career batting average, 475 home runs, 1,951 runs batted in, and was eventually inducted into the Baseball Hall of Fame. He was called "baseball's perfect knight." He is pictured here in front of his statue at Busch Stadium in St. Louis. (Courtesy Stan Musial.)

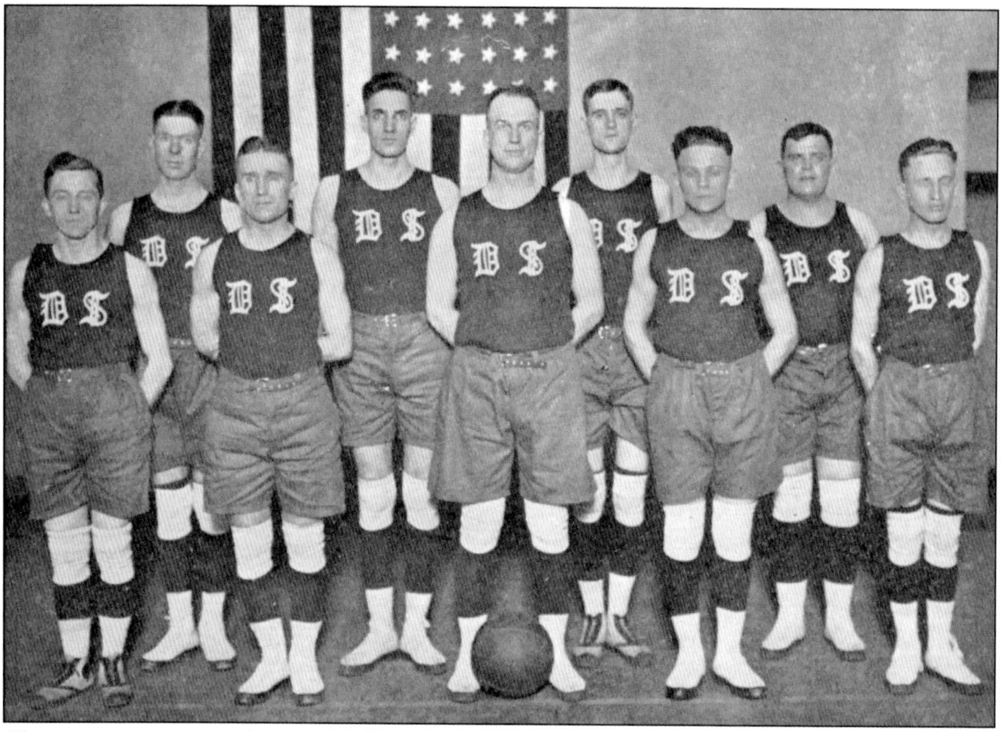

There was a strong rivalry among the various athletic teams sponsored by the Mon-Valley steel mills. In 1921, the Donora Americo Club Steel Workers defeated a highly touted team from Rankin in basketball by the score of 60-17. Judging from the photograph, the muscular physiques of the team's players may have been a contributing factor in the lopsided victory.

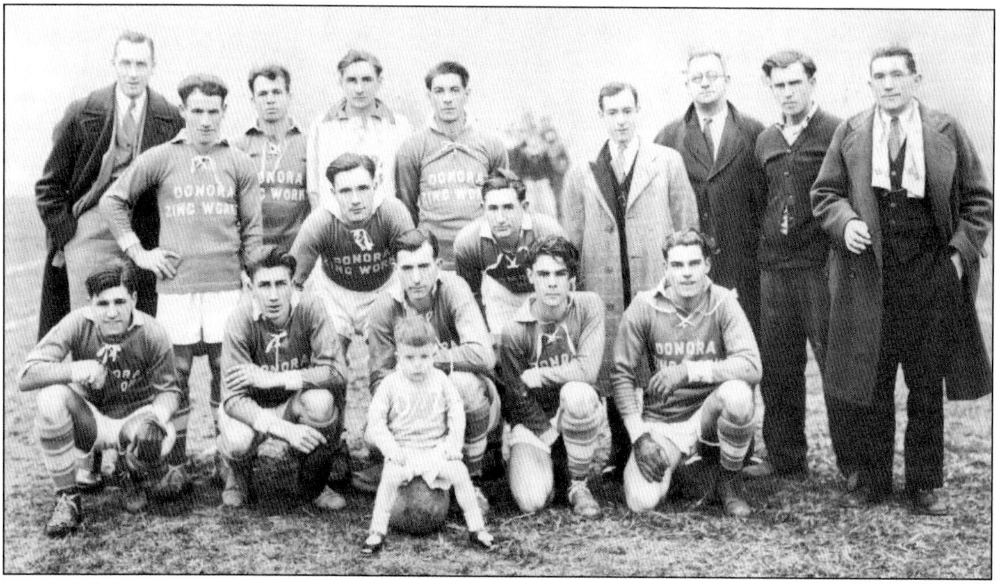

Zinc workers of Spanish descent had a strong interest in soccer and formed teams that competed successfully throughout the state. One of the highlights of the annual Spanish Club picnic held in July was a soccer game between the Donora team and opponents who came from as far away as St. Louis.

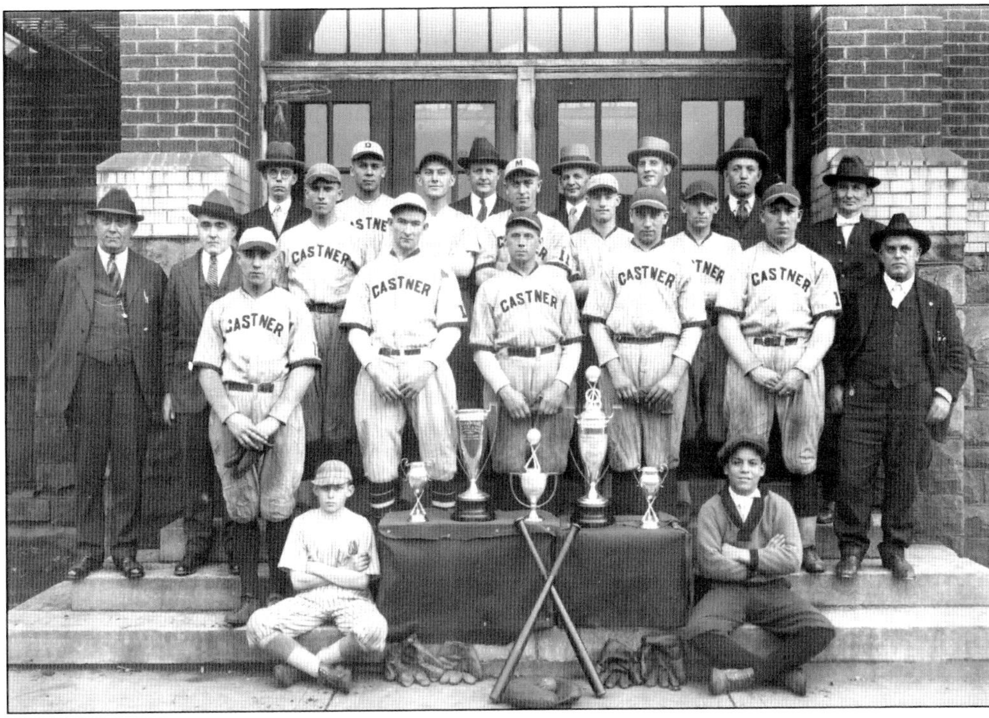

Pictured here is the 1920 Castner baseball team. The physical maturity of the players and the variety of ball caps indicates this was an adult all-star team. The number of trophies on display suggests the team had some success, but not much else is known about its record. The stories of neighborhood teams such as this are part of Donora's lost history.

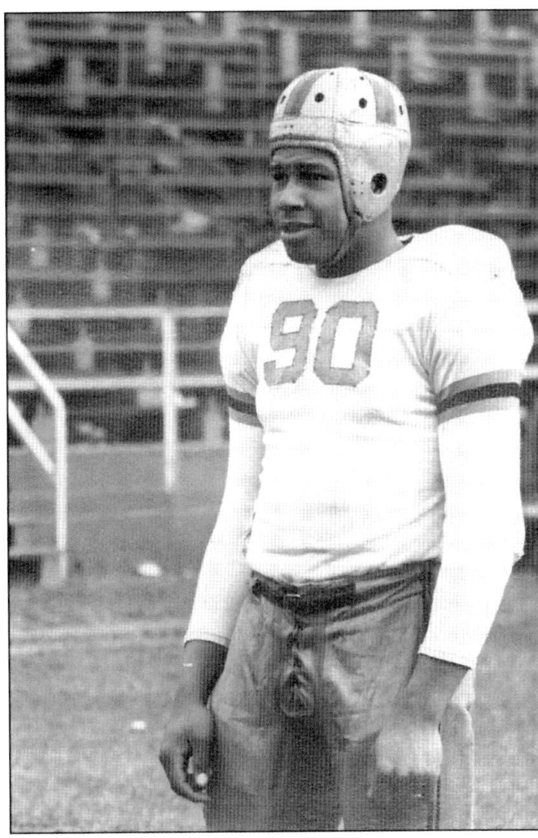

After playing fullback on the 1944 and 1945 Donora High School championship teams, "Deacon" Dan Towler went on to outstanding collegiate and professional careers. As a member of the Los Angeles Rams, he won the National Football League championship, led the league in rushing, and was named Most Valuable Player in the Pro Bowl. Later he earned a doctorate in theology and became pastor of a large Baptist church in Los Angeles.

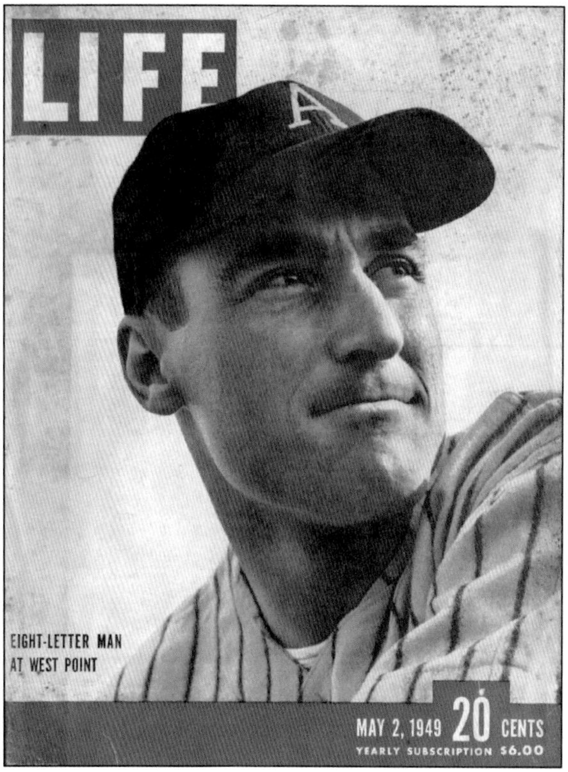

Arnold "Pope" Galiffa earned all-state honors in football and basketball at Donora High School, and then he won 11 varsity letters in sports at the United States Military Academy. After his senior year, he was selected as first-team all-American quarterback and then served with distinction during the Korean War. After his military discharge, he played professional football and then returned to reside in Donora, where he became a respected member of the borough council. (Courtesy Time-Warner Company.)

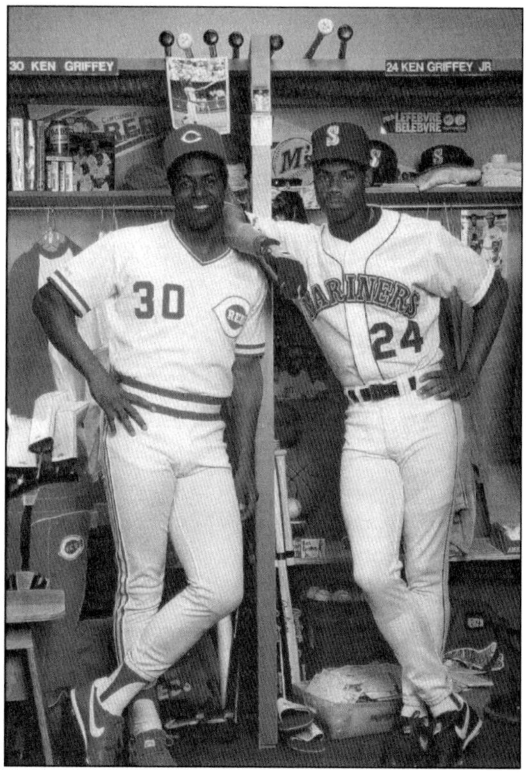

Donora natives Ken Griffey Sr. and Ken Griffey Jr. have been Major League Baseball stars for the past four decades. Griffey Sr. played for the Cincinnati Reds, the New York Yankees, the Atlanta Braves, and the Seattle Mariners and was named Most Valuable Player of the All-Star Game in 1980. Griffey Jr. was named All-Star Game Most Valuable Player in 1992, American League Most Valuable Player in 1997, and player of the decade for the 1990s. They were the first father/son tandem to play on the same team and hit back-to-back home runs. (Courtesy Casey Perrotta.)

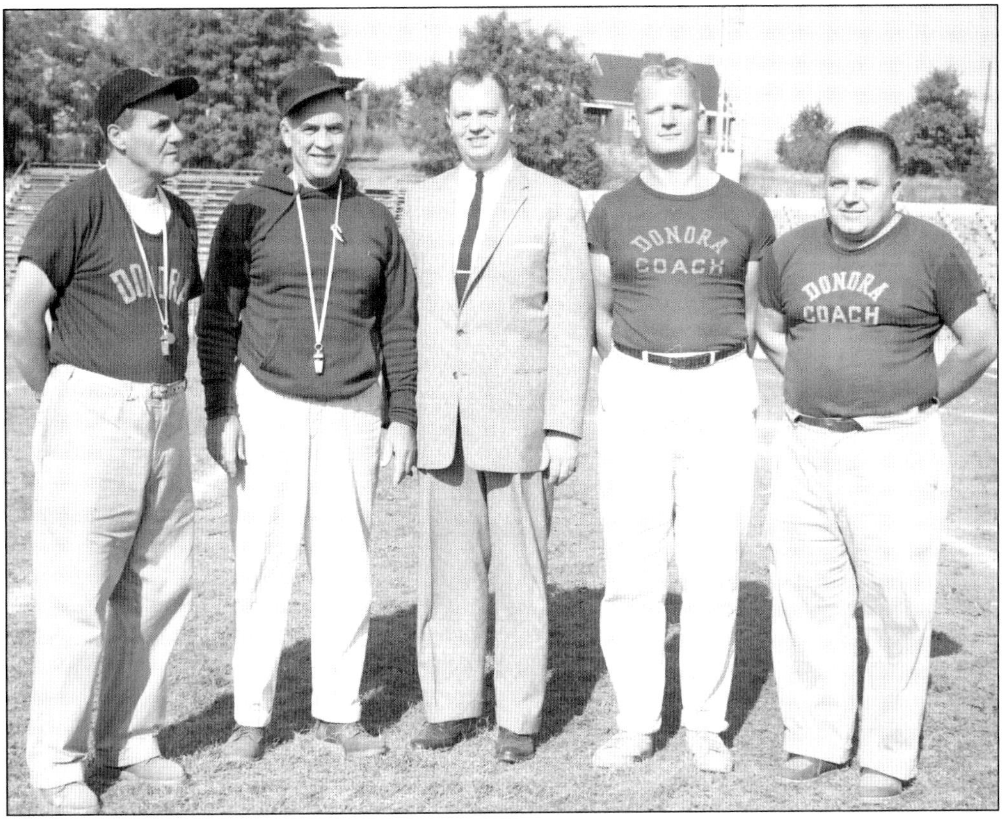

Some of Donora High School's outstanding coaches pose in this 1960s photograph. Included from left to right are James K. Russell, John P. "Moon" Clark, Dr. Michael J. Herk, Rudy Andabaker, and Bill Pykosh.

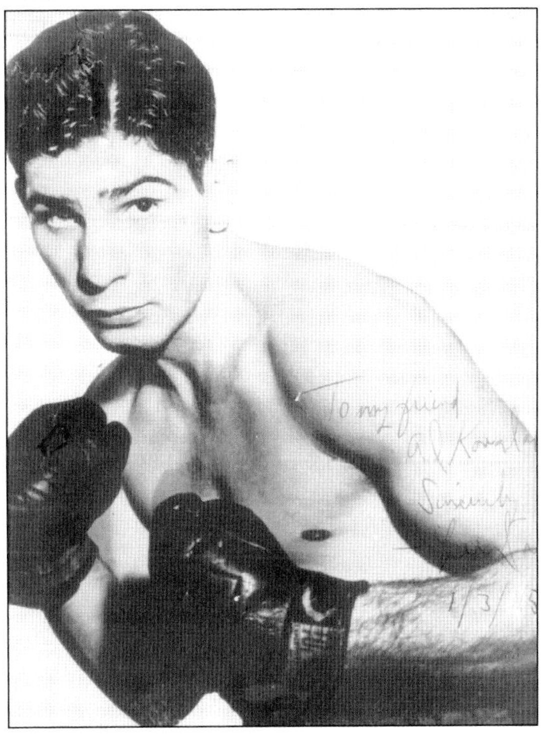

Lee Sala was the most famous of Donora's family of boxers. After returning from military service during World War II, he won 48 straight bouts and achieved a *Ring* magazine ranking as one of the top 10 middleweight fighters in the world. After retiring from boxing, he moved to Florida and worked as a police officer. (Courtesy Albert Kovalik.)

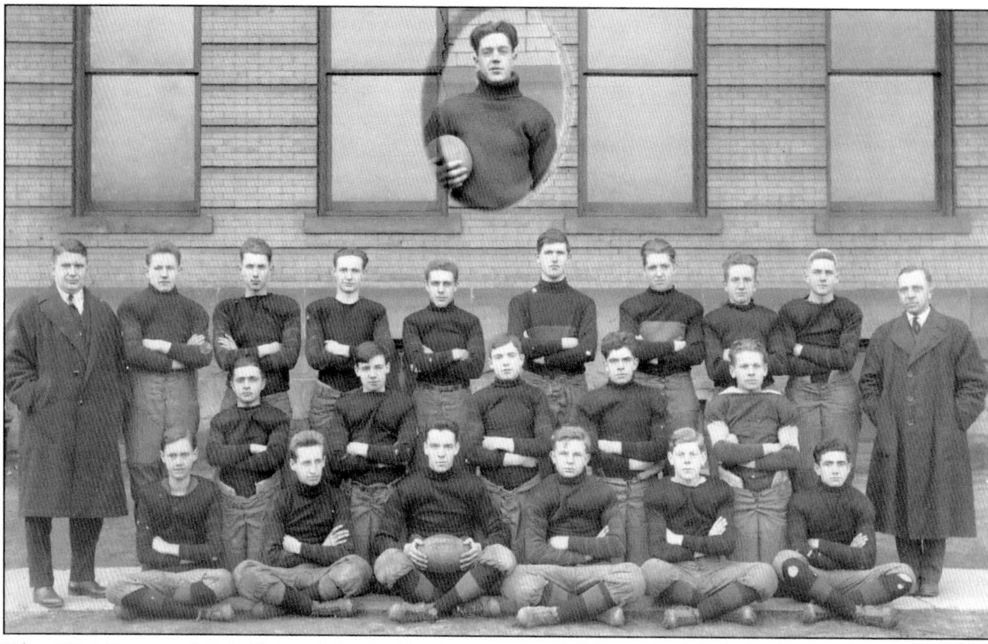

The 1914 Donora High School football team is pictured here outside Castner School with A. J. Martin (far left), the first salaried school football coach. In the first row (far right) is Max Heatter, who later became a prominent physician in town. The third player from the left in the back row is George Frazier, who became a well-known attorney. This team actually practiced and played at Gilmore Field on Fourteenth Street.

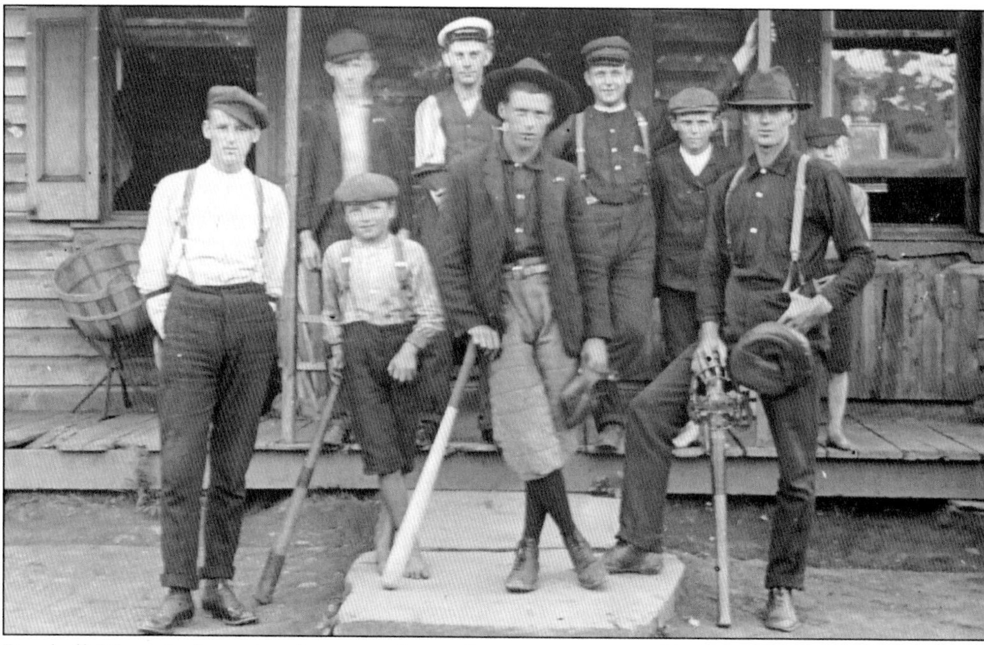

Baseball, "America's pastime," was one form of recreation enjoyed by Donora workers during time off from their long hours in the mill. This group of players poses on the front steps of Watkins General Store in the first decade of the 20th century. Note the lack of uniforms and the condition of the bats and catcher's equipment.

Seven

ENTER TO LEARN

The community of Donora has always had a strong commitment to education. Education has been perceived as the means of acquiring the knowledge, skills, and credentials necessary to advance economically, socially, and professionally. Parents told their children that formal schooling could prepare them for employment in fields other than the mills and mines of the Monongahela River Valley.

Donorans also imbued their children with a strong work ethic that carried into the classroom. Students were expected to study hard, follow the direction of the teacher, and behave in school. This pattern was seen as the key to successfully improving their lot in life. This combination of student work values, community support, parental encouragement, and dedicated teachers produced an extraordinary number of successful Donorans. Therefore, education, as much as any other factor, has truly made this small community the "Home of Champions."

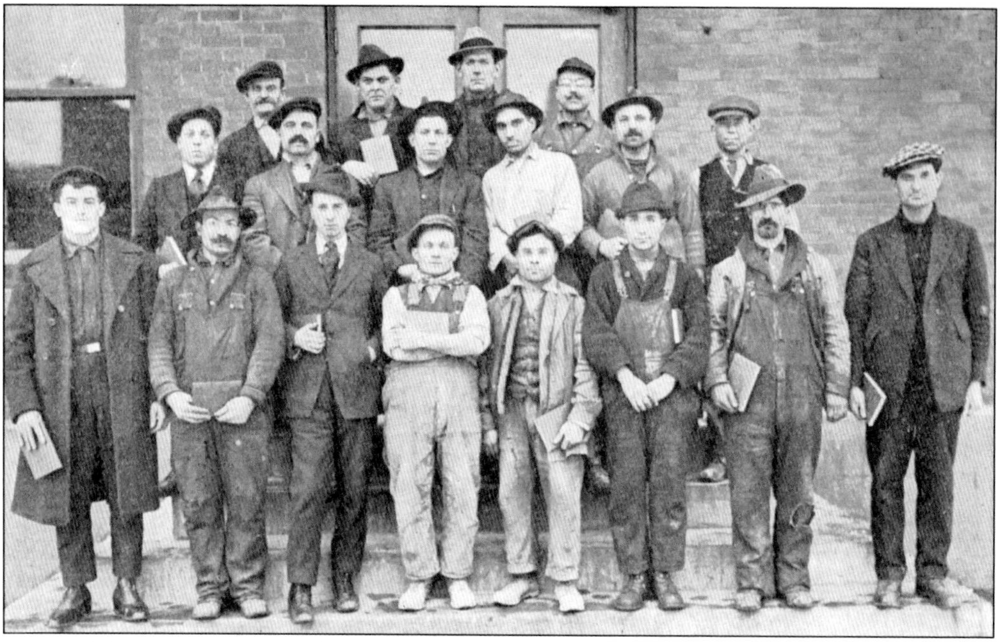

Many of the early residents of Donora who emigrated from southeastern Europe spoke little English and were unfamiliar with the customs of their new homeland. Citizenship classes were held to help these individuals become full-fledged American citizens. Pictured here is a group of workers enrolled in such a class in 1921.

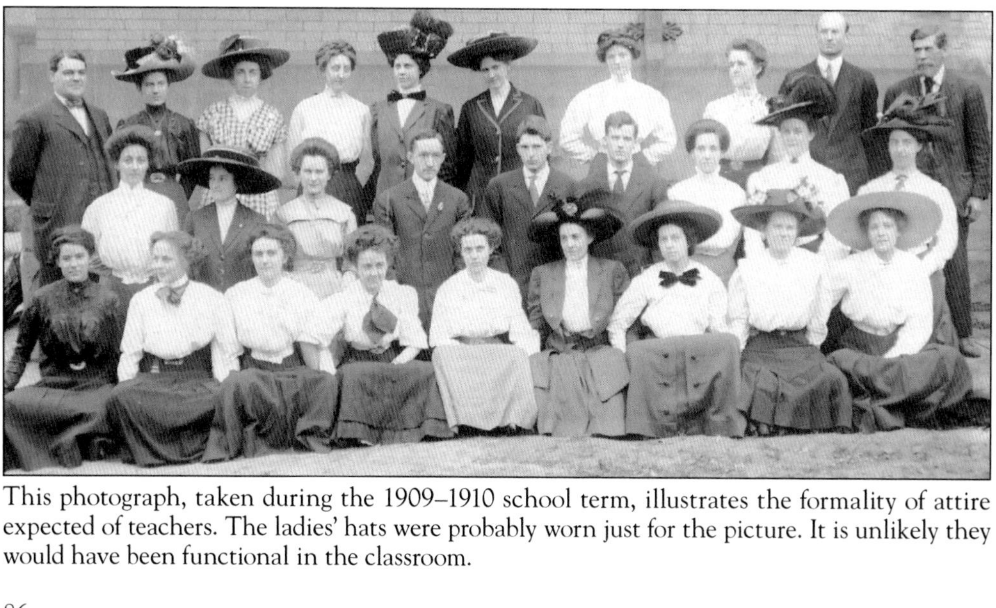

This photograph, taken during the 1909–1910 school term, illustrates the formality of attire expected of teachers. The ladies' hats were probably worn just for the picture. It is unlikely they would have been functional in the classroom.

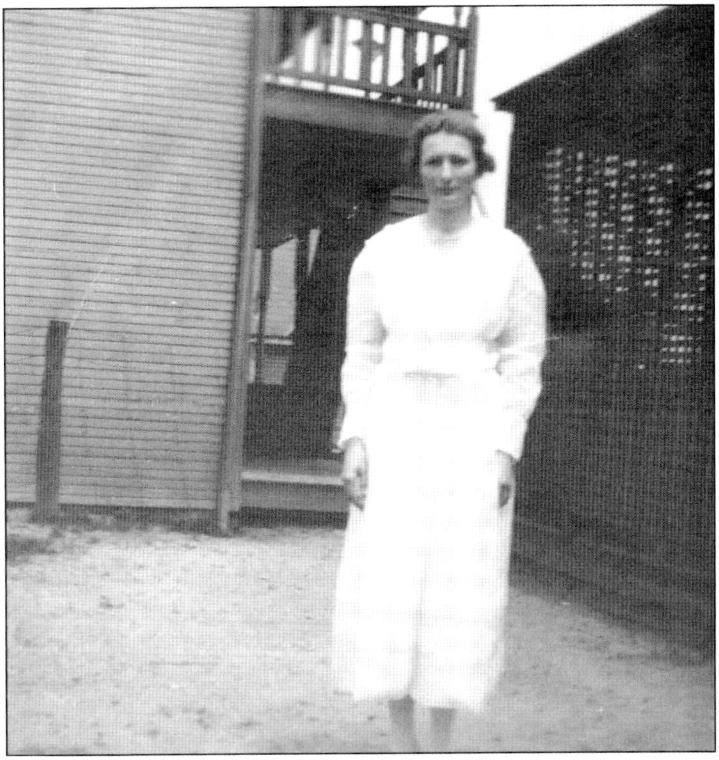

Margaret Gillingham attended Castner School. She is the third girl from the left in the second row in the 1906 picture (below) of the first-grade class. In 1918, she finished high school and posed for a picture in her graduation dress (right). The picture, taken outside her home, shows the ever-present mill smoke.

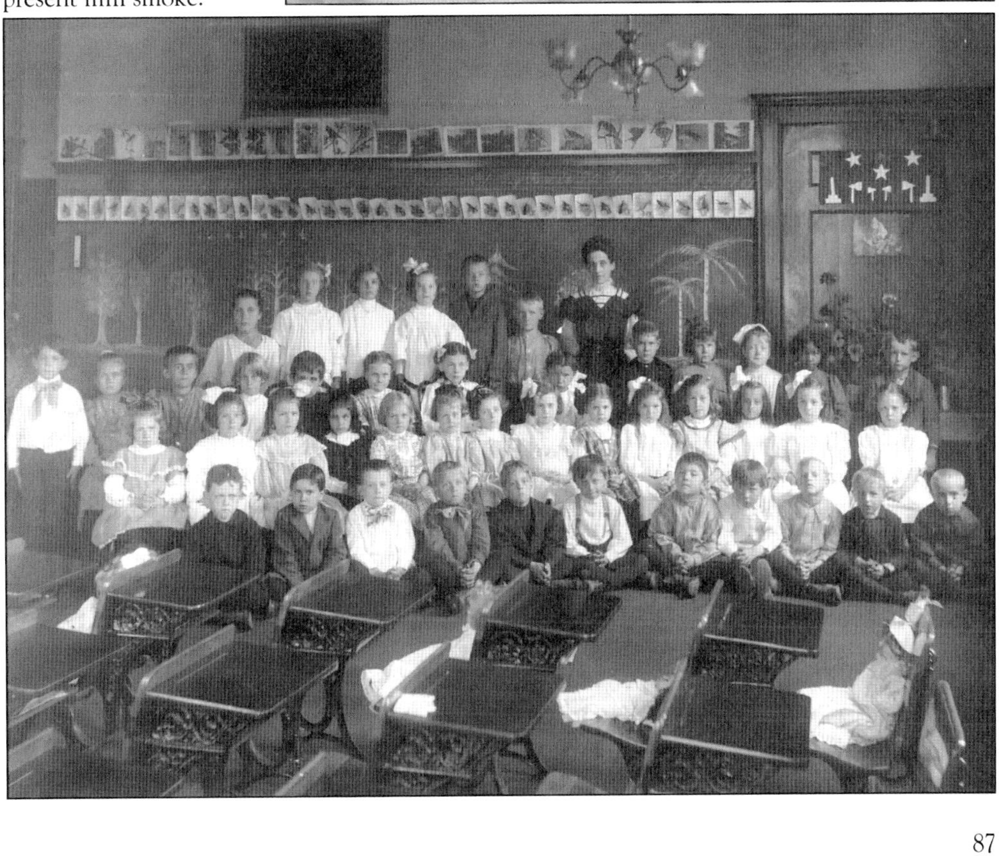

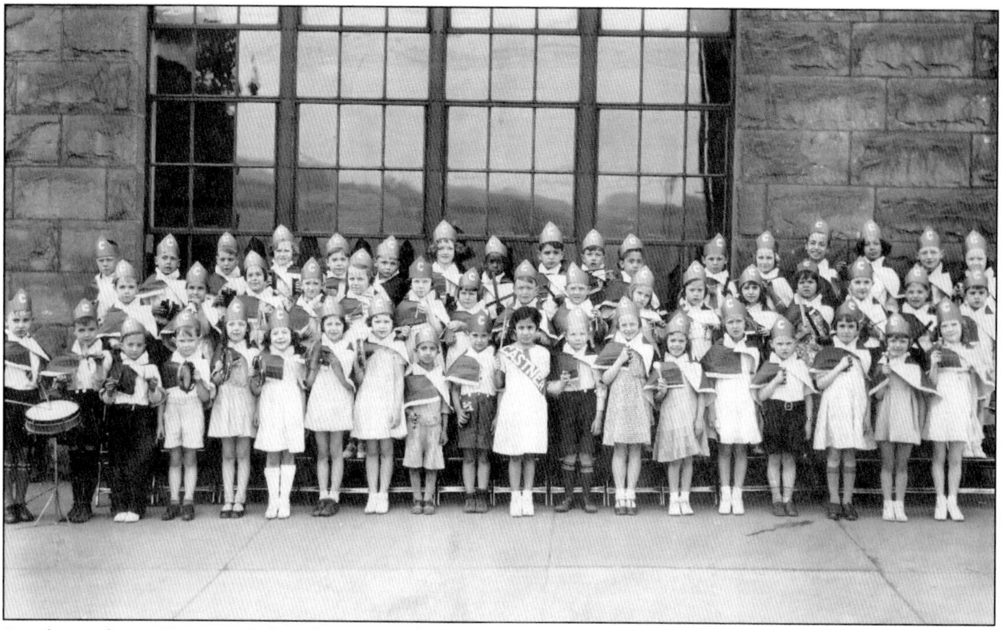

Students from Castner School are seen holding a variety of percussion instruments in this 1935 photograph. To help develop strength, stamina, and coordination, the students marched around the school yard "playing" these instruments. Some of these youngsters doubtlessly went on to become members of the high school marching band.

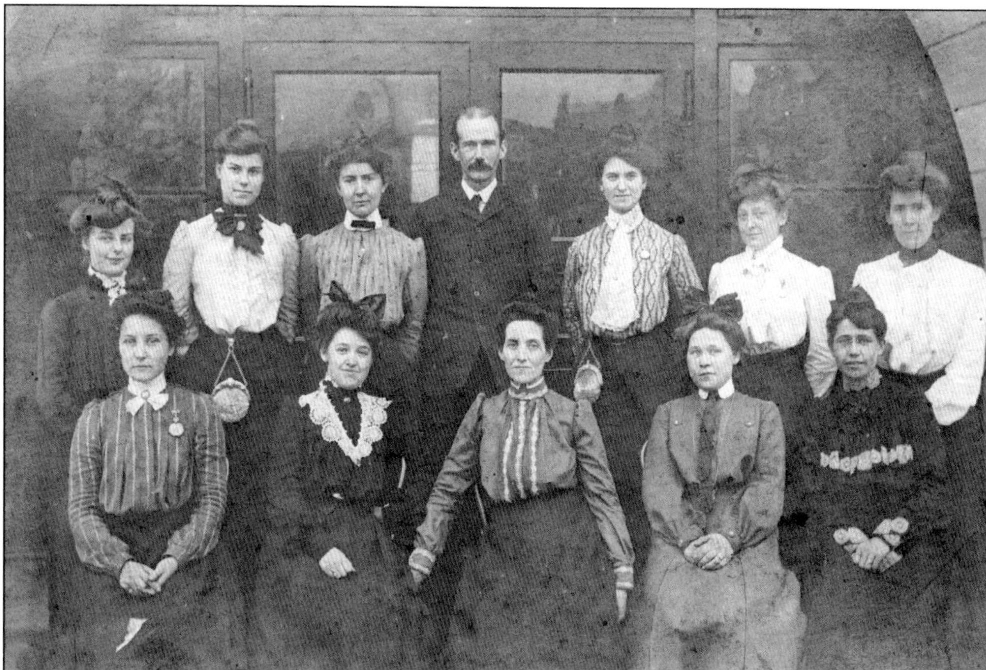

As this photograph of the first faculty of Castner School shows, basic education in the first half of the 20th century was dominated by female teachers. Teacher licensing requirements mandated only two years of college. Most of these women were probably unmarried, another common requirement of local school boards.

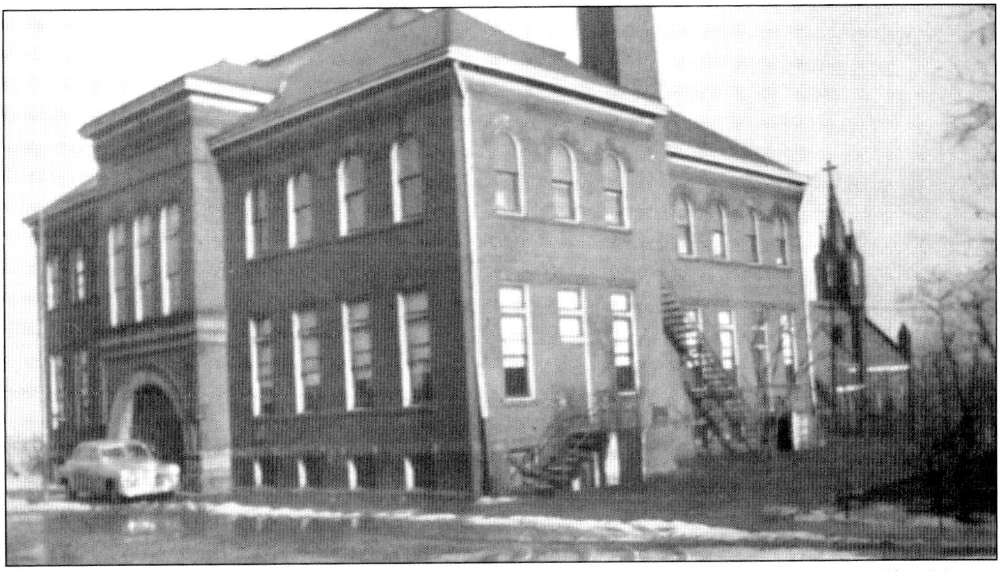

Allen School was the first one built after the borough's incorporation in 1901. The Union Improvement Company donated a large tract of land at the crest of Second Street for construction of an elementary school. The brick structure with eight classrooms opened in September 1901 with an enrollment of 252. The next year's enrollment swelled to 625. Note St. Mary's Church in the background.

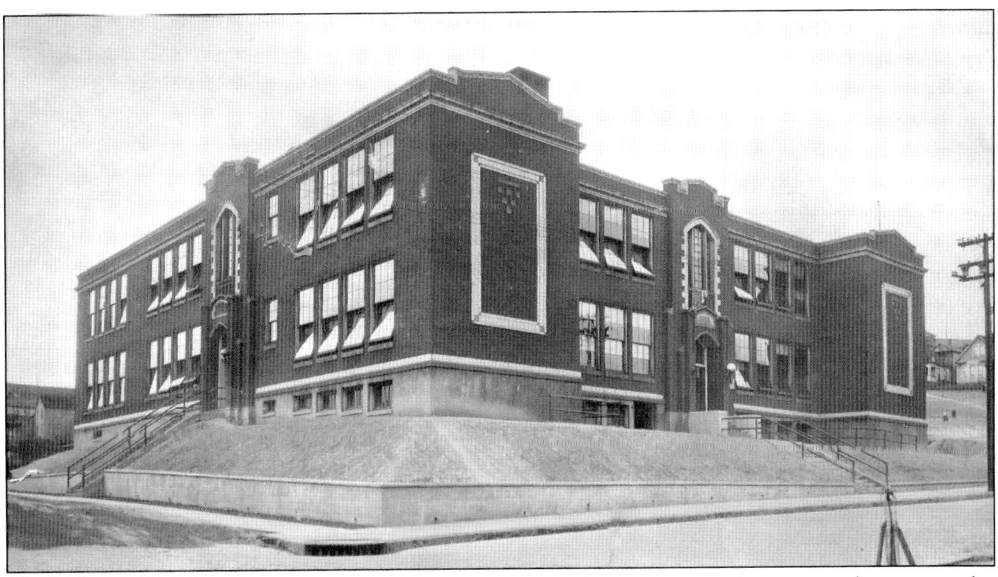

Sixth Street School opened in 1920 to accommodate the children living in new homes on the hill above town. The construction site was created by leveling a steep slope. The school's small playground can be seen at the back of the building. This structure, like all of Donora's schools, became a part of the consolidated Ringgold School District in 1964. Sixth Street School was eventually closed and razed.

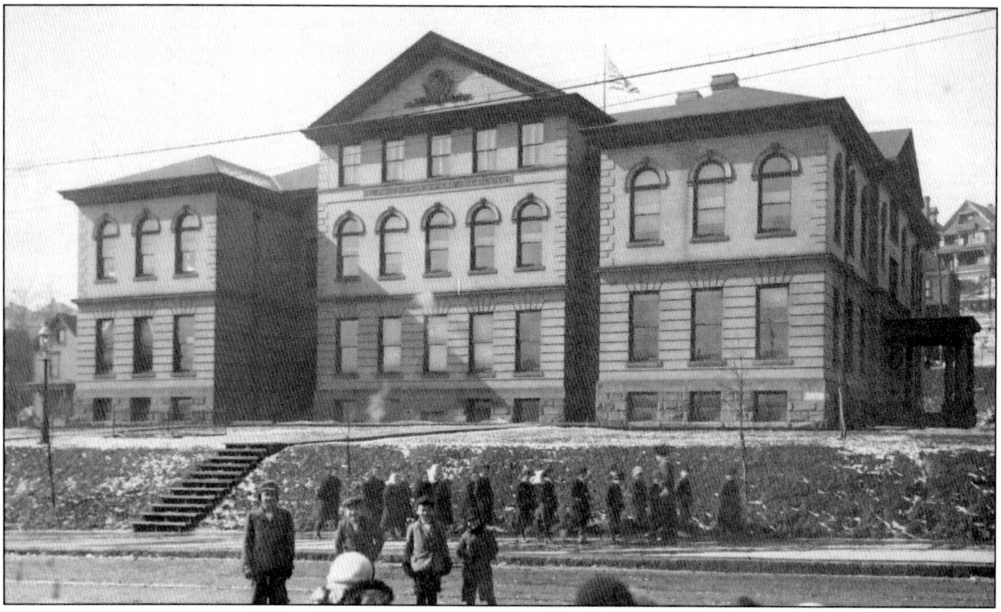

Castner School was built in 1903 in the northeast quadrant of Donora on McKean Avenue to educate the children of families living in the newly annexed land between Eighth and Tenth Streets. It had 12 classrooms and a spacious auditorium. For several years, it served as both an elementary school and a high school.

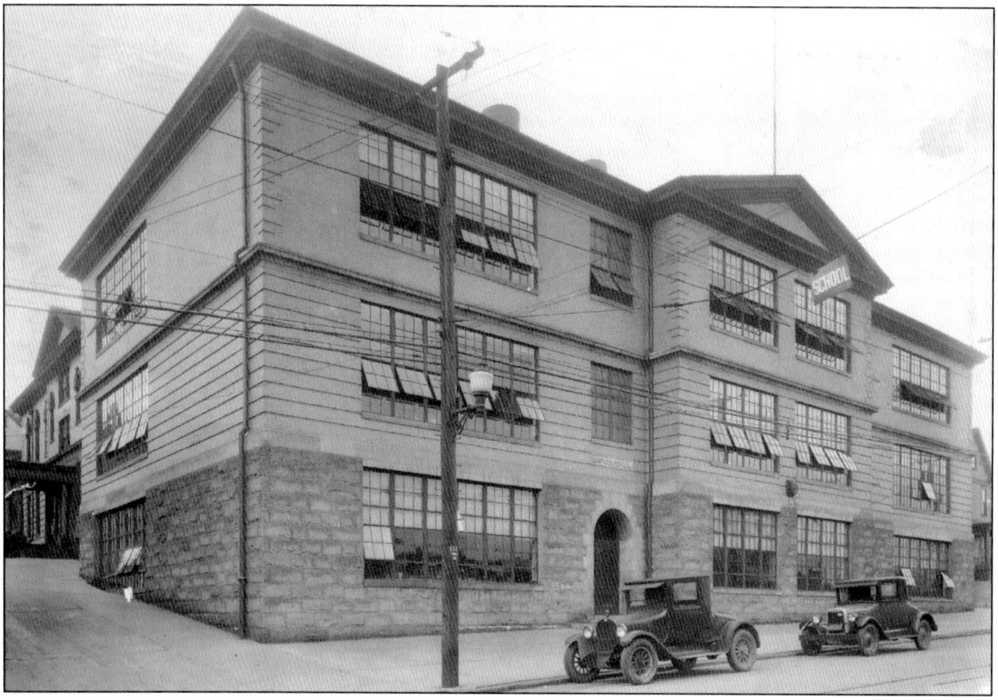

In 1926, the population growth in Donora necessitated making major changes to Castner School. The new addition contained several classrooms and three rooms used as gymnasiums. The auditorium was relocated to the street area in the new section. Castner School has been demolished and modern townhouses now occupy the site.

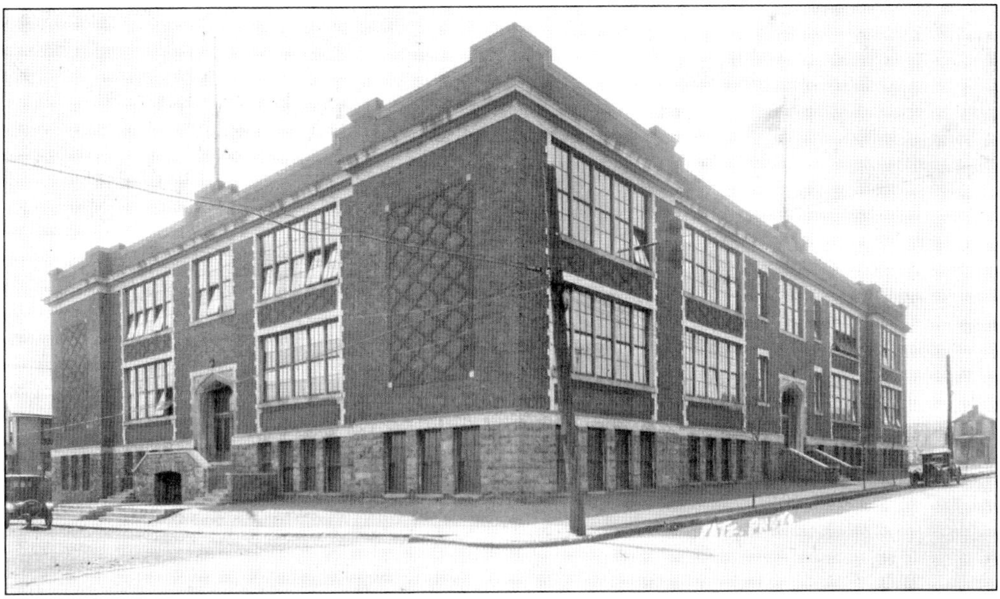

The First Street School, which later became the junior high school, was opened in 1913. The dedication ceremony for the new school was a gala occasion attended by Pennsylvania governor Martin Brumbaugh. From 1920 until 1931, when the new high school was constructed, the building served as a combination junior-senior high.

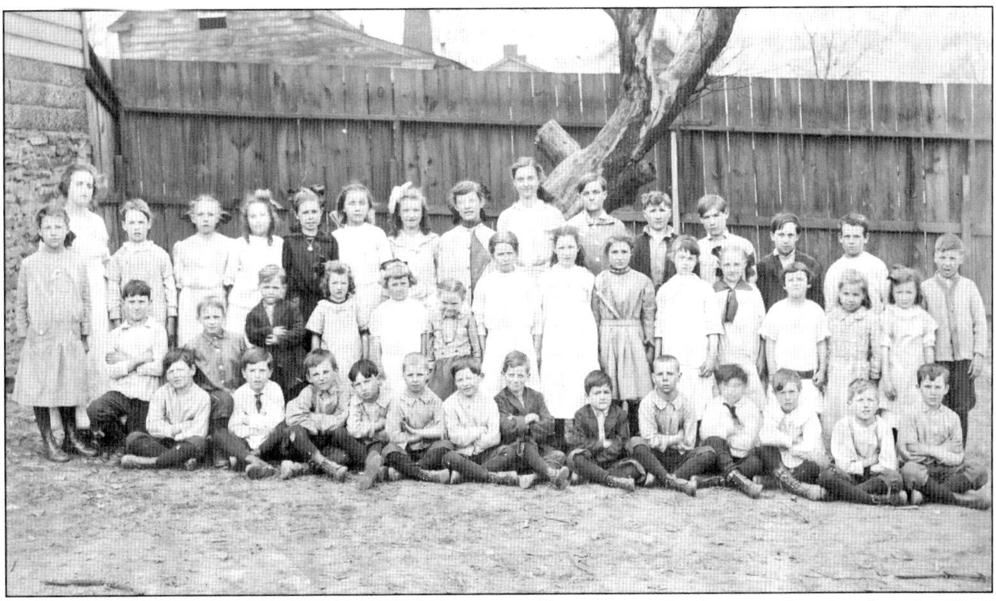

It is believed the first school in the area that became Donora was built immediately after the Civil War on what is now the corner of Fifteenth Street and Meldon Avenue. It was named in honor of steamboat owner Capt. James Gilmore. This picture of the backyard playground of Gilmore School was taken in 1914. A small portion of the building is visible on the far left.

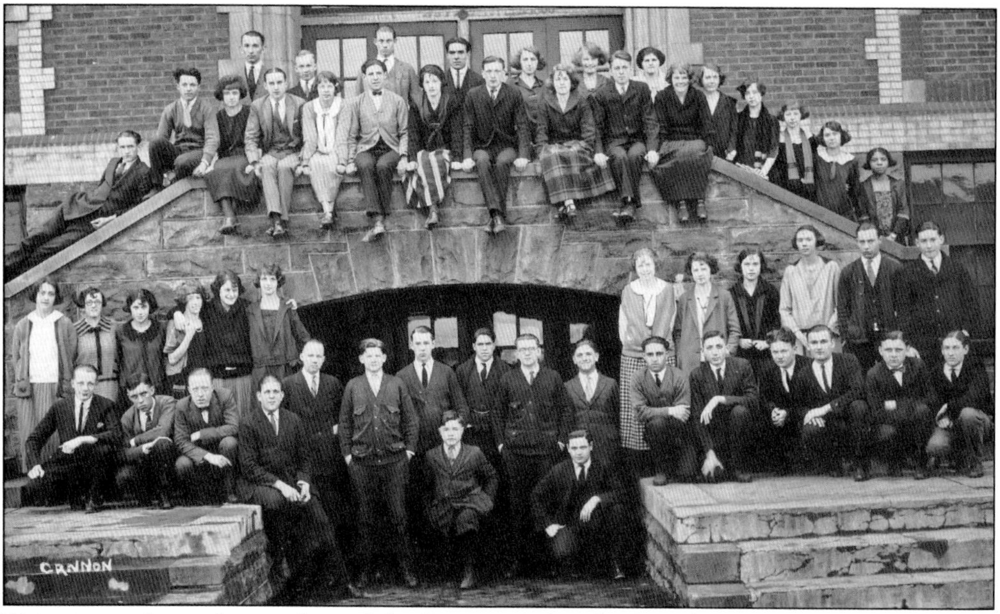

This picture shows the members of the Donora High School graduating class of 1922. In spite of Donora's growing population, the number of graduates is small because, at the time, very few young people opted to continue their education past the eighth grade.

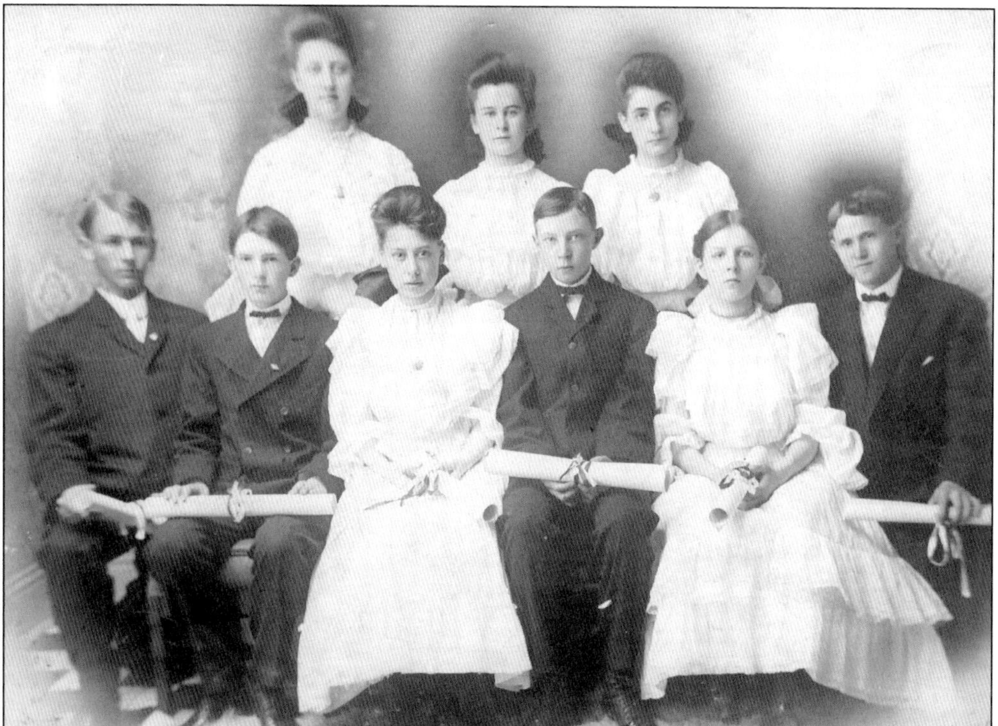

This is believed to be a picture of the graduating class of 1904. At that time, the two-year high school program was located in Castner School. Very few of the children of working-class families pursued schooling beyond the basic literacy and mathematical requirements.

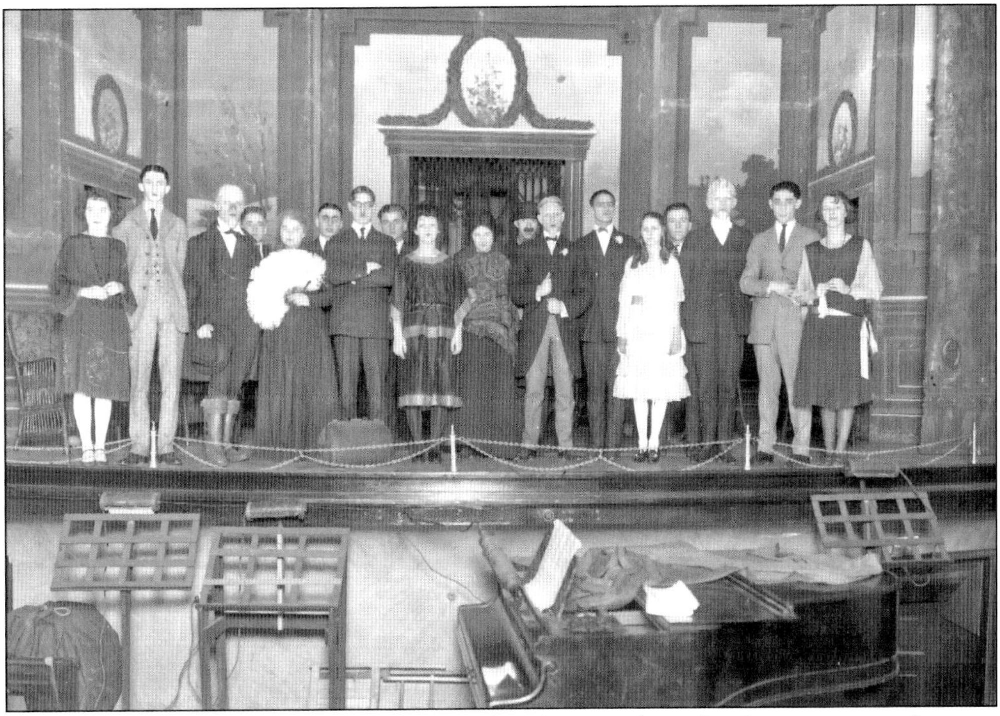

Forensics, speech, debate, and drama were vital to the secondary school experience in the years prior to World War II. This picture shows the cast of a high school play in 1920. This production was staged in the auditorium of the newly built Sixth Street School.

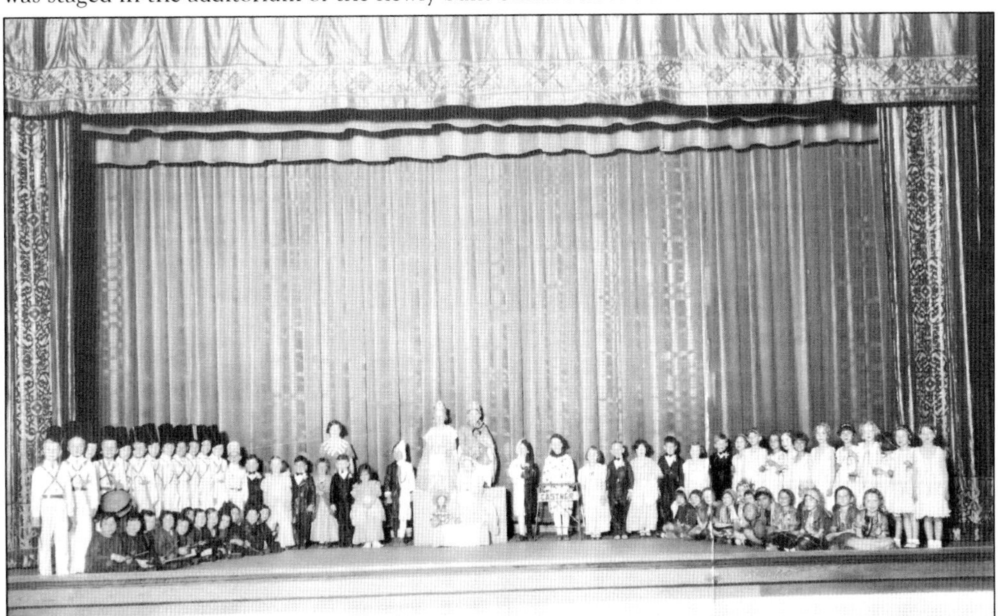

It was traditional spring practice for students at each of Donora's elementary schools to produce a musical program to be performed for the town's other students and the community at large. This picture was taken in 1933 and shows Castner School students as they prepare to conduct one of these performances at the high school auditorium.

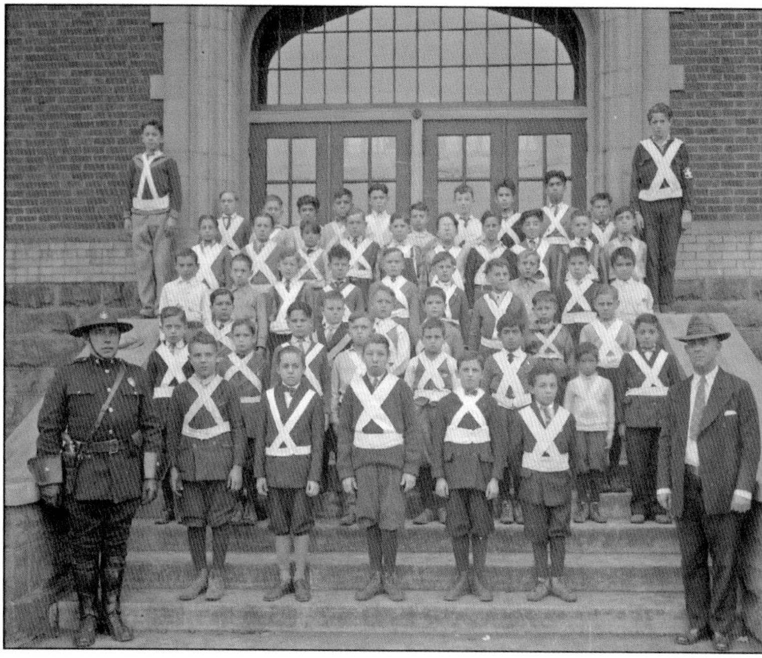

Because most Donora students walked to school, patrols were created to help ensure the safety of the pupils. Patrol boys were easily recognized because of their wide white belts and shoulder straps. Pictured are the junior high patrol boys.

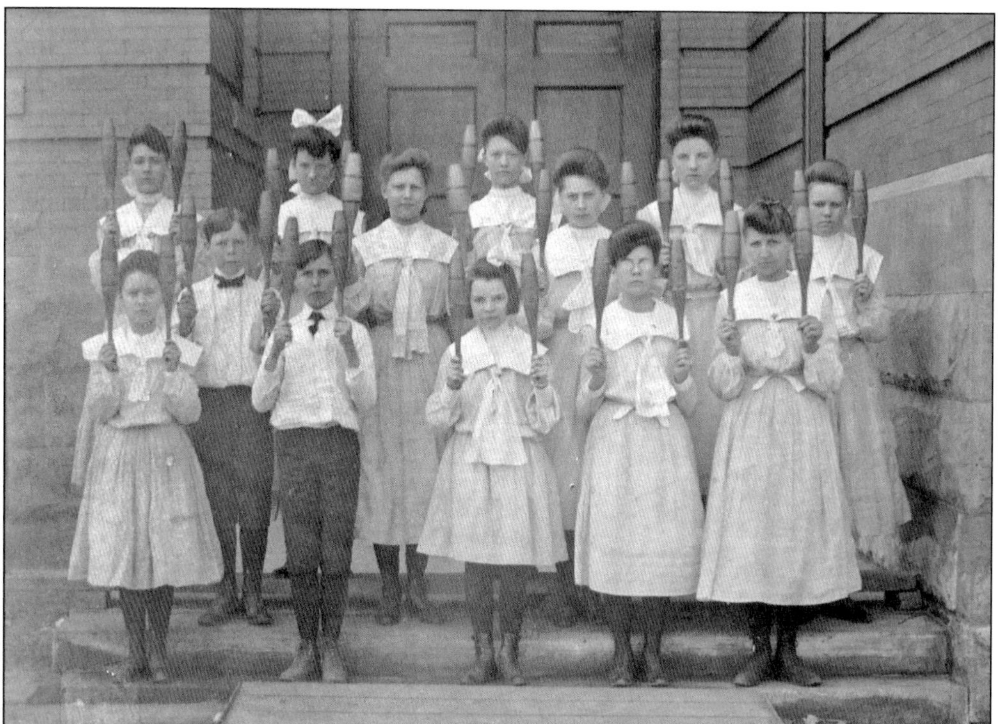

One form of exercise designed to develop arm and shoulder muscles involved the use of "Indian Clubs." These wooden artifacts, being demonstrated by the boys and girls in this picture, were lifted and swung in unison to enhance strength and coordination.

Dr. Michael Duda had a long and illustrious career in education. After graduating from Donora High School and St. Vincent College, he served as a teacher and principal at Donora High School. He was later elected superintendent of the Monessen School District and then went on to serve as president of California State Teachers College. He died suddenly in 1968. He is pictured here with his wife, Veronica. (Courtesy California University of Pennsylvania Archives.)

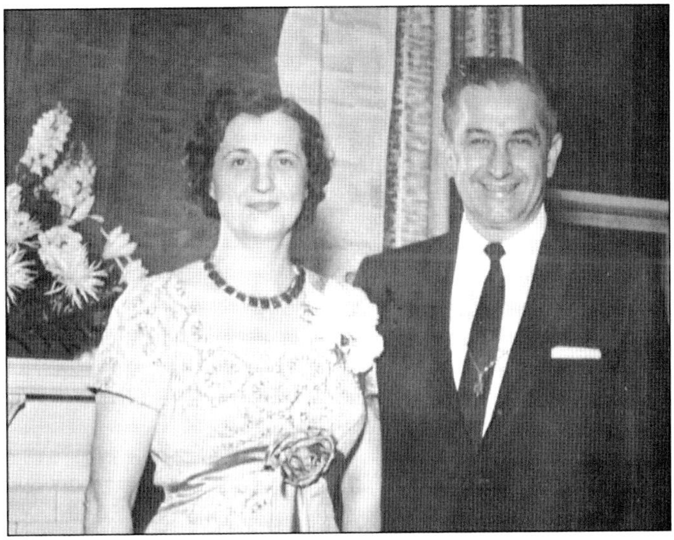

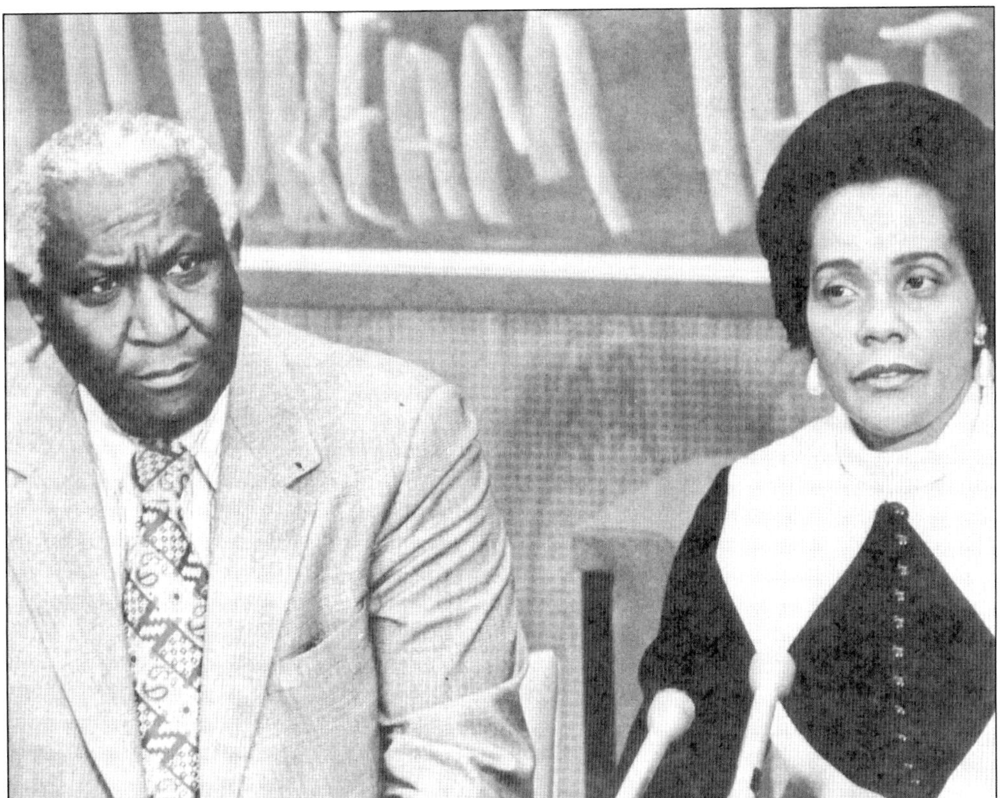

Dr. Wade Wilson moved to Donora when he was a young child. After high school, he worked in the steel mill to pay his way through Cheyney State College. He earned his doctorate from New York University and in 1968 became president of Cheyney, where he served until 1981. Throughout his professional career, he was an enthusiastic advocate of civil rights. He is pictured here with Coretta Scott King. (Courtesy Cheyney University of Pennsylvania Public Relations Department.)

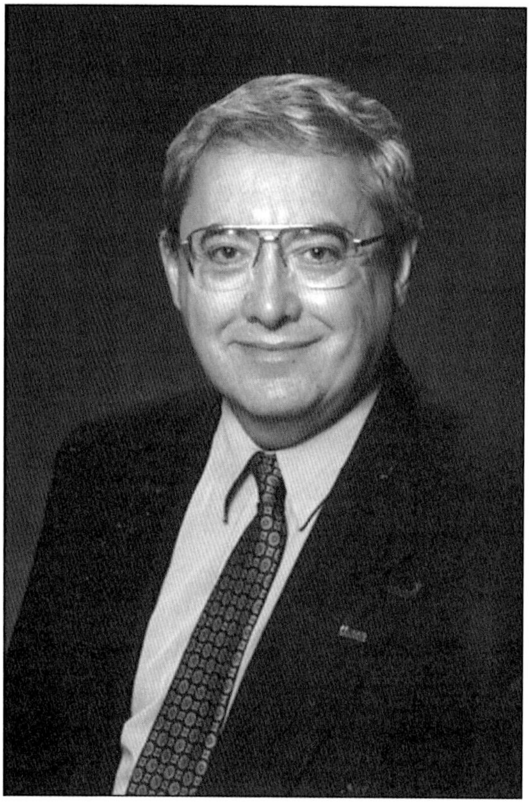

After earning degrees from Wilmington College and Pennsylvania State University, Dr. Manuel Ibanez taught biology and biochemistry at different universities. From 1989 to 1998, he served as president of Texas A&M University. In 1994, he was appointed as a regent to the Smithsonian Institution. His studies led him to the Amazon Valley, where he discovered a new type of beetle, which was named after him. (Courtesy Texas A&M University Kingsville.)

These students at Allen School posed for this picture around 1902. The wooden plank sidewalk shown in the foreground was typical of many such walkways in Donora. The muddy boots of the students indicate they must have traveled across unpaved streets on their way to school.

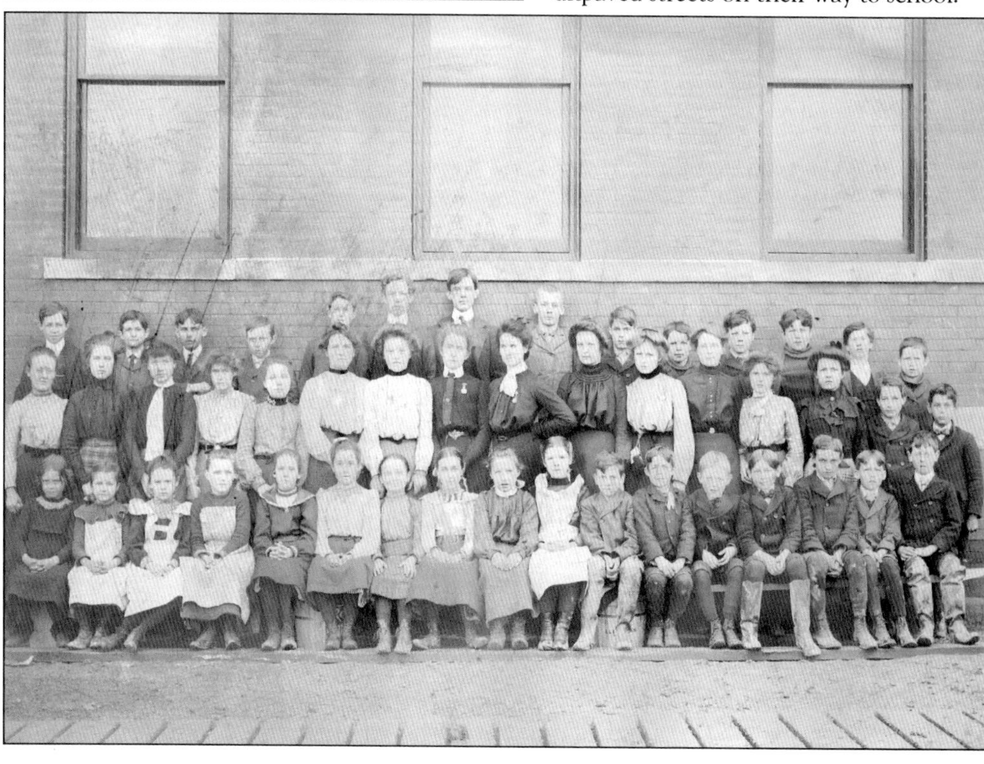

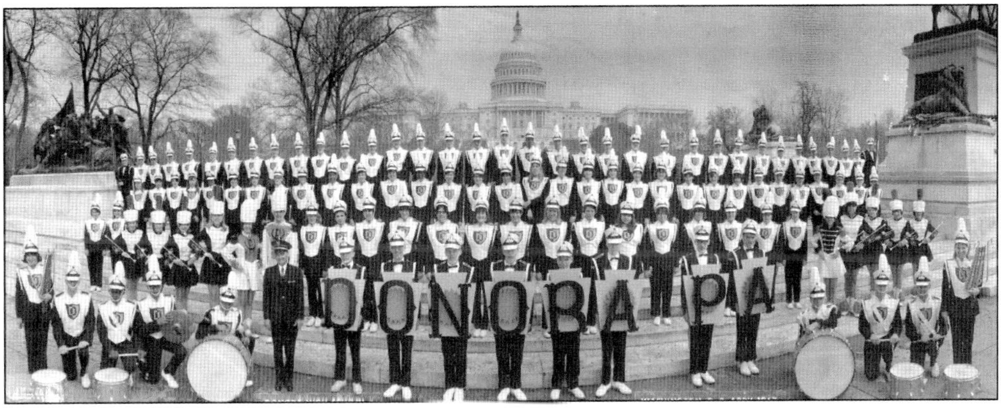

In the spring of 1967, the Donora High School band traveled to Washington, D.C., to perform in the nation's capital. The band members stand in their orange and black uniforms against the backdrop of the Capitol building. Band director Guy Corno is seen in the front row on the left.

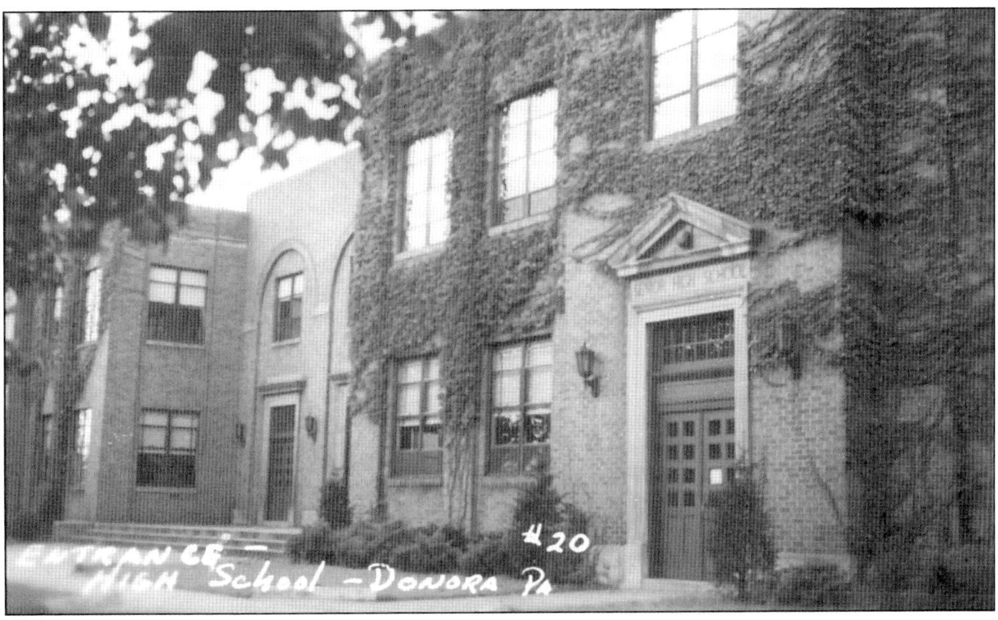

The Donora Senior High School was opened in 1930 to accommodate the growing student enrollment in the school district. The building was originally planned to be a combination junior-senior high school, but financial problems connected with the Great Depression resulted in the building being downsized. The school was remodeled in 1977–1978 and became the Donora Elementary Center of the Ringgold School District in 1979.

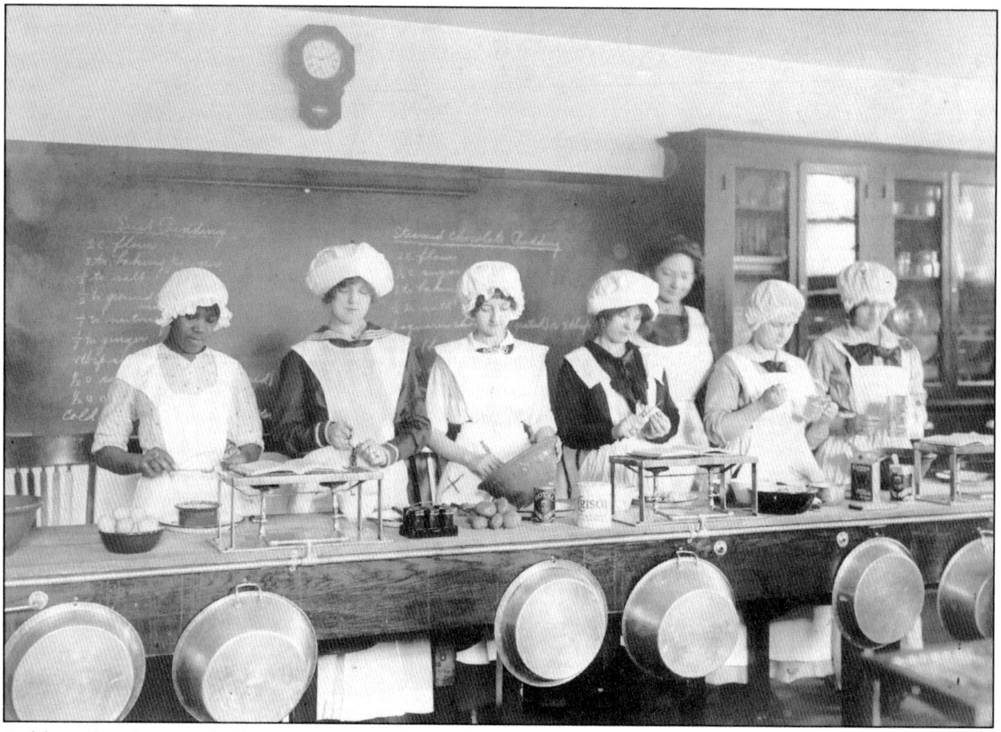

Public schools in early Donora took on the responsibility of training young girls to cook, sew, and develop the other skills needed to successfully follow careers as wives and homemakers. These photographs show a group of girls in a home economics cooking class in Donora Junior-Senior High School in 1915. Their male counterparts took industrial arts classes.

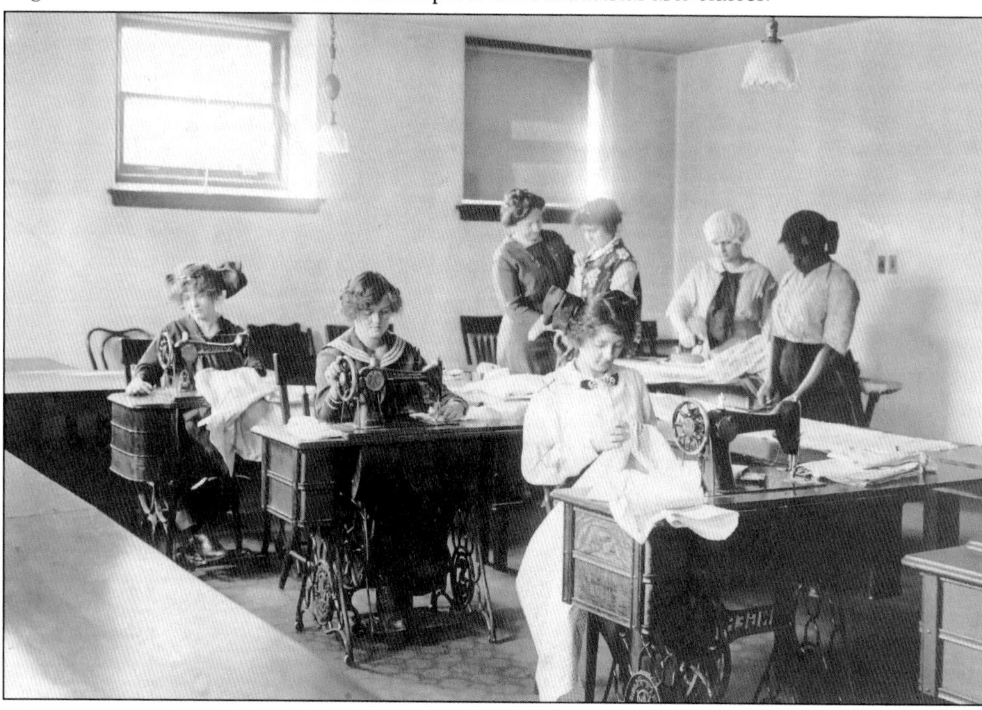

Eight

Go Forth and Serve

Since its incorporation as a borough in 1901, the citizens of Donora have demonstrated a keen interest in the governance of their community. The civic involvement of Donorans manifests their belief that active participation in governmental processes ensures the continuance of freedom and liberty. As a result of this enthusiasm, the political atmosphere in Donora has been broad based and spirited.

For the first three decades of the borough's history, the Progressive Republican Party remained dominant. However, the coming of Pres. Franklin D. Roosevelt and the New Deal brought a dramatic shift of political allegiance. Donora has remained an overwhelmingly Democratic town since the 1930s.

Throughout the years, Donora's residents have shown their commitment to the ideals of the democratic process in another important way. During the century of its existence, significant numbers of the town's sons and daughters have served in the various branches of the country's military. Many of these soldiers were wounded or killed while serving. Furthermore, the town has always supported its military personnel and respected its veterans.

Donora has always been a community of intense patriotism that has had faith in popular rule and been a supporter of just causes.

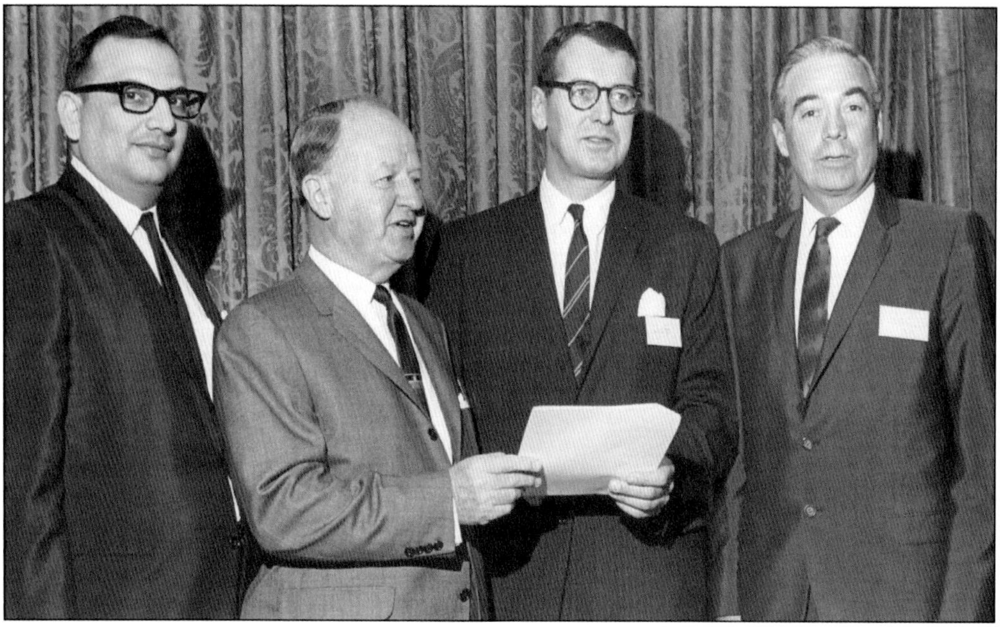

Hercules Power was one of the first tenants of the Monongahela Industrial Development Association (MIDA), which took over the former steel mill site along the river. Here Leslie Worthington (second from the right), president of U.S. Steel, hands a deed to James Booth of Hercules Power. They are flanked by Donora council president Anthony Massafra (far left) and Pennsylvania governor William Scranton (far right). (Courtesy Anthony Massafra.)

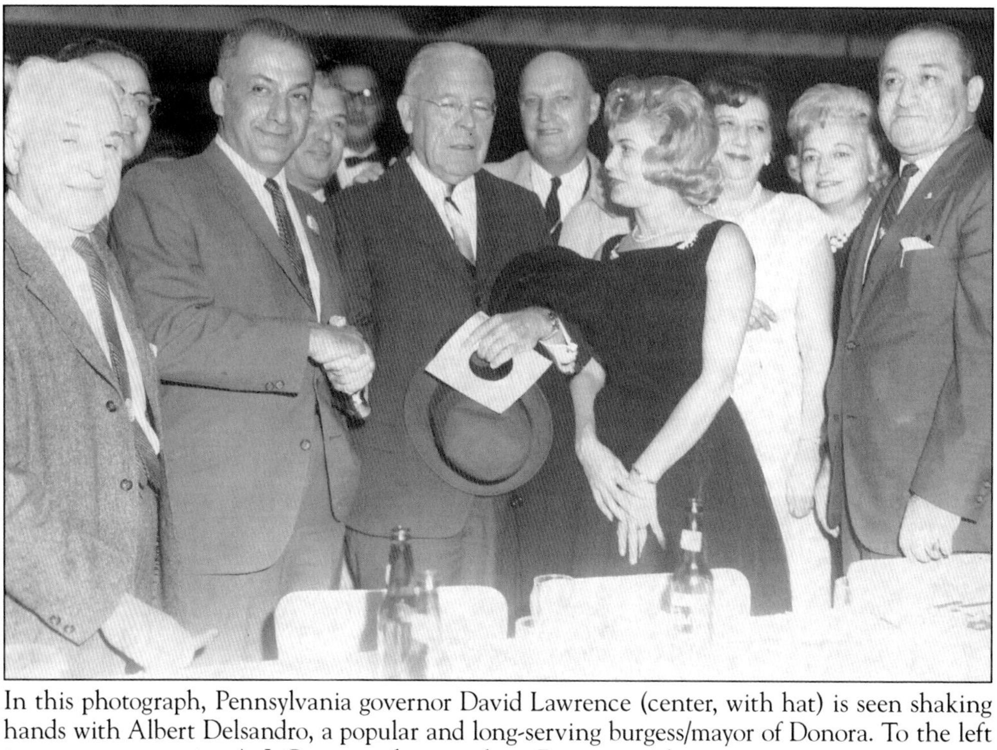

In this photograph, Pennsylvania governor David Lawrence (center, with hat) is seen shaking hands with Albert Delsandro, a popular and long-serving burgess/mayor of Donora. To the left is state representative A. J. Capano, who was also a Donora resident.

In 1993, Gov. Robert P. Casey designated Donora as "Pennsylvania Capital for a Day." The town was chosen for this honor because of its efforts toward community revitalization in the decades after the closing of the mill. Casey, Lt. Gov. Mark Singel, and the entire state cabinet moved their operations into the borough on April 15. This picture shows Casey (right) with local restaurant owners Anthony and Theresa DiDonato. (Courtesy Anthony DiDonato.)

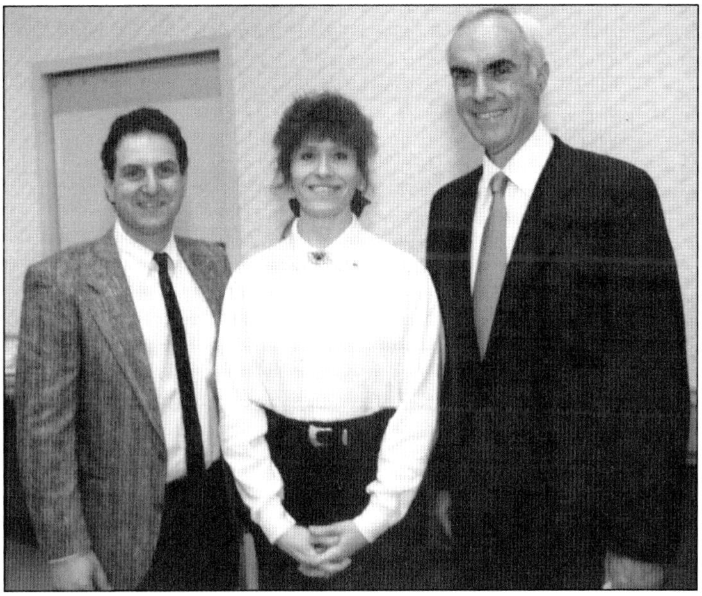

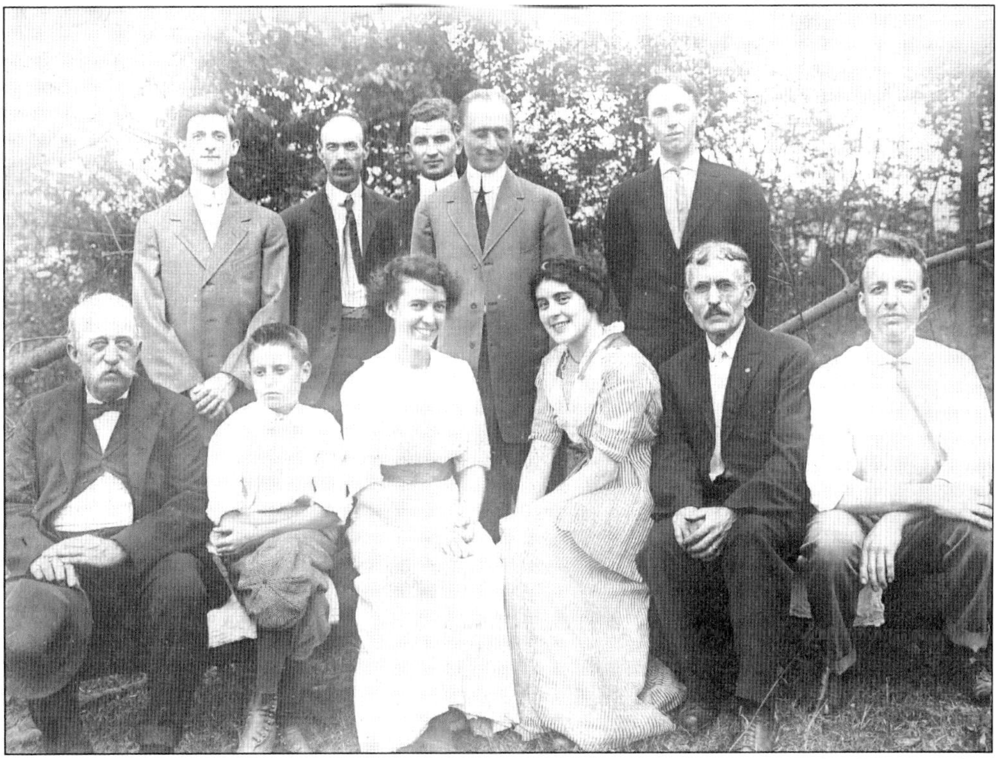

The *Donora American*, the town's first newspaper, began publication in 1901 under the ownership of Vernon Hazard. Roman Koehler (pictured here in the center with the post office staff), who was the editor, manager, and eventual owner of the newspaper, served as the borough council clerk and was responsible for preserving much of the history of early Donora. He was the first president of the Donora Historical Society in 1946.

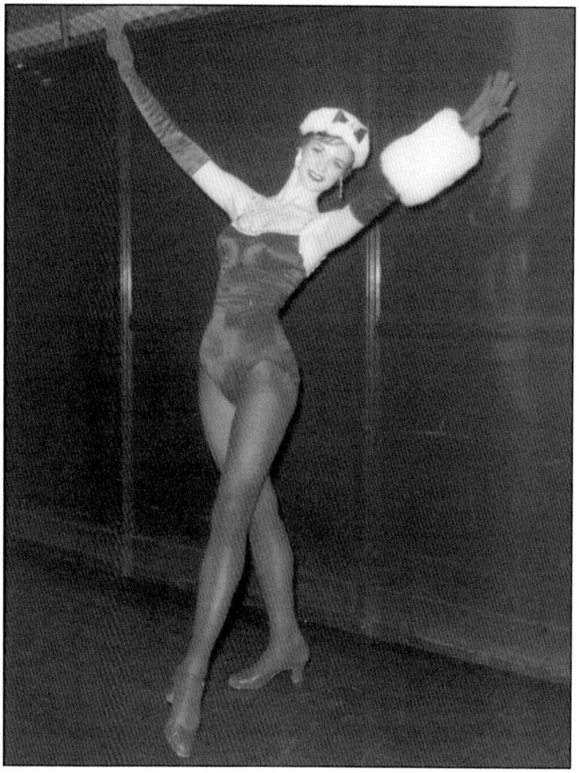

After she graduated from Donora High School, Trudy Carson left for New York City to pursue a career in dancing. She quickly became a member of the Radio City Music Hall Rockettes and the June Taylor Dancers. She appeared in several Broadway musicals and married comedian Soupy Sales. (Courtesy Kathy O'Connell.)

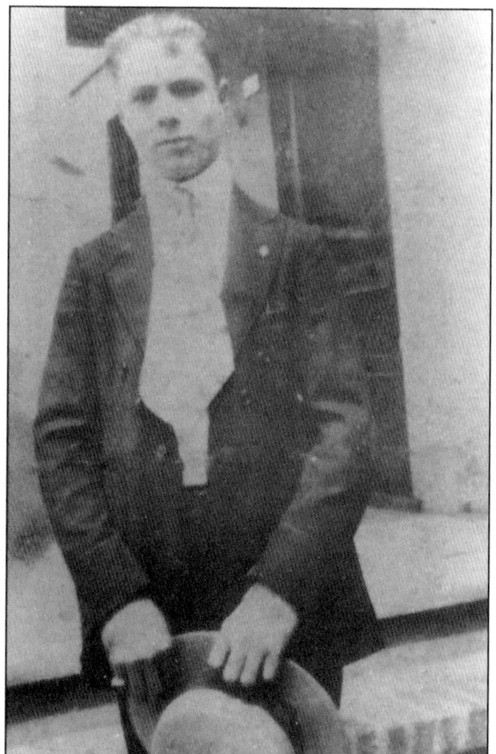

Joe Joy was not a native son but spent many of his formative years in Donora. While working in a local coal mine, he came up with many ideas, such as power loading cars and roof support systems, to make the mining process both safer and more efficient. Eventually he founded Joy Mining Company, which contributed to the revolution in coal mining production. (Courtesy Charles Stacey.)

Donora businessman John S. McCans was master of Donora Freemason Lodge 626 and was elected potentate of Pittsburgh's Syria Shrine Temple, the second-largest Shrine temple in North America, in 1966. McCans and his fellow Shriners were active in many charitable projects, especially building and maintaining hospitals for severely burned children. (Courtesy John McCans Jr.)

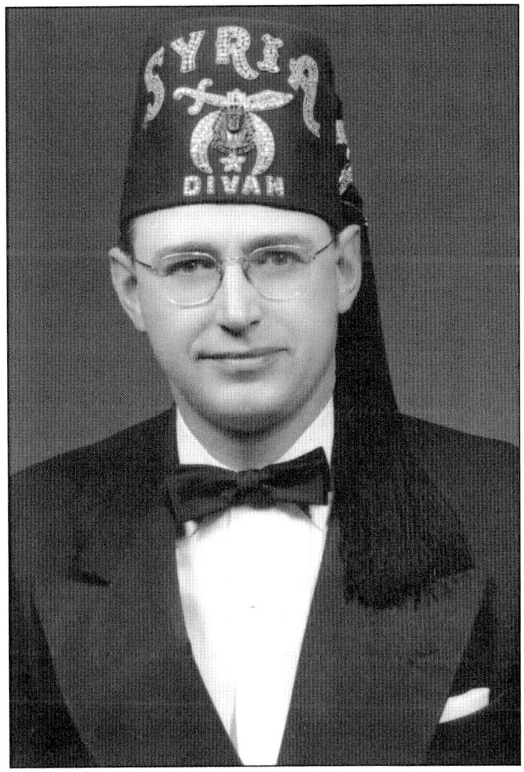

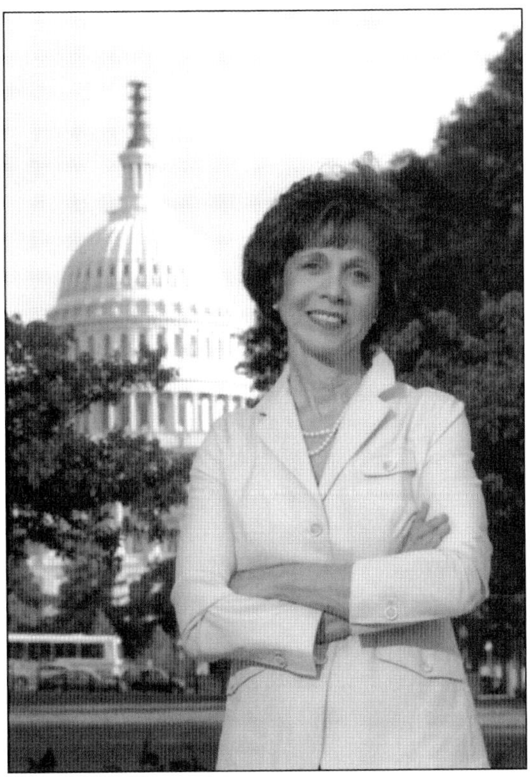

Dr. Devra Davis, considered one of the world's leading authorities on epidemiology and public health, spent her younger years in Donora. In 2010, Davis serves as director of the Center for Environmental Oncology at the University of Pittsburgh Medical Center. She is the author of the highly acclaimed books *When Smoke Ran Like Water* and *The Secret History of the War on Cancer.* (Courtesy University of Pittsburgh.)

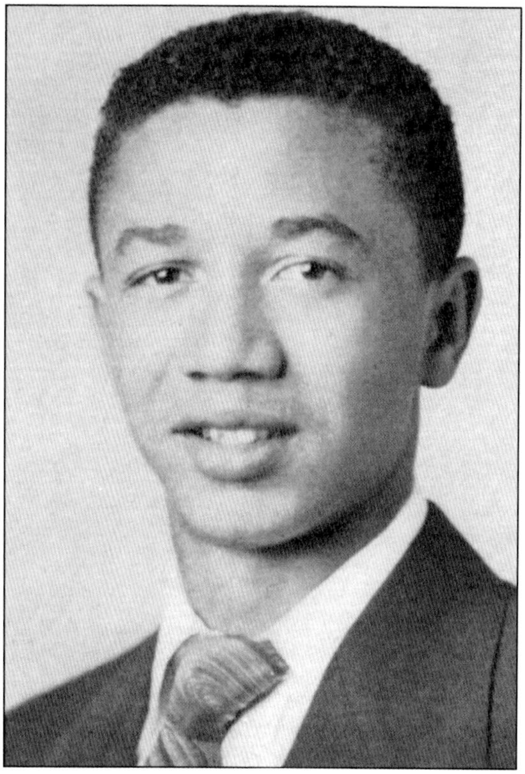

Donora native Dr. Dorval Carter was a Phi Beta Kappa graduate of the Howard University Medical School. He practiced obstetrics and gynecology in Chicago for five decades, during which time he delivered "thousands of babies." In 2007, Chicago's St. Anthony's Hospital renamed its maternity facility the Dorval and Vivian Carter Birthing Center.

After starring in basketball at Donora High School, Ulice Payne attended Marquette University and was a member of the 1977 National Collegiate Athletic Association (NCAA) national championship team. He graduated from Marquette Law School and became the first African American to lead a major-league baseball team, when he was named president and chief executive officer of the Milwaukee Brewers. In 2010, Payne was named the national president of the YMCA. (Courtesy Loretta Manus.)

Loretta Ross Jones Manus has devoted much of her life to altruistic community activities designed to improve the lives of young people. In 2009, she was recognized by the Pennsylvania State Police for her efforts in reducing juvenile crime. In this picture, she is being honored by the Deborah Grand Chapter of the Eastern Star as she completed her term as state grand matron. (Courtesy Loretta Manus.)

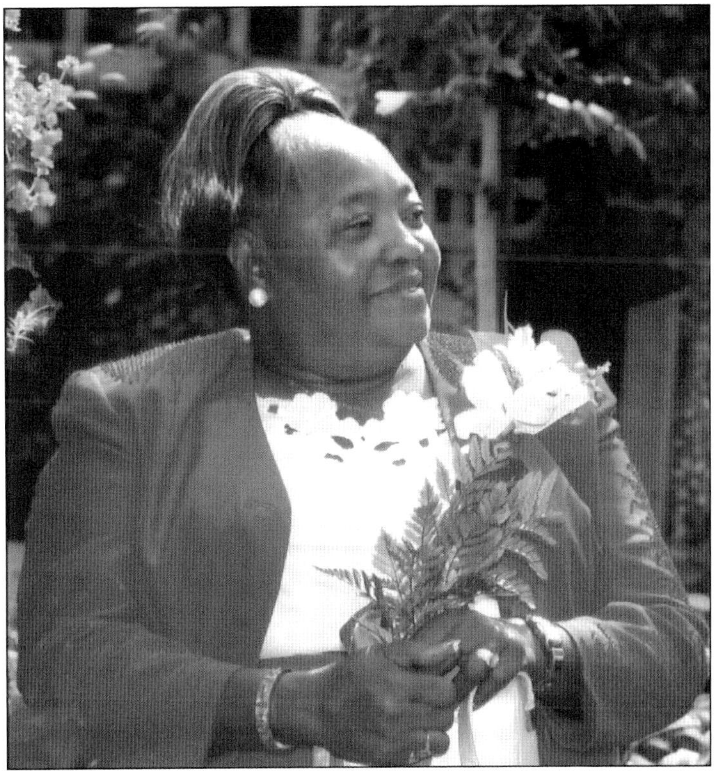

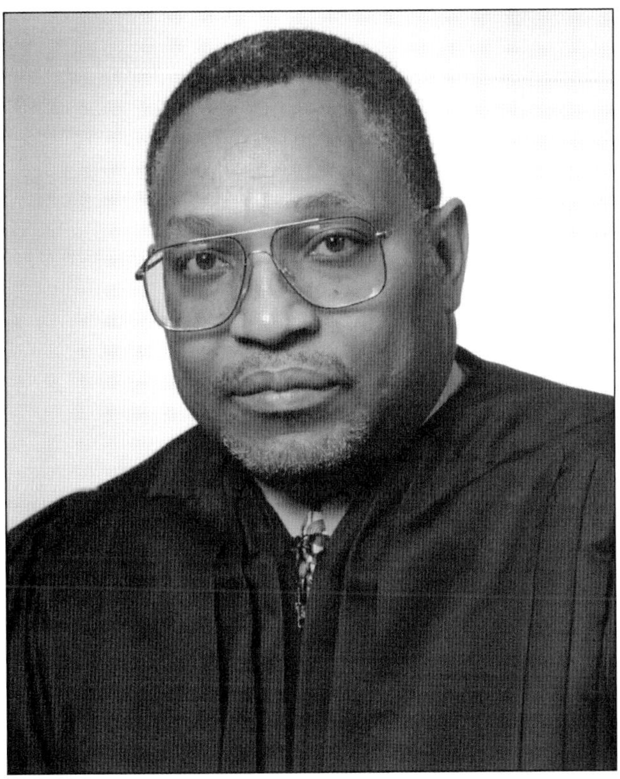

U.S. District Court Judge Reggie Walton is an alumnus of Donora High School. His government and legal career includes service with the National Drug Control Policy Office, the U.S. Attorney's Office, and Harvard Law School. He presided over the perjury trial of Lewis "Scooter" Libby and was recently appointed to the U.S. Foreign Intelligence Surveillance Court by chief justice of the United States John Roberts. (Courtesy Reggie Walton.)

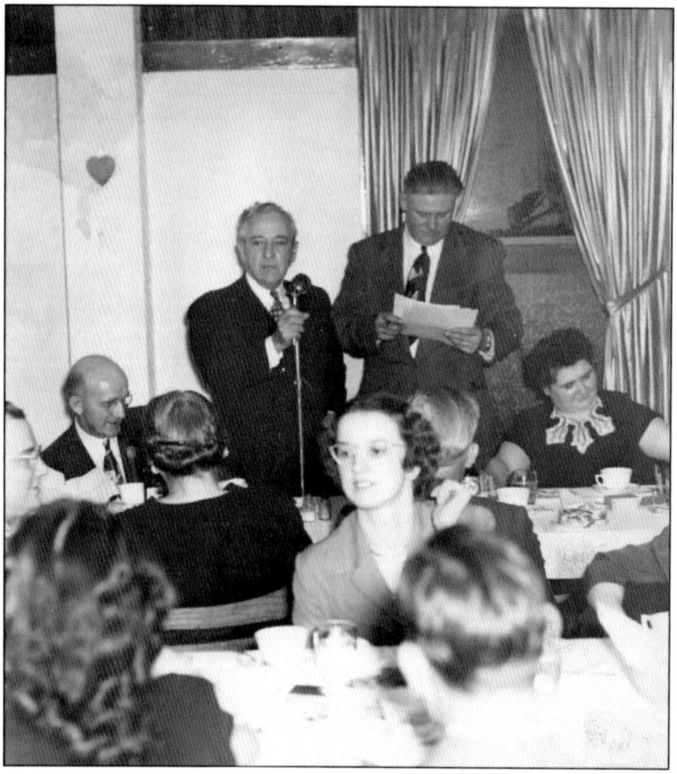

Along with his medical practice, Dr. Grant Furlong (left) also had a remarkable and versatile political career. He served as burgess, postmaster, state assemblyman, county sheriff, and U.S. congressman. He is seen in this photograph speaking to a group of the town's citizens with Burgess August Chambon in 1949.

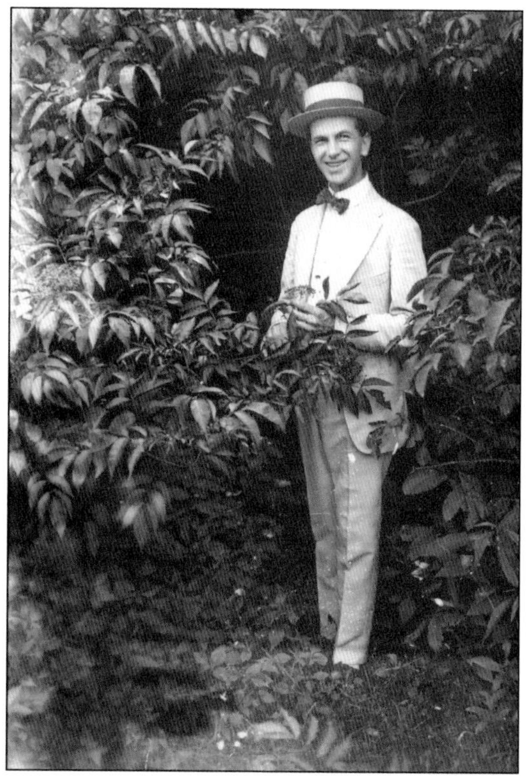

Bruce Dreisbach, who compiled a comprehensive pictorial history of Donora, came to town in 1906 and found work as a packer in the American Steel and Wire Company plant. The Donora Historical Society holds hundreds of his impressive photographs in its archives.

William C. Jones graduated from the United States Air Force Academy, became a fighter pilot, and flew 189 combat missions during the Vietnam War. By the time of his retirement, he had attained the rank of brigadier general. He is believed to be the highest-ranking military officer from Donora. (Courtesy William Jones.)

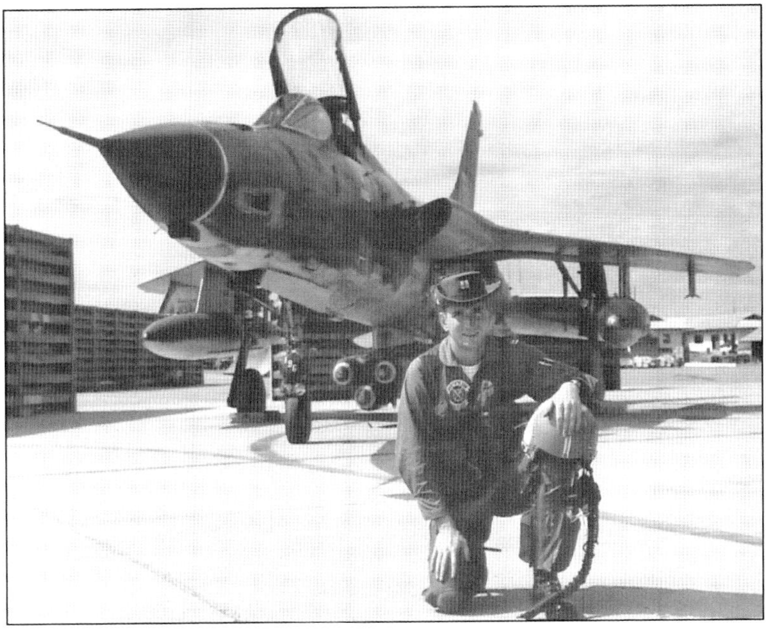

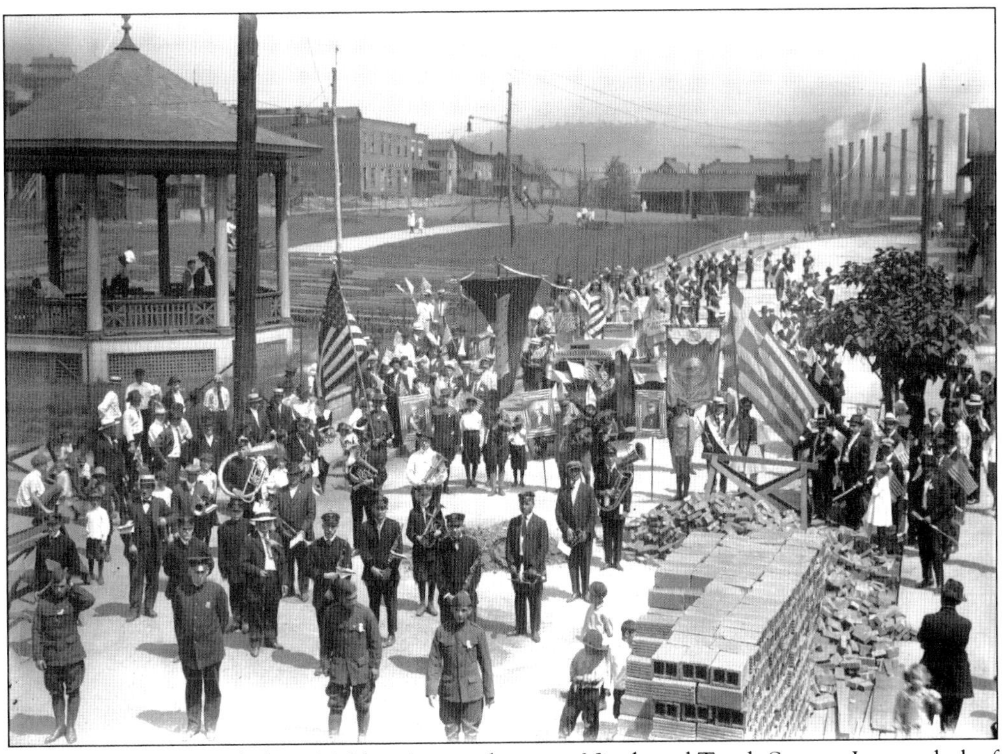

Donner Park is located along Meldon Avenue between Ninth and Tenth Streets. It was a hub of civic and recreational activity in early Donora. In this picture, borough and mill police, military veterans, Boy Scouts, and representatives of fraternal organizations parade in the park. In the background beyond the bandstand and playground are the Donora Zinc Works smokestacks.

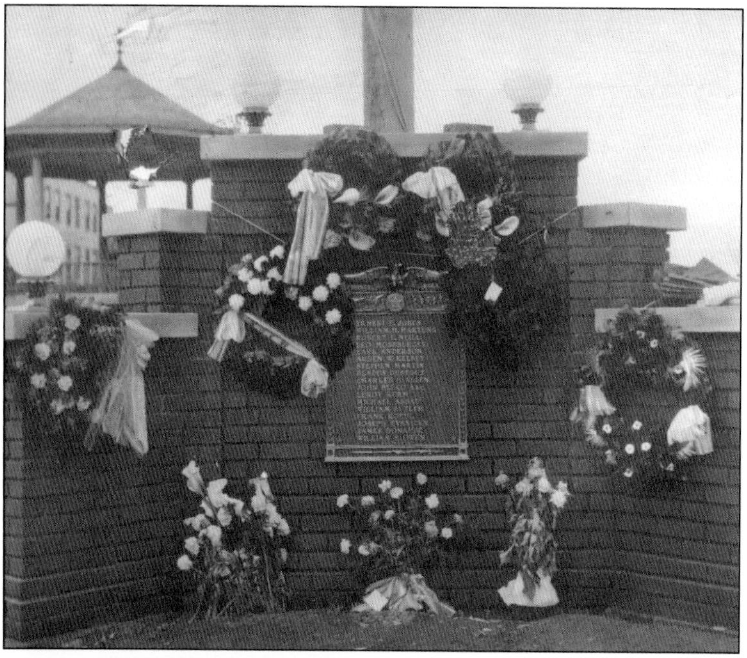

Pictured here is an impressive brick and stone memorial in Donner Park dedicated to the town's veterans who served during World War I. Later a memorial that included names of both World War I and World War II veterans was erected in the central business district. Today a monument that includes all the names of those Donorans who served in the military stands at the southern entrance of the town.

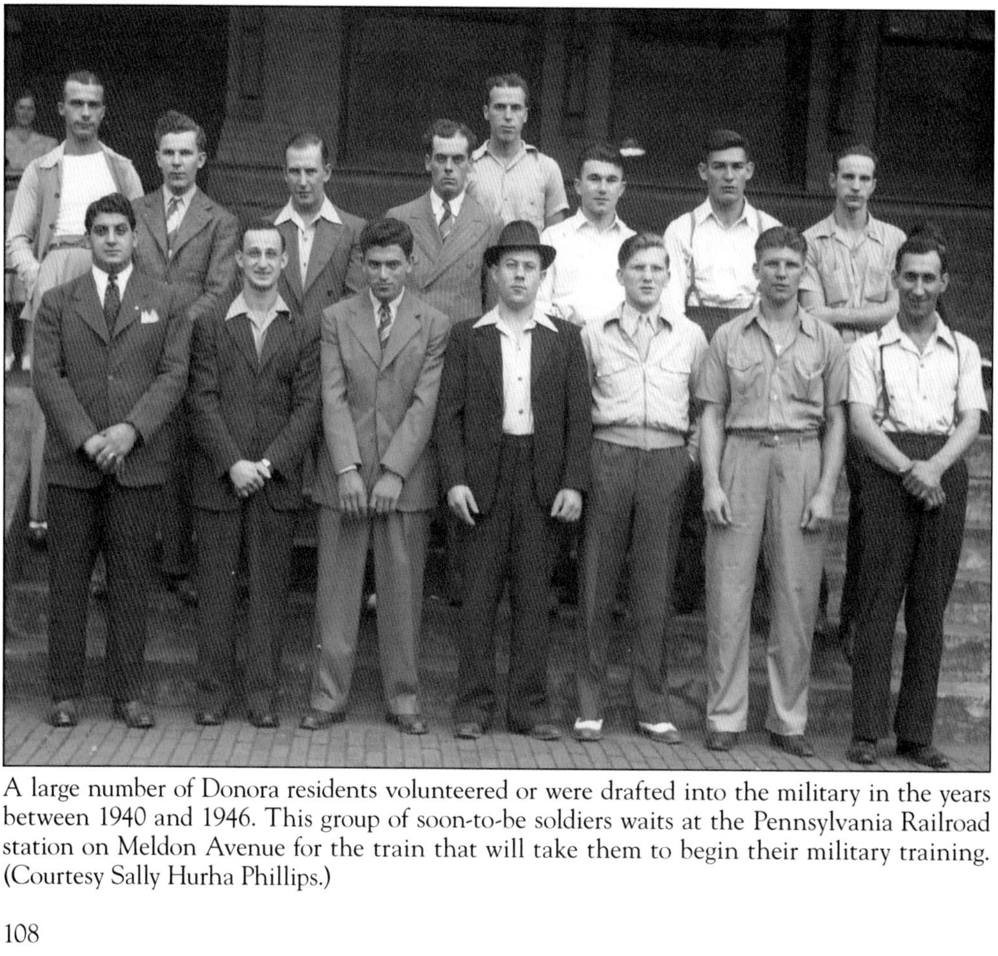

A large number of Donora residents volunteered or were drafted into the military in the years between 1940 and 1946. This group of soon-to-be soldiers waits at the Pennsylvania Railroad station on Meldon Avenue for the train that will take them to begin their military training. (Courtesy Sally Hurha Phillips.)

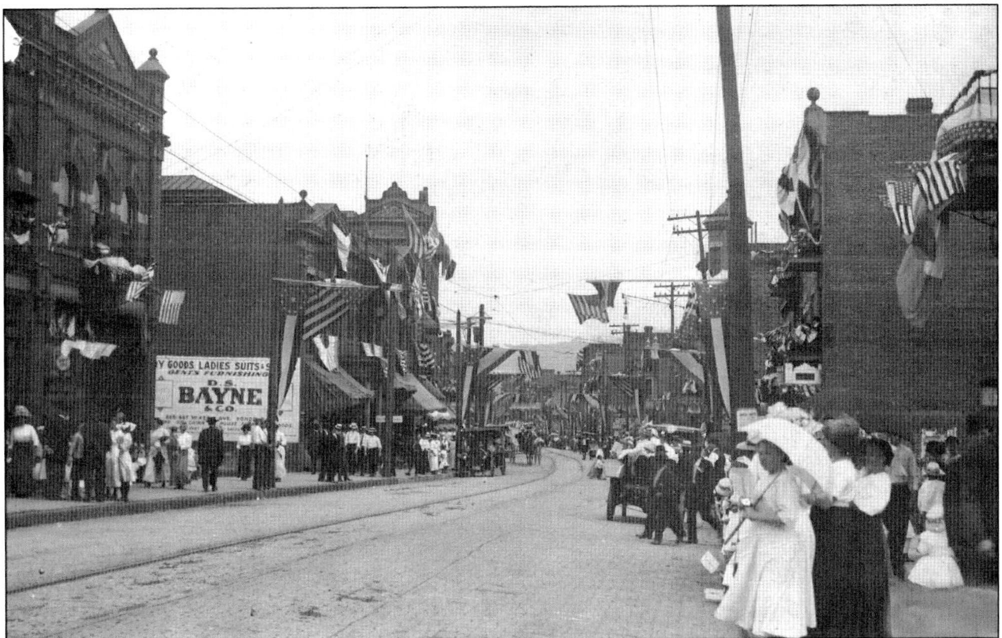

Many Donorans served in the military in World War I, and when the "war to end all wars" ended, the town celebrated with a great parade. Returning troops, along with accompanying musical groups, marched down McKean Avenue.

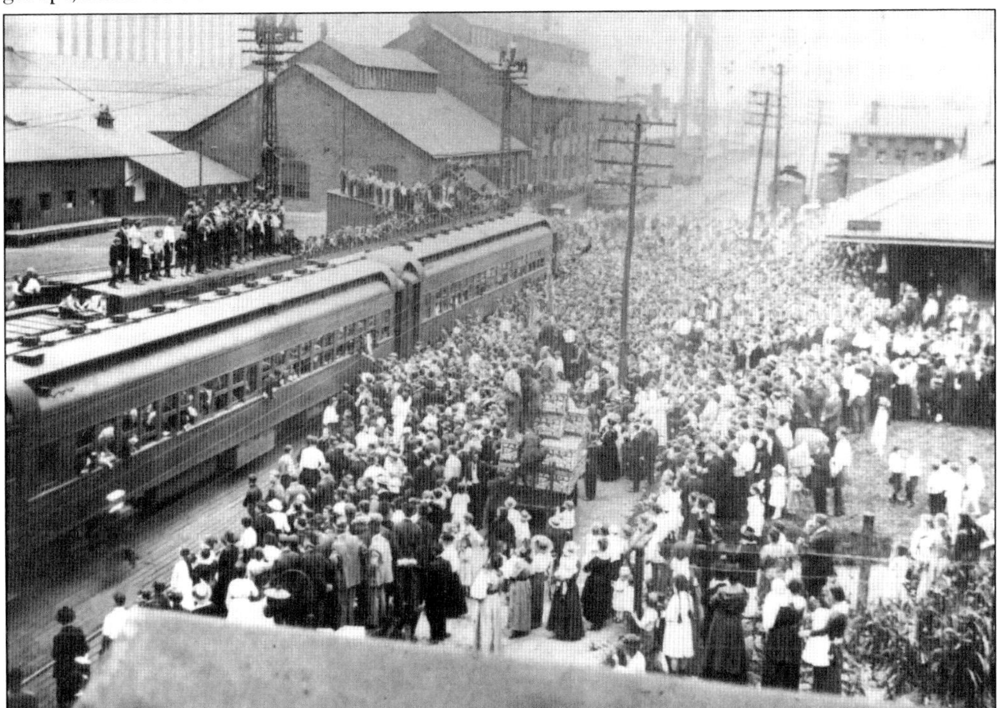

This remarkable photograph shows hundreds of Donora residents at the Pennsylvania Railroad Station bidding farewell to a group of World War I draftees. The enthusiasm of the crowd indicates they truly seem to believe Donora's sons were going off to "make the world safe for democracy."

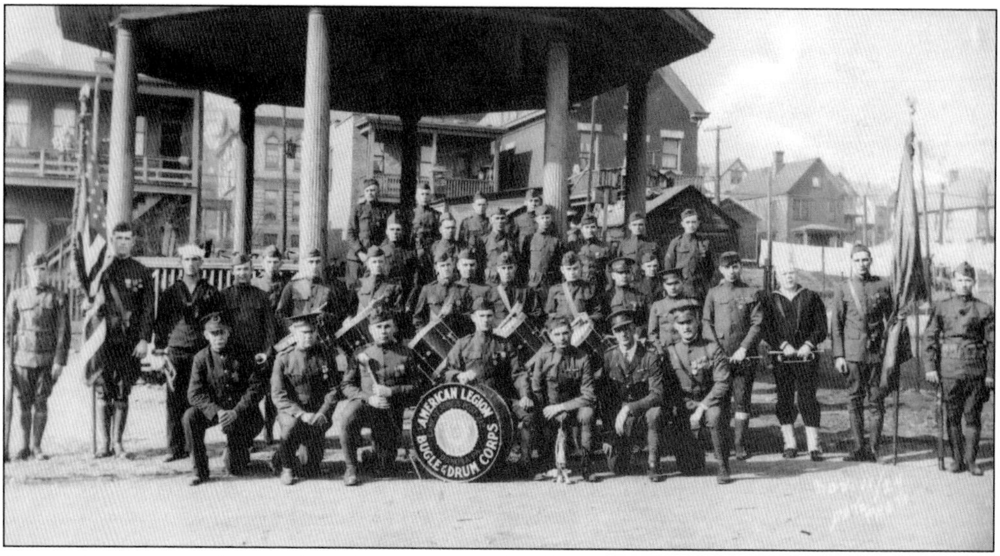

Donora's American Legion Post 212 was named in honor of Ernest E. Jobes, the first Donora citizen killed in World War I. This 1924 photograph shows the Sons of the Legion Drum and Bugle Corps and the Color Guard near the bandstand in Donner Park. Ironically, some of these young men served in the military in World War II.

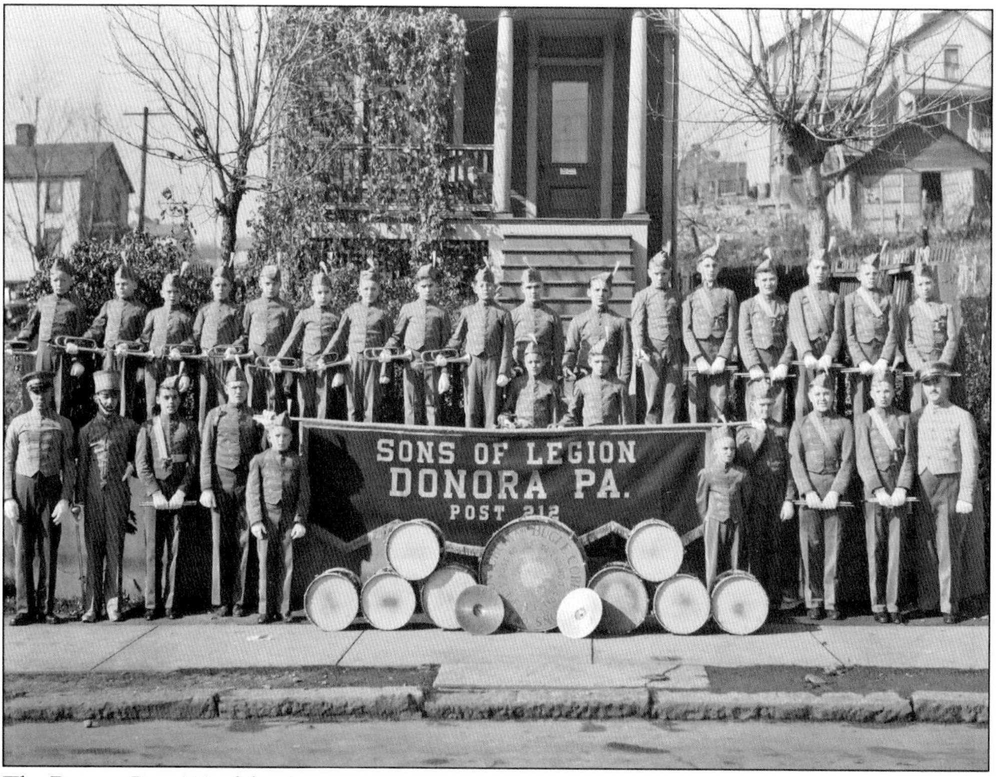

The Donora Post 212 of the American Legion had a women's auxiliary and a youth group. Pictured here is the Sons of the Legion youth military band. This group marched in many community parades before it was disbanded in the late 1930s.

Nine

Smoke Near the Water

For the first half of the 20th century, the Donora industrial plant was a vital part of the greatest steel-producing region in the world. At the Donora site, raw materials were turned into steel rods, beams, rails, wire, and nails. The local zinc works produced the material used to coat the steel and prevent oxidation. The products made in Donora were used in such ambitious projects as the Golden Gate, Mackinac, and Verrazano-Narrows Bridges. Donora steel was also used to construct the canons, tanks, bullets, and bombs that supplied the nation's military during the century's wars. The manufacture of these steel and zinc products brought steady employment, good wages, and a high degree of personal and community pride to the people of Donora.

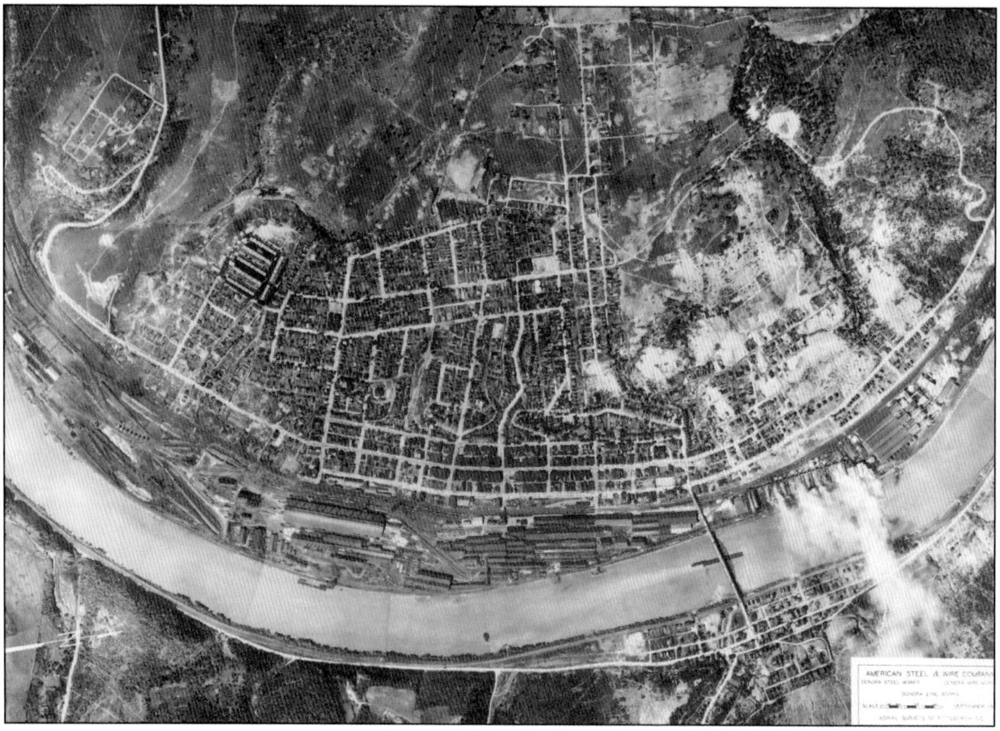

The U.S. Department of Defense took this aerial view of Donora in 1941 as part of Pres. Franklin D. Roosevelt's "Arsenal of Democracy" program. The Donora mill provided zinc, acid, and other materials that made it a potential target for foreign enemies. Note the impact of the zinc works smoke on the surrounding landscape.

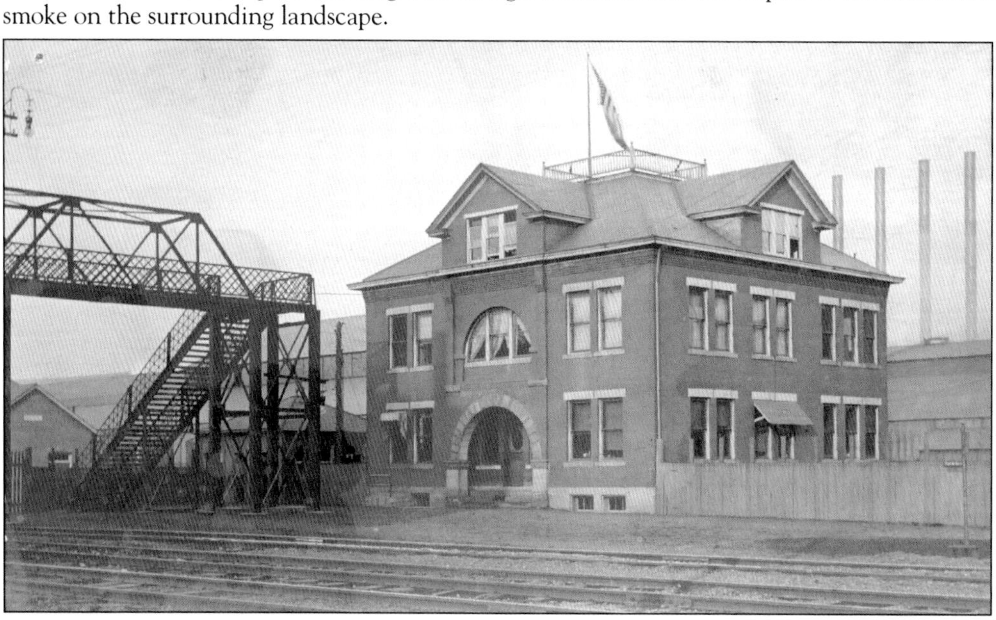

Over the years, thousands of employees of American Steel and Wire walked across the bridge over the railroad tracks at the Sixth Street gate to pass by or through the main office building to punch the time clock. The bridge was an efficient time-saver as well as safety measure in avoiding the constant rail traffic.

Major Goggins was born into slavery in Virginia but was given his freedom at age 18. After attending Hampton Normal Institute, he moved to Donora, where he became one of the first African Americans to work in the steel mill. He purchased a home, and his family became one of the pillars of the community. A relative, Perry Goggins, served as Donora's postmaster.

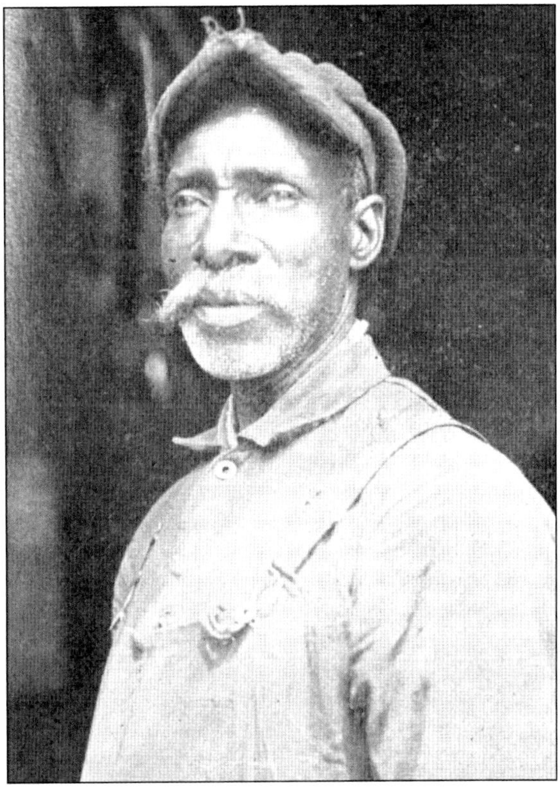

The American Steel and Wire Company encouraged the celebration of patriotic holidays. In this picture, workers of various ethnic backgrounds proclaim their feelings for the United States as they participate in a 1921 Flag Day ceremony.

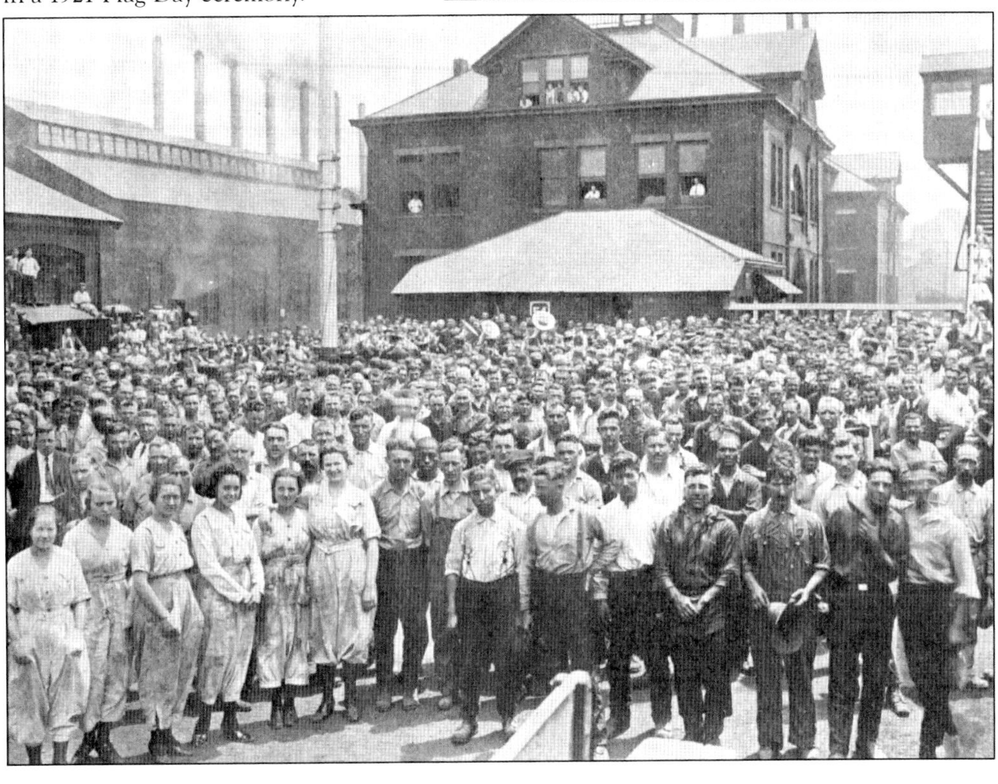

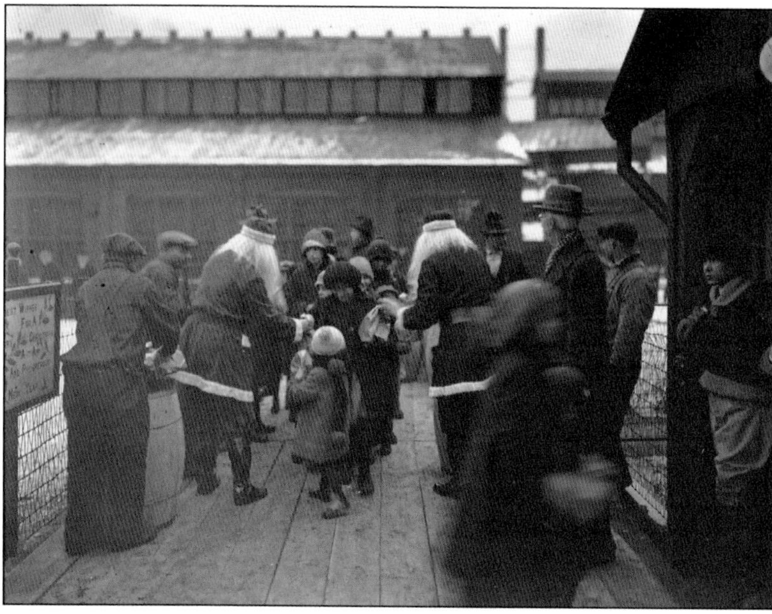

One of Donora's traditions was the distribution of candy treats during the holiday season. During economic downturns, these sweets were the only gifts some children received. This picture shows a typical line of youngsters waiting to receive their gift bags from Santa's helpers at the mill gate.

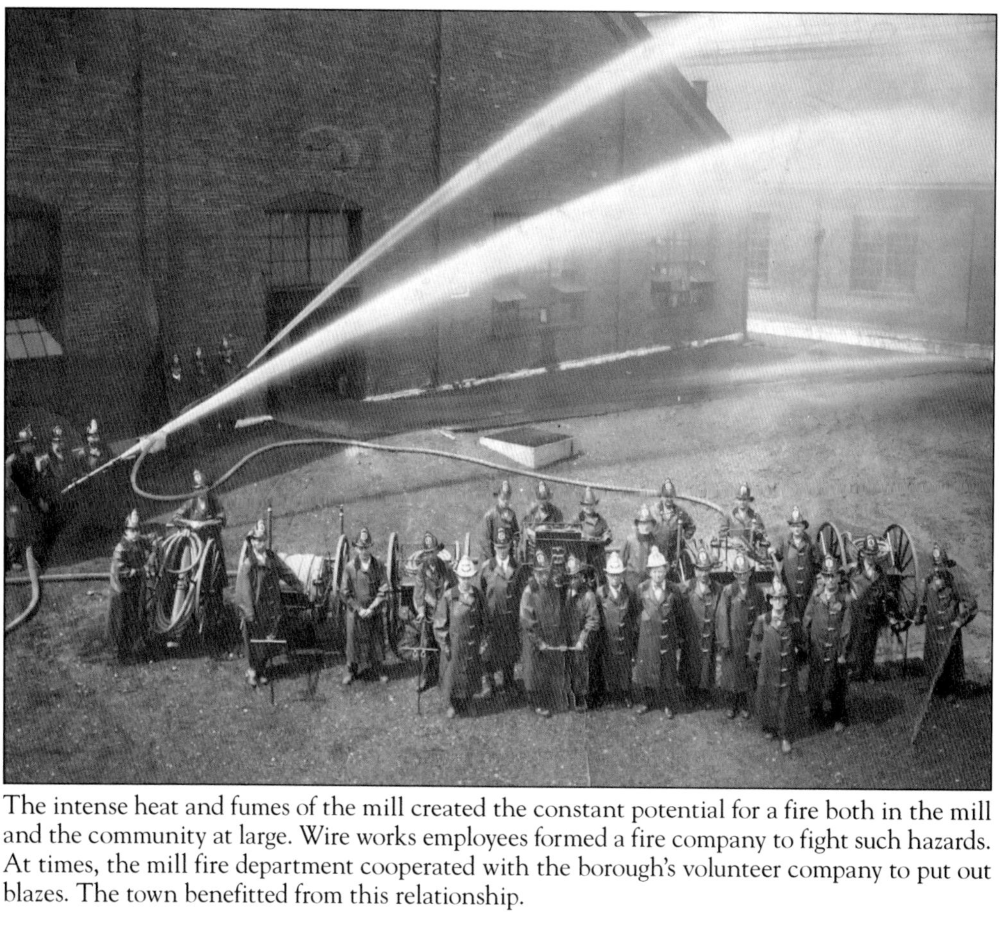

The intense heat and fumes of the mill created the constant potential for a fire both in the mill and the community at large. Wire works employees formed a fire company to fight such hazards. At times, the mill fire department cooperated with the borough's volunteer company to put out blazes. The town benefitted from this relationship.

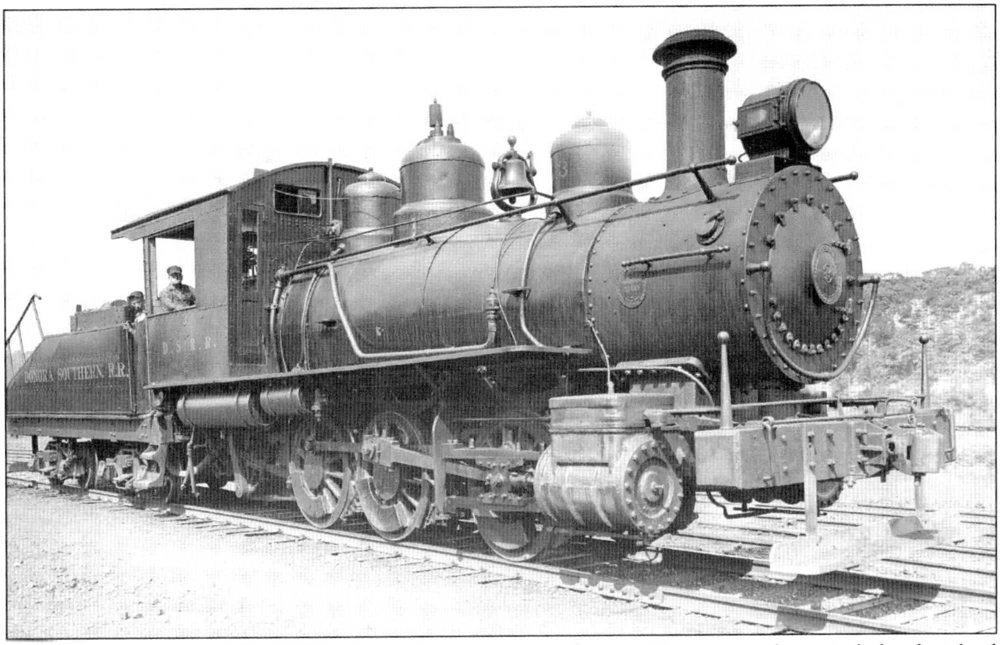

The Pennsylvania Railroad line brought raw materials into Donora and carried the finished products to all parts of the eastern United States. The Donora Southern Railroad, owned by the American Steel and Wire Company, operated exclusively within the mill on its own track system. Pictured here is one of the railroads early steam locomotives.

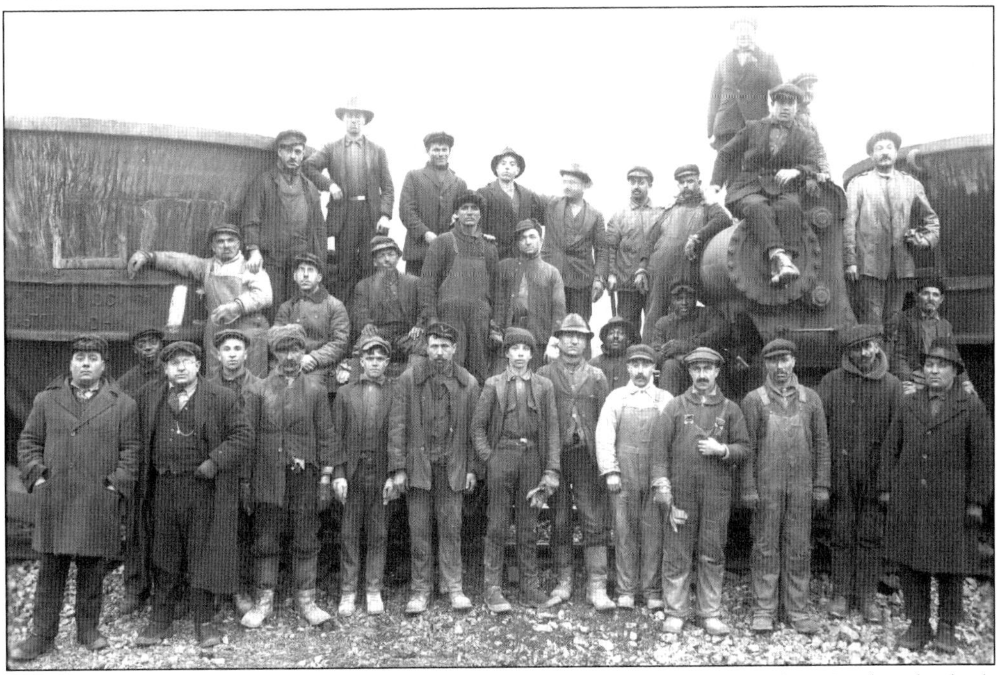

Note the racial and ethnic diversity of these employees of the Donora Southern Railroad, which had over 20 miles of track running through the mill and borough. The employees are posing in front of slag and cinder pots. Slag was dumped along the river to raise the floodplain and later deposited in an area near Palmer Park.

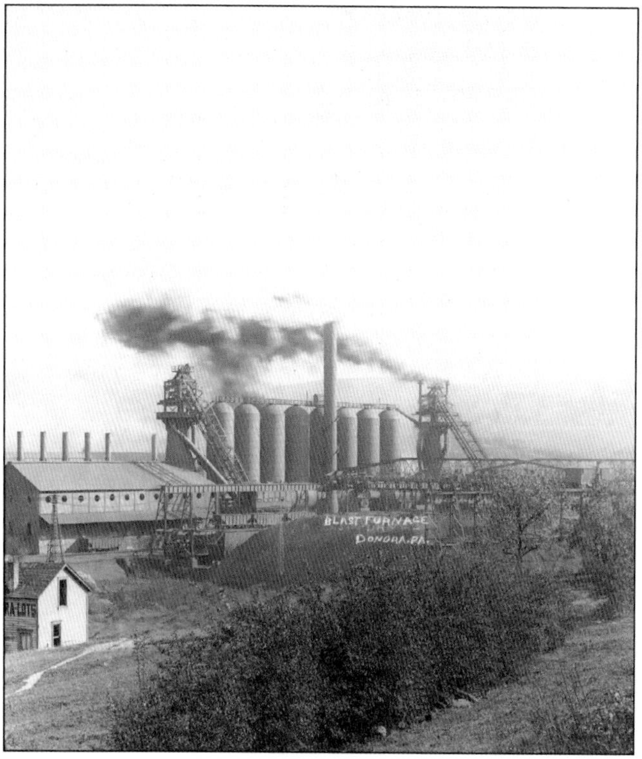

Donora's blast furnaces were constructed in 1907 and 1908 under the auspices of the Carnegie Steel Company. Iron ore and limestone were melted at extremely high temperatures, and the molten metal was tapped from the furnace several times a day. This photograph shows the dense smoke and red iron ore dust emitted from the furnace.

One of the commodities produced in the Donora mill was steel rods. This photograph shows thousands of these rods ready to be shipped throughout the country and across the world. The crane operator (far right) stacked the rods into bundles and placed them on railroad cars for transport.

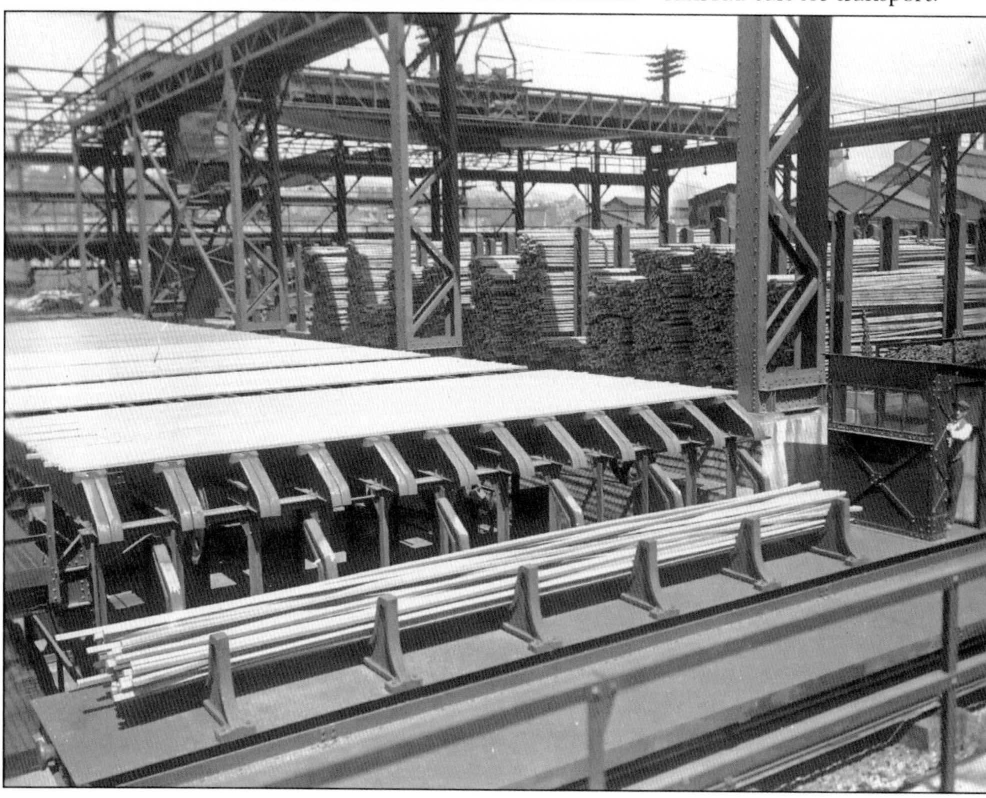

This photograph shows several young female employees of the nail mill in 1928. The dirt and grime on their clothes and hands indicates they were hard workers. Note the comparatively clean appearance of almost all of the male workers.

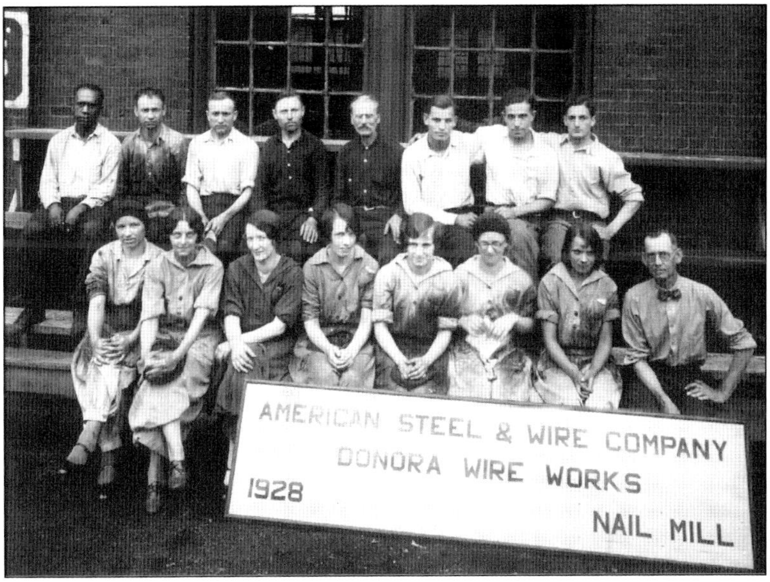

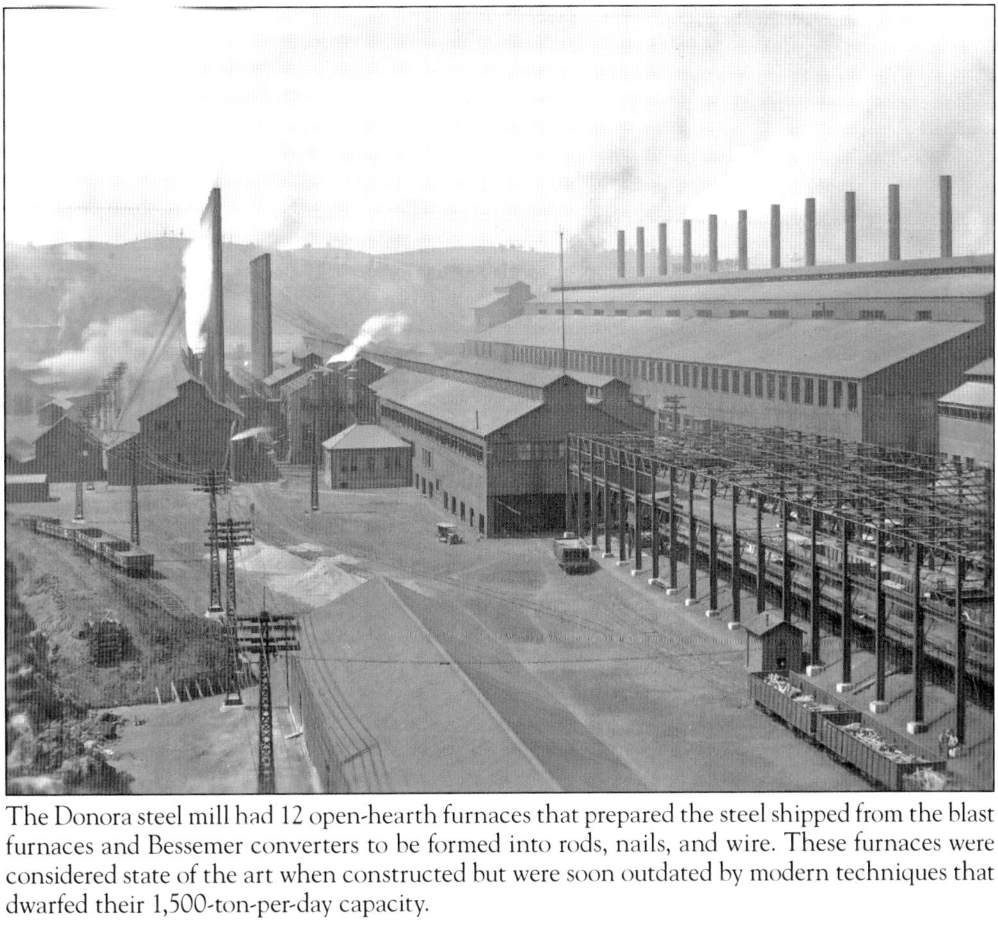

The Donora steel mill had 12 open-hearth furnaces that prepared the steel shipped from the blast furnaces and Bessemer converters to be formed into rods, nails, and wire. These furnaces were considered state of the art when constructed but were soon outdated by modern techniques that dwarfed their 1,500-ton-per-day capacity.

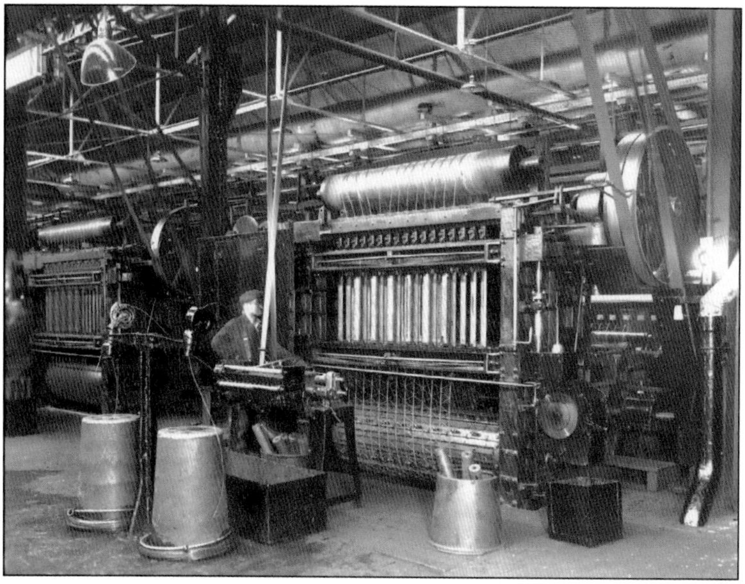

This machine produced what was known as Elwood fence. This type of fence was very popular in western states for confining livestock. Donora products not only contributed to the construction of the nation's bridges but also helped feed the country's population.

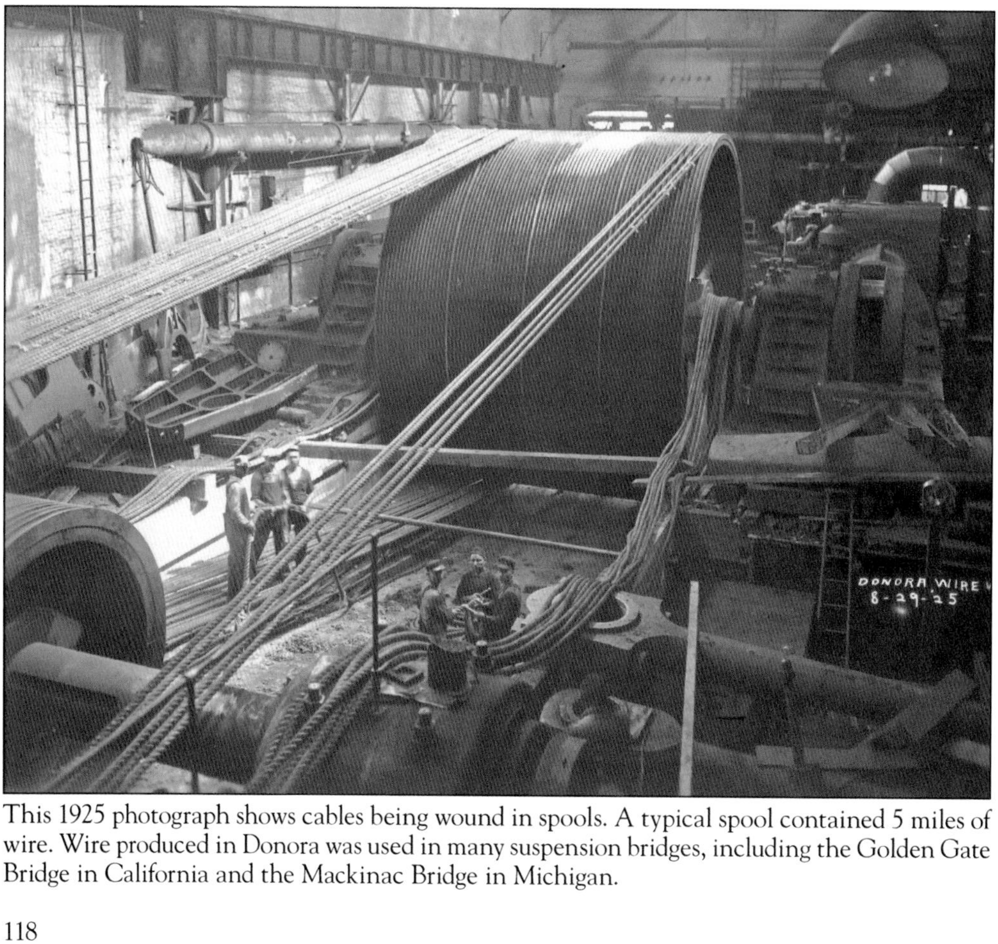

This 1925 photograph shows cables being wound in spools. A typical spool contained 5 miles of wire. Wire produced in Donora was used in many suspension bridges, including the Golden Gate Bridge in California and the Mackinac Bridge in Michigan.

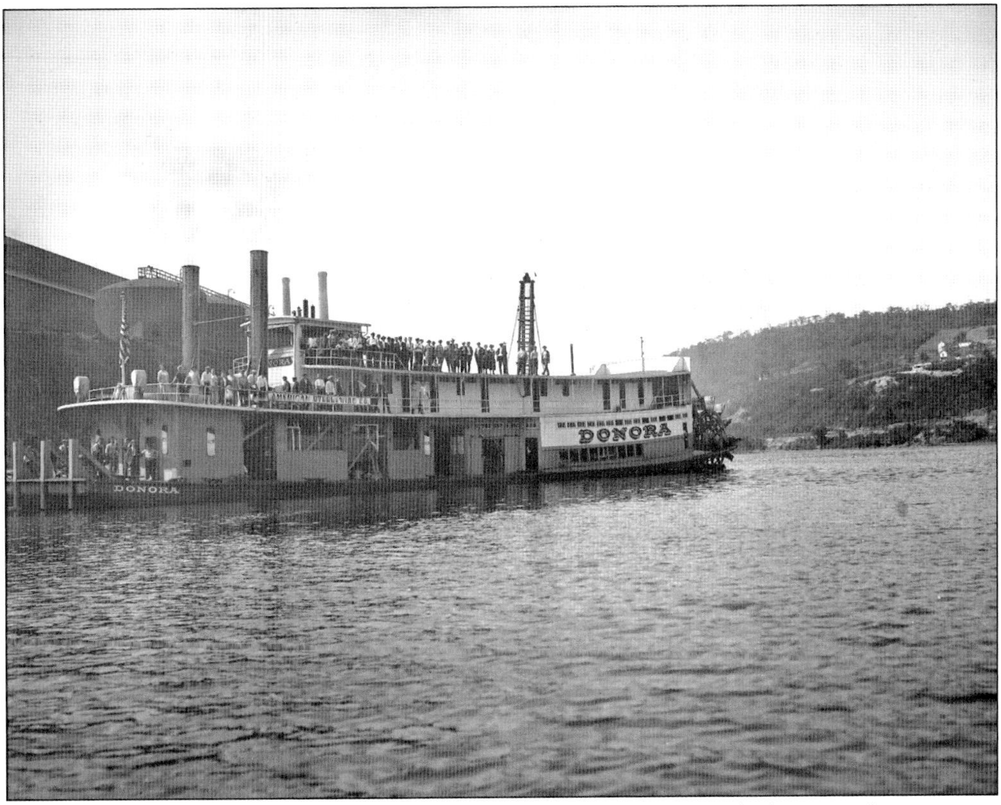

Barges carried raw materials and finished products between Donora and other sites along western Pennsylvania's rivers. Pictured here is the steamboat *Donora*, which was owned and operated by the American Steel and Wire Company. In addition to its industrial duties, the vessel was at times used for excursions.

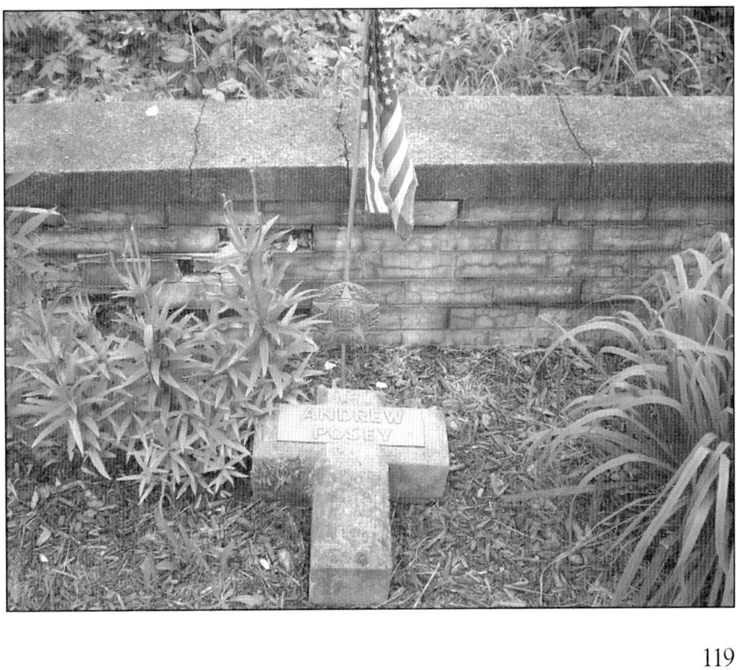

On January 20, 1920, World War I veteran Andrew Posey, age 22, was performing his job as a ladle checker. A stopper cracked, and 60 tons of 3,000-degree molten steel poured over him. His remains, sealed within the hardened steel mass, were transported by rail to a location on the mill property and buried. His brother Steven constructed a memorial grave site.

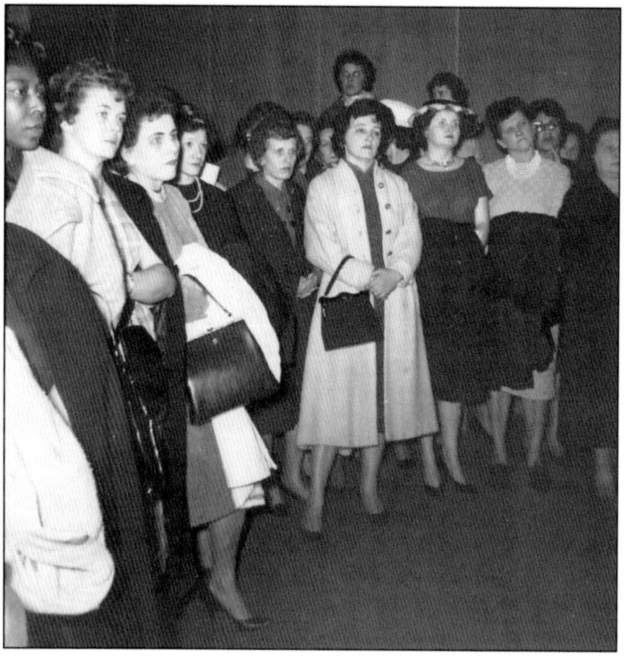

On May 7, 1962, a group of Donora's women, responding to anxiety about the future of the steel mill, traveled to Pittsburgh to speak at the U.S. Steel Corporation stockholders meeting. The women also met with secretary of labor Arthur Goldberg. Their efforts were for naught, as the steel mill closed three years later.

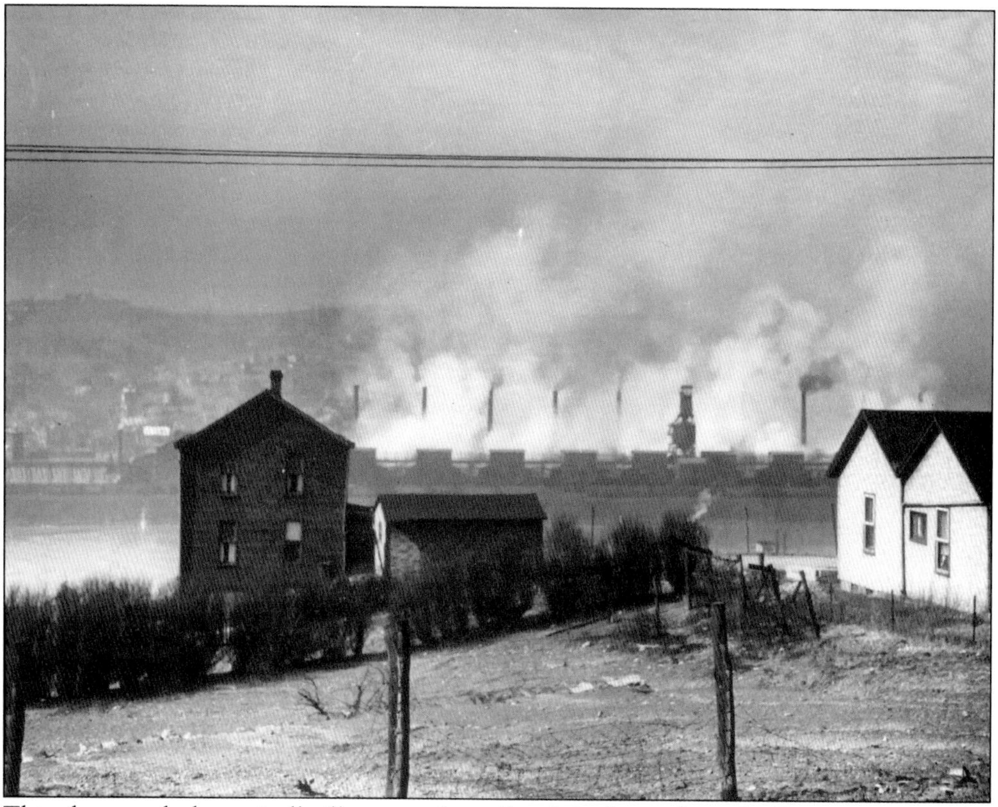

This photograph dramatically illustrates the polluted discharge from the Donora Zinc Works. After the zinc works closed in the late 1950s, grass and vegetation returned to the soil of Donora and Webster.

The sulfurous and fluoride gases that were emitted from the zinc works furnaces killed the vegetation in Gilmore Cemetery and other sections of northern Donora. Water running down the steep hillside eroded the soil, displaced the gravestones, and, according to some sources, exposed coffins.

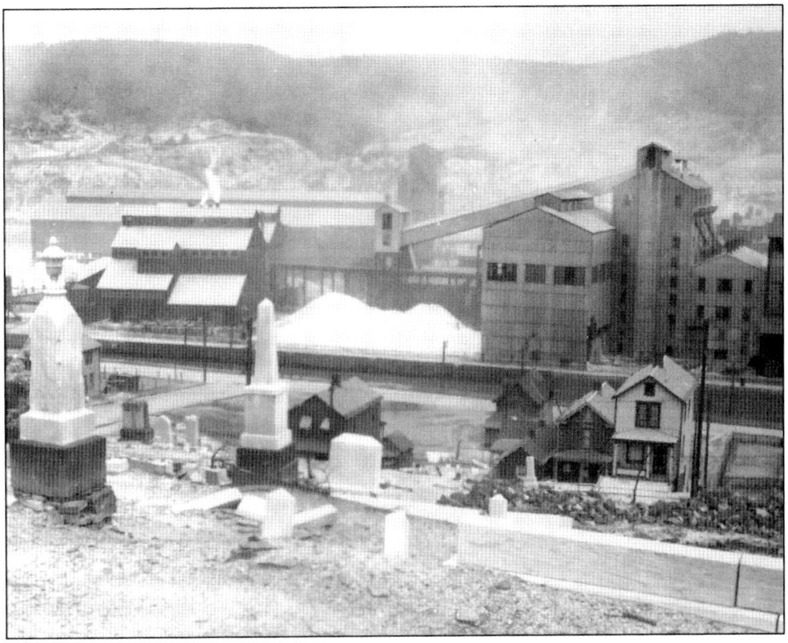

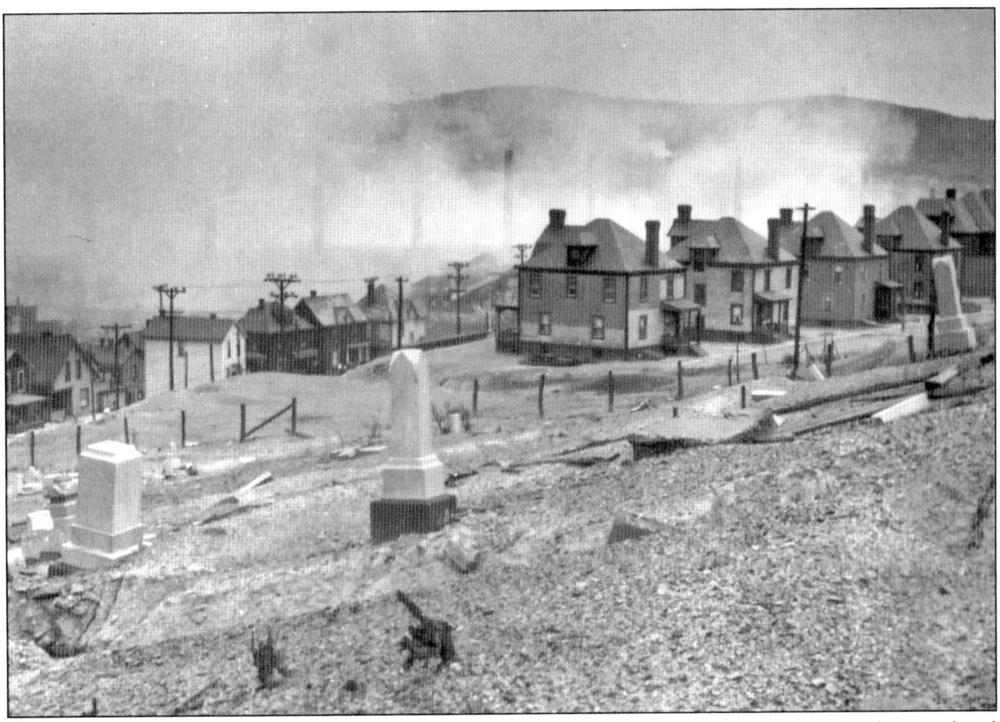

The large homes on Overlook Terrace were originally built for the superintendent and upper-level managers of the mill. However, the polluted air caused superintendent M. M. Neil to abandon the residence and move several blocks away. The building was then acquired by a group of workers and became the Spanish Club.

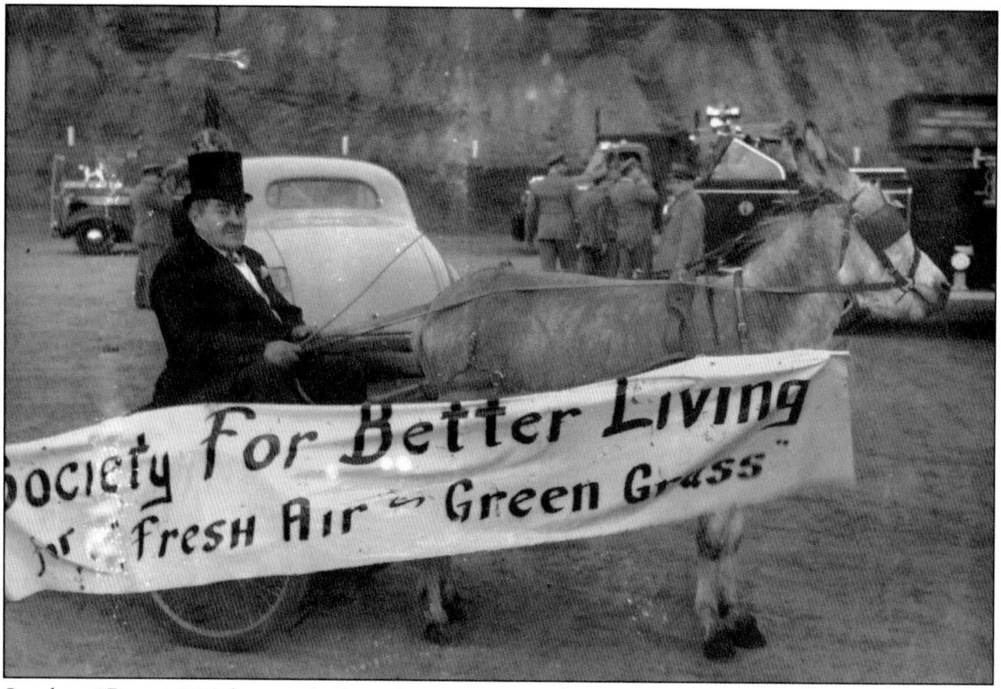

Stephen "Beanie" Huhra worked in the accounting department at American Steel and Wire. He and his donkey-drawn cart were frequent participants in Donora parades and were among the favorites of local children. This photograph shows Huhra promoting Webster's antipollution Society for Better Living. (Courtesy Sally Hurha Phillips.)

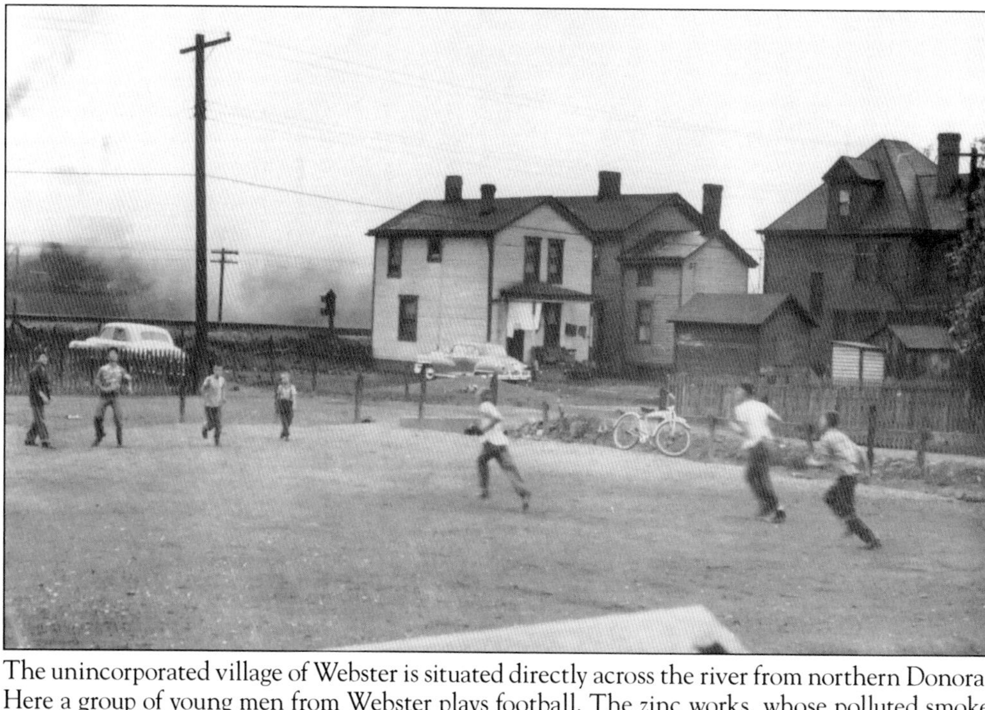
The unincorporated village of Webster is situated directly across the river from northern Donora. Here a group of young men from Webster plays football. The zinc works, whose polluted smoke blew regularly over to Webster, is visible in the background. (Courtesy Jerry Dran.)

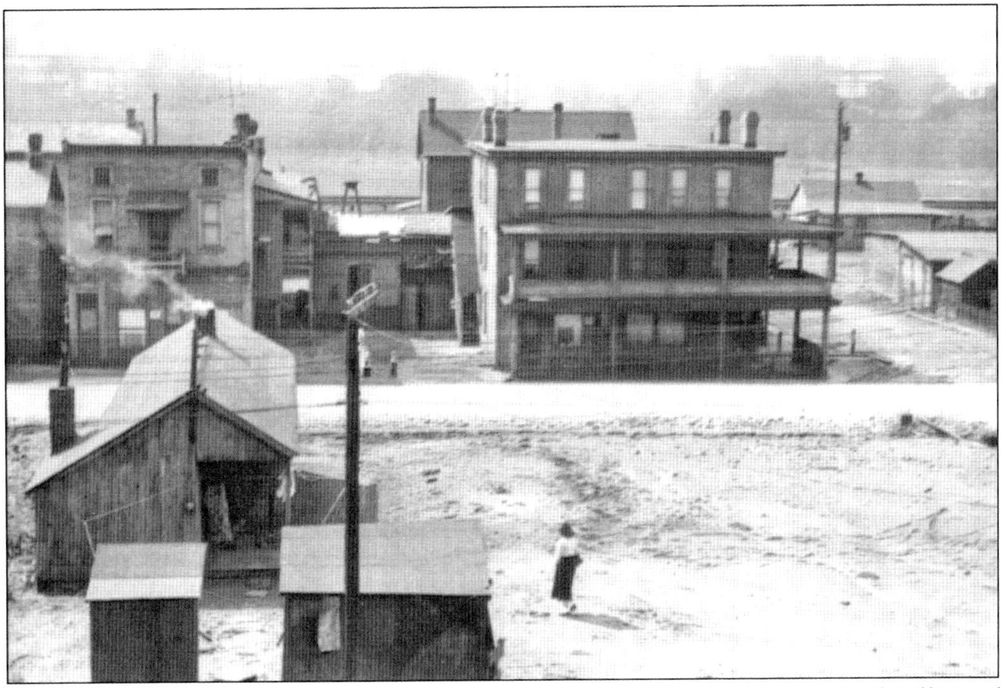

The faded paint on these Webster buildings is another example of the negative side effects of the discharge from the zinc works smokestacks. The residents of Webster were quite aware of the environmental health hazards posed by the zinc works and were among the first to call for an investigation of the dangers.

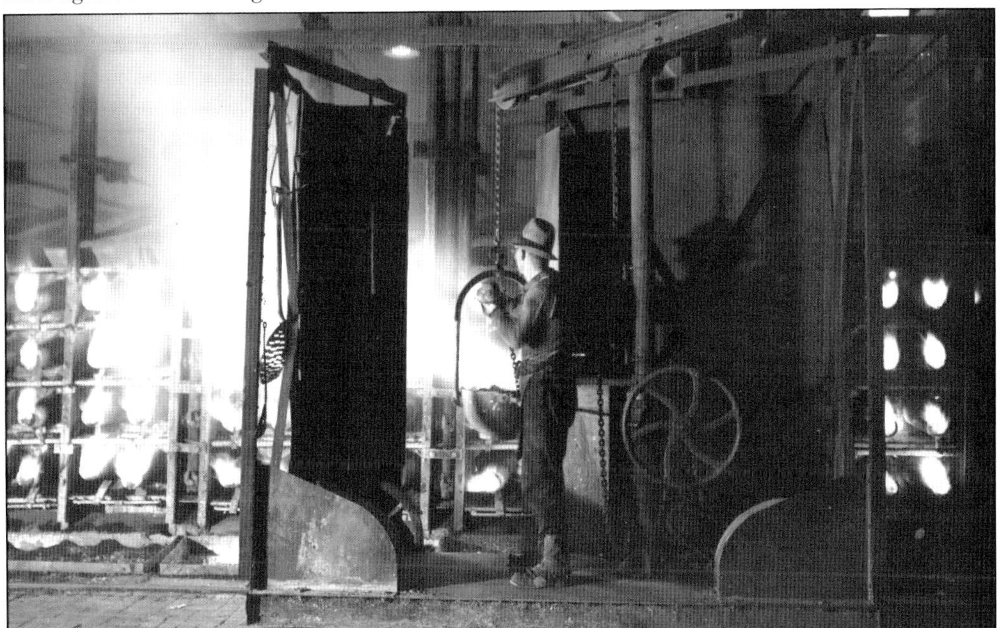

Because the labor in the zinc works spelter furnaces was so hot and hazardous, many employees were paid eight hours of wages for only three to five hours on the job. Their job cycle consisted of tapping the spelters, pouring the molten zinc into molds, then recharging the furnace for the next heat.

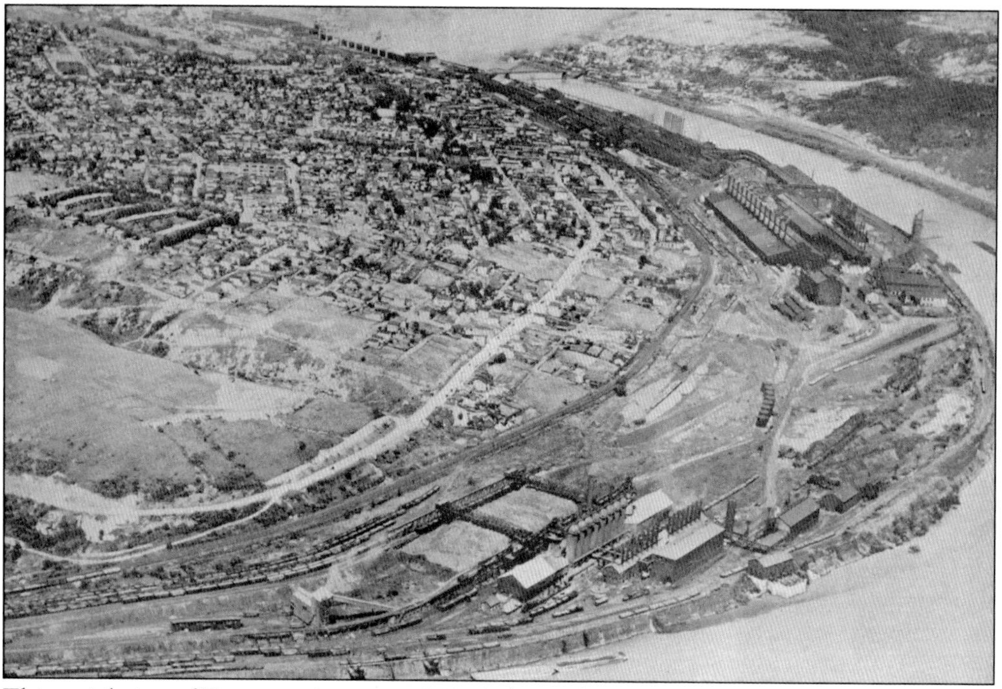

This aerial view of Donora, taken around 1946, shows the concentrated industrial development along the horseshoe bend in the Monongahela River. The blast furnace, where the steel-making process started, is in the foreground. The zinc works, spewing the smoke that had a negative impact on the vegetation of both Donora and Webster, is seen at the top of the photograph.

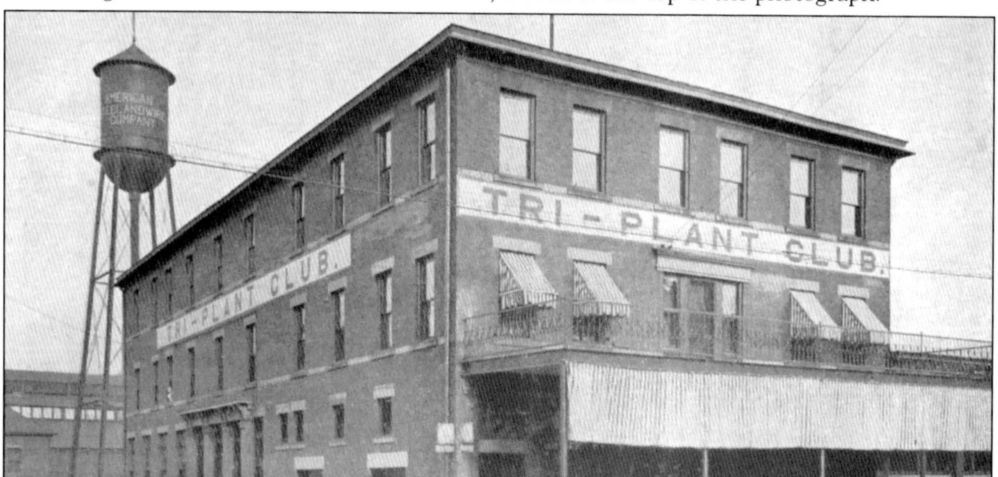

The Tri-Plant Club, originally the Hotel Indiana, was located on Sixth Street and Meldon Avenue at the main entrance to the wire mill. This building became the social meeting place of management of the steel mill and zinc works. This 1921 picture shows the proximity of the building to the mill.

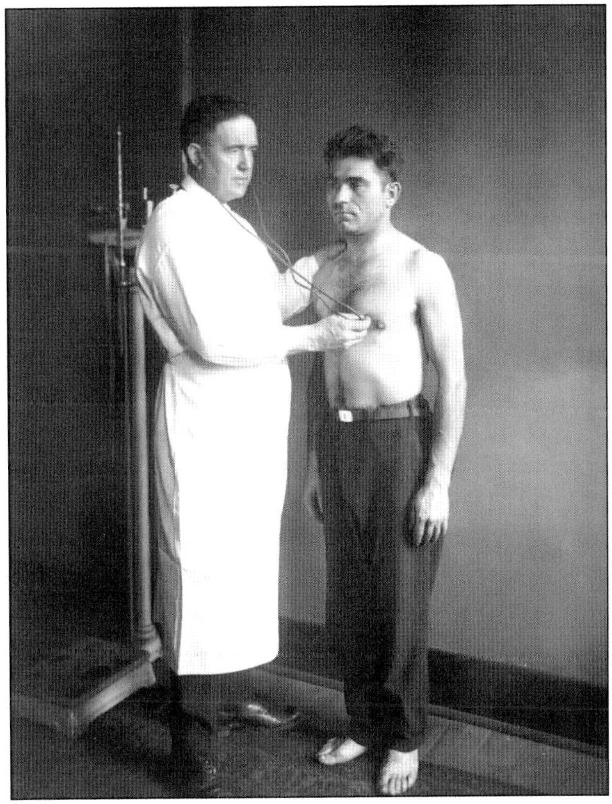

During the smog episode, Donora's doctors were overwhelmed with calls from sick and dying residents. Dr. William Rongaus responded to the emergency by advising patients to "get the hell out of town." Rongaus was vocal in his belief that pollution from the mill, particularly the zinc works, was responsible for the tragedy. Here Dr. Minor Day examines a steelworker.

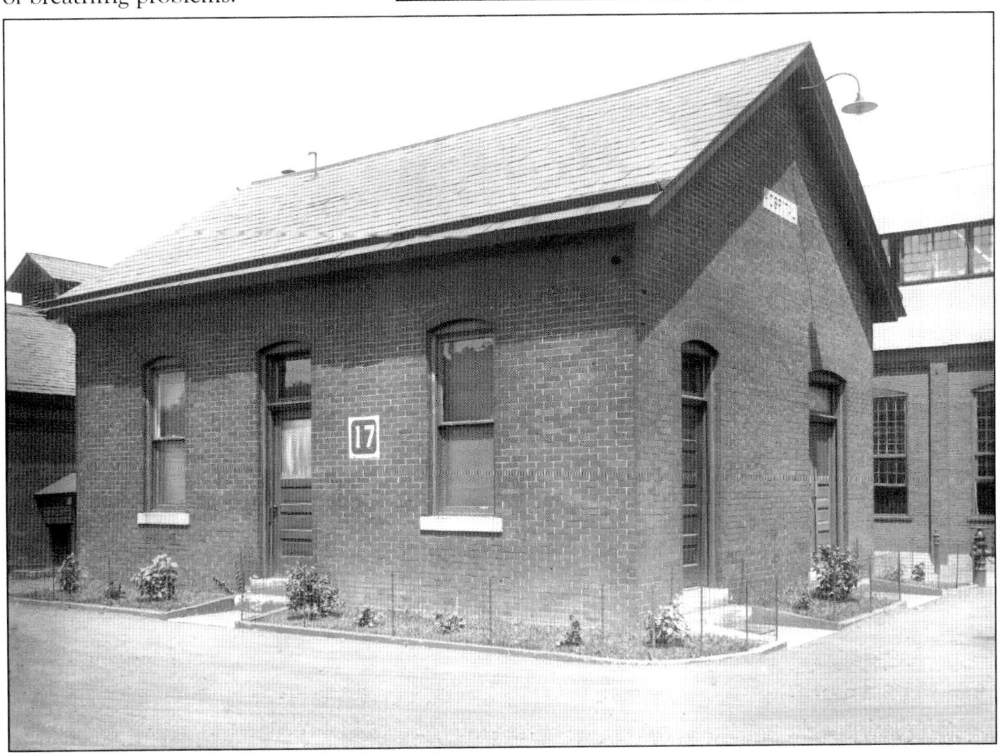

The American Steel and Wire Company hospital, built on the grounds of the steel mill, was staffed by dedicated, well-trained nurses who worked with company and local physicians. During the week of the smog, the hospital was inundated with workers complaining of breathing problems.

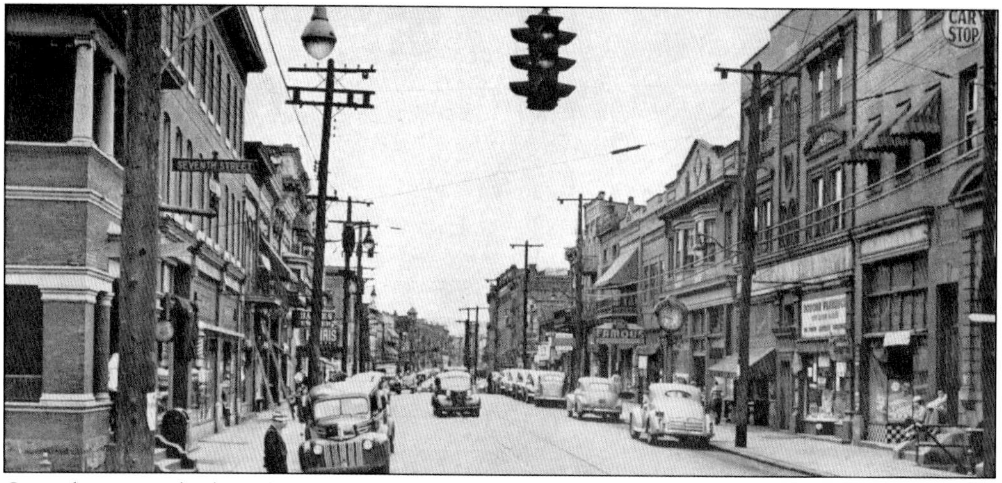

Over the years, the large brick building on the corner of Seventh and McKean Avenue housed a hotel, the public library, and the town's community center. During the last week of October in 1948, when the smog caused an overflow at both local doctor's offices and funeral parlors, it also served as a temporary hospital and morgue.

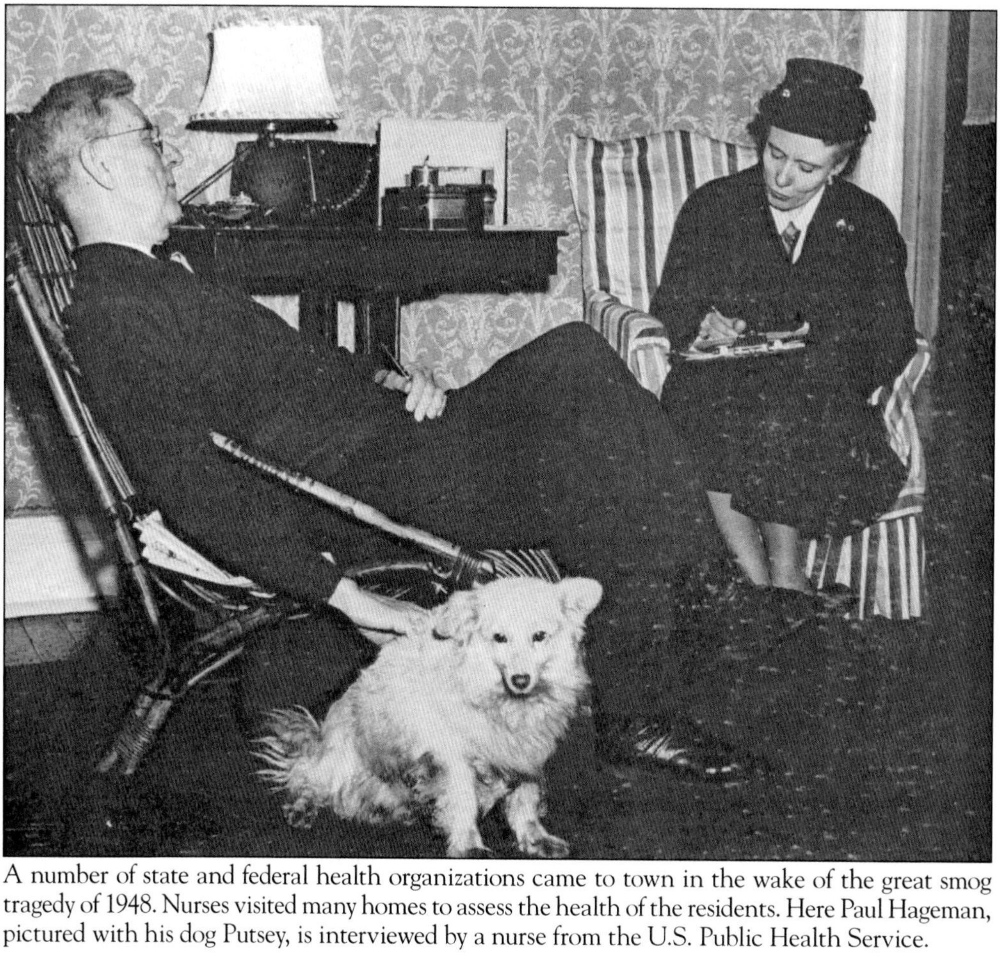

A number of state and federal health organizations came to town in the wake of the great smog tragedy of 1948. Nurses visited many homes to assess the health of the residents. Here Paul Hageman, pictured with his dog Putsey, is interviewed by a nurse from the U.S. Public Health Service.

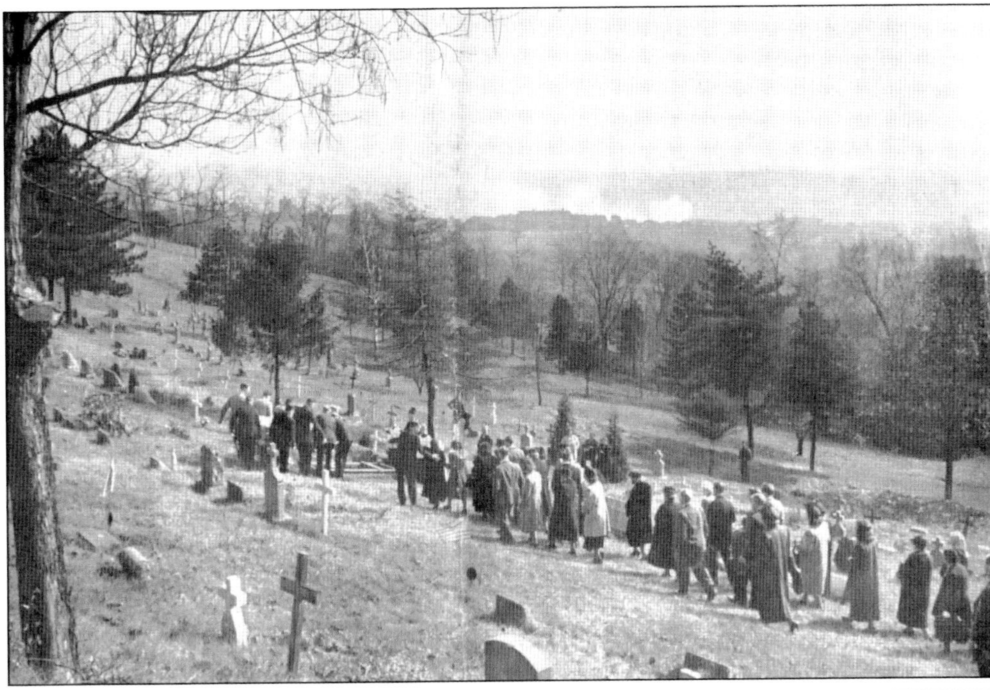

Many funerals were conducted during the aftermath of the great smog. One of the most poignant pictures of a smog victim (Peter Stancovich) being laid to rest appeared in *Life* magazine. A line of mourners follows the body to the grave in St. Dominic Cemetery, while the white smoke from the zinc works can be seen in the background. (Courtesy Time-Warner Company.)

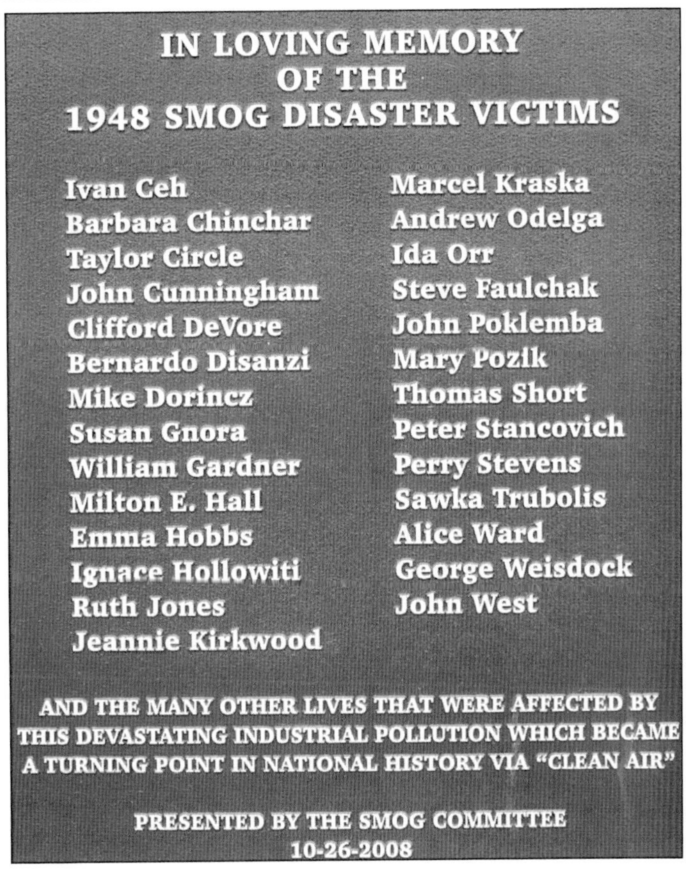

In October 2008, as part of the commemoration of the 60th anniversary of the great smog, a plaque listing the names of 27 victims was dedicated in south Donora. There has been an ongoing controversy about how many people actually died as a result of the tragedy. Some believe the number is much higher than the 27 listed.

Consistent with our mission to preserve history on a local level, this book was printed in South Carolina on American-made paper and manufactured entirely in the United States. Products carrying the accredited Forest Stewardship Council (FSC) label are printed on 100 percent FSC-certified paper.

MADE IN THE USA